Thrice-Greatest Hermes

Studies in Hellenistic Theosophy and Gnosis

Being a Translation of the Extant Sermons and Fragments of the Trismegistic
Literature, with Prolegomena, Commentaries, and Notes

By
G. R. S. Mead

Volume II.—Sermons

I

Corpus Hermeticum

CORPUS HERMETICUM I.

PŒMANDRES, THE SHEPHERD OF MEN

(Text: R. 328-338; P. 1-18; Pat. 5b-8.) [1]

1. IT chanced once on a time my mind was meditating on the things that are, [2] my thought was raised to a great height, the senses of my body being held back—just as men are who are weighed down with sleep after a fill of food, or from fatigue of body.

Methought a Being more than vast, in size beyond all bounds, called out my name and saith: What wouldst thou hear and see, and what hast thou in mind to learn and know?

2. And I do say: Who art thou?

He saith: I am Man-Shepherd, [3] Mind of all-masterhood [4]; I know what thou desirest and I'm with thee everywhere.

3. [And] I reply: I long to learn the things that are, and comprehend their nature, and know God. This is, I said, what I desire to hear.

He answered back to me: Hold in thy mind all thou wouldst know, and I will teach thee.

4. E'en with these words His aspect changed, [5] and straightway, in the twinkling of an eye, all things were opened to me, and I see a Vision limitless, all things turned into Light,—sweet, joyous [Light]. And I became transported as I gazed.

But in a little while Darkness came settling down on part [of it], awesome and gloomy, coiling in sinuous folds, [6] so that methought it like unto a snake. [7]

---

[1] P. = Parthey (G.), *Hermetis Trismegisti Poemander* (Berlin; 1854). Pat. = Patrizzi (F.), *Nova de Universis Philosophia* (Venice; 1593).

[2] περὶ τῶν ὄντων.

[3] Ποιμάνδρης.

[4] ὁ τῆς αὐθεντίας νοῦς. The αὐθεντία was the *summa potestas* of all things; see R. 8, n. 1; and § 30 below. Cf. also *C. H.*, xiii. (xiv.) 15.

[5] ἠλλάγη τῇ ἰδέᾳ.

[6] σκολιῶς ἐσπειραμένον. The sense is by no means certain. Ménard translates "*de forme sinueuse*"; Everard, "coming down obliquely"; Chambers, "sinuously terminated." But cf. in the Sethian system "the sinuous Water—that is, Darkness (see Hipp., *Philos.*, v. 19).

[7] Cf. Hipp., *Philos.*, v. 9 (S. 170, 71): "They say the Serpent is the Moist Essence."

And then the Darkness changed into some sort of a Moist Nature, tossed about beyond all power of words, belching out smoke as from a fire, and groaning forth a wailing sound that beggars all description.

[And] after that an outcry inarticulate came forth from it, as though it were a Voice of Fire.

5. [Thereon] out of the Light . . . [8] a Holy Word (*Logos*) [9] descended on that Nature. And upwards to the height from the Moist Nature leaped forth pure Fire; light was it, swift and active too.

The Air, too, being light, followed after the Fire; from out the Earth-and-Water rising up to Fire so that it seemed to hang therefrom.

But Earth-and-Water stayed so mingled each with other, that Earth from Water no one could discern. [10] Yet were they moved to hear by reason of the Spirit-Word (*Logos*) pervading them.

6. Then saith to me Man-Shepherd: Didst understand this Vision what it means?

Nay; that *shall* I know, I said.

That Light, He said, am I, thy God, Mind, prior to Moist Nature which appeared from Darkness; the Light-Word (*Logos*) [that appeared] from Mind is Son of God.

What then?—say I.

Know that what sees in thee [11] and hears is the Lord's Word (*Logos*); but Mind is Father-God. Not separate are they the one from other; just in their union [rather] is it Life consists.

Thanks be to Thee, I said.

So, understand the Light [He answered], and make friends with it.

7. And speaking thus He gazed for long into my eyes,[12] so that I trembled at the look of Him.

But when He raised His head, I see in Mind the Light, [but] now in Powers no man could number, and Cosmos [13] grown beyond all bounds, and that the Fire was compassed round about by a most mighty Power, and [now] subdued had come unto a stand.

And when I saw these things I understood by reason of Man-Shepherd's Word (*Logos*).

---

[8] A lacuna of six letters in the text.

[9] The idea of the Logos was the central concept of Hellenistic theology; it was thus a word of many meanings, signifying chiefly Reason and Word, but also much else. I have accordingly throughout added the term *Logos* after the English equivalent most suitable to the context.

[10] Cf. II., vii. 99, as quoted by Apion in the chapter "Concerning the Æon" as Comment, on *C. H.*, xi. (xii.).

[11] That is, in vision.

[12] Cf. *C. H.*, xi (xii) 6.

[13] κόσμον. The word *kosmos* (world-order) means either "order" or "world"; and in the original there is frequently a play upon the two meanings, as in the case of *logos*.

8. But as I was in great astonishment, He saith to me again: Thou didst behold in Mind the Archetypal Form whose being is before beginning without end. Thus spake to me Man-Shepherd.

And I say: Whence then have Nature's elements their being?

To this He answer gives: From Will of God. [Nature[14]] received the Word (*Logos*), and gazing on the Cosmos Beautiful [15] did copy it, making herself into a cosmos, by means of her own elements and by the births of souls.

9. And God-the-Mind, being male and female both, as Light and Life subsisting, brought forth another Mind to give things form, who, God as he was of Fire and Spirit, [16] formed Seven Rulers who enclose the cosmos that the sense perceives. [17] Men call their ruling Fate. [18]

10. Straightway from out the downward elements God's Reason (*Logos*)[19] leaped up to Nature's pure formation, and was at-oned with the Formative Mind; for it was co-essential with it. [20] And Nature's downward elements were thus left reason-less, so as to be pure matter.

11. Then the Formative Mind ([at-oned] with Reason), he who surrounds the spheres and spins them with his whirl, set turning his formations, and let them turn from a beginning boundless unto an endless end. For that the circulation of these [spheres] begins where it doth end, as Mind doth will.

And from the downward elements Nature brought forth lives reason-less; for He did not extend the Reason (*Logos*) [to them]. The Air brought forth things winged; the Water things that swim, and Earth-and-Water one from another parted, as Mind willed. And from her bosom Earth produced what lives she had, four-footed things and reptiles, beasts wild and tame.

12. But All-Father Mind, being Life and Light, did bring forth Man [21] co-equal to Himself, with whom He fell in love, as being His own child; for he was beautiful beyond compare, the Image of his Sire. In very truth, God fell in love with His own Form [22]; and on him did bestow all of His own formations.

---

[14] Nature and God's Will are identical.
[15] That is, the ideal world-order in the realms of reality.
[16] Presumably the Pure Air of § 3.
[17] τὸν αἰσθητὸν κόσμον. The sensible or manifested world, our present universe, as distinguished from the ideal eternal universe, the type of all universes.
[18] εἱμαρμένη.
[19] The Logos which had previously descended into Nature.
[20] ὁμοούσιος, usually translated "consubstantial"; but οὐσία is "essence" and "being" rather than "substance."
[21] The Prototype, Cosmic, Ideal or Perfect Man.
[22] Or Beauty (μορφῆς).

13. And when he gazed upon what the Enformer had created in the Father, [Man] too wished to enform; and [so] assent was given him by the Father. [23]

Changing his state to the formative sphere, [24] in that he was to have his whole authority, [25] he gazed upon his Brother's creatures. [26] They fell in love with him, and gave him each a share of his own ordering. [27]

And after that he had well-learned their essence and had become a sharer in their nature, he had a mind to break right through the Boundary of their spheres, and to subdue [28]the might of that which pressed upon the Fire. [29]

14. So he who hath the whole authority o'er [all] the mortals in the cosmos and o'er its lives irrational, bent his face downwards through [30]the Harmony, [31] breaking right through its strength, and showed to downward Nature God's fair Form.

And when she saw that Form of beauty which can never satiate, and him who [now] possessed within himself each single energy of [all seven] Rulers as well as God's [own] Form, she smiled with love; for 'twas as though she'd seen the image of Man's fairest form upon her Water, his shadow on her Earth.

He in his turn beholding the form like to himself, existing in her, in her Water, loved it and willed to live in it; and with the will came act,[32] and [so] he vivified the form devoid of reason.

And Nature took the object of her love and wound herself completely round him, and they were intermingled, for they were lovers.

15. And this is why beyond all creatures on the earth man is twofold; mortal because of body, but because of the essential Man immortal.

Though deathless and possessed of sway o'er all, yet doth he suffer as a mortal doth, subject to Fate.

Thus though above the Harmony, within the Harmony he hath become a slave. Though male-female, [33] as from a Father male-female, and though he's sleepless from a sleepless [Sire], yet is he overcome [by sleep].

---

[23] Cf. *The Gospel of Mary* in the Akhmīm Codex: "He nodded, and when He had thus nodded assent . . . ." (*F. F. F.*, 586).
[24] The Eighth Sphere bounding the Seven.
[25] For note on ἐξουσία, see R. *in loc.* and 48, n. 3.
[26] That is the Seven Spheres fashioned by his Brother.
[27] τάξις, rank or order.
[28] Or "wear down" (καταπονῆσαι). The reading κατανοῆσαι, however, may be more correct; "he had a mind to come to knowledge of" this Boundary or Ring Pass not. See R. 49, n. 1.
[29] *Sc.* the Mighty Power of § 9.
[30] παρέκυψεν. Cf. Cyril, *C. J.*, i. 33 (Frag. xiii.); R. 50: "*beugt sich . . . nieder*" But compare especially Plato, *Phædrus*, 249 C., where he speaks of the soul "raising up her face (ἀνακύψασα) to That which is." Cf. also Apion in *Clement. Hom.*, vi. 4, in Comment. *C. H.*, xi. (xii.).
[31] That is, the harmonious interplay, concord or system of the spheres ruled by the Rulers; in other words, the cosmos of Fate.
[32] ἐνέργεια, energy, and realization.

16. Thereon [I say: Teach on], ³⁴ O Mind of me, for I myself as well ³⁵am amorous of the Word (*Logos*).

The Shepherd said: This is the mystery kept hid until this day. Nature embraced by Man brought forth a wonder, oh so wonderful. For as he had the nature of the Concord ³⁶of the Seven, who, as I said to thee, [were made] of Fire and Spirit ³⁷—Nature delayed not, but immediately brought forth seven "men," in correspondence with the natures of the Seven, male-female and moving in the air. ³⁸

Thereon [I said]: O Shepherd, . . . ³⁹; for now I'm filled with great desire and long to hear; do not run off. ⁴⁰

The Shepherd said: Keep silence, for not as yet have I unrolled for thee the first discourse (*logos*).

Lo! I am still, I said.

17. In such wise then, as I have said, the generation of these seven came to pass. Earth was as woman, her Water filled with longing; ripeness she took from Fire, spirit from Æther. Nature thus brought forth frames to suit the form of Man.

And Man from Life and Light changed into soul and mind,—from Life to soul, from Light to mind.

And thus continued all the sense-world's parts ⁴¹until the period of their end and new beginnings.

18. Now listen to the rest of the discourse (*logos*) which thou dost long to hear.

The period being ended, the bond that bound them all was loosened by God's Will. For all the animals being male-female, at the same time with man were loosed apart; some became partly male, some in like fashion [partly] female. And straightway God spake by His Holy Word (*Logos*):

"Increase ye in increasing, and multiply in multitude, ye creatures and creations all; and man that hath Mind in him, let him learn to know that he himself is deathless, and that the cause of death is love, ⁴² though Love is all."⁴³

---

³³ That is "a-sexual" but having the potentiality of both sexes.
³⁴ For the various suggestions for filling up this lacuna, see R. *in loc.*; and for that of Keil, see R. 367.
³⁵ *Sc.* as well as Nature.
³⁶ Harmony.
³⁷ See § 9.
³⁸ μεταρσίους. A term that must have a more definite meaning than the vague "sublime" by which it is generally translated.
³⁹ For Keil's completion of the lacuna, see R. 368.
⁴⁰ μὴ ἔκτρεχε, perhaps meaning diverge from the subject, or go too fast; lit., it means "do not run away."
⁴¹ That is, the parts of what Hermes elsewhere calls the "cosmic man."
⁴² *Cf. C. H.*, xvi. 16.

19. When He said this, His Forethought [44]did by means of Fate and Harmony effect their couplings and their generations founded. And so all things were multiplied according to their kind.

And he who thus hath learned to know himself, hath reached that Good which doth transcend abundance; but he who through a love that leads astray, expends his love upon his body,—he stays in Darkness wandering, [45] and suffering through his senses things of Death.

20. What is the so great fault, said I, the ignorant commit, that they should be deprived of deathlessness?

Thou seem'st, he said, O thou, not to have given heed to what thou heardest. Did not I bid thee *think?*

Yea do I think, and I remember, and therefore give Thee thanks.

If thou didst think [thereon], [said He], tell me: Why do they merit death who are in Death?

It is because the gloomy Darkness is the root and base of the material frame; from it [46]came the Moist Nature; from this [47] the body in the sense-world was composed; and from this [body] Death doth the Water drain.

21. Right was thy thought, O thou! But how doth "he who knows himself, go unto Him," as God's Word (*Logos*) hath declared?

And I reply: the Father of the universals doth consist of Light and Life, and from Him Man was born.

Thou sayest well, [thus] speaking. Light and Life is Father-God, and from Him Man was born.

If then thou learnest that thou *art* thyself of Life and Light, and that thou [only] *happen'st* to be out of them, thou shalt return again to Life. Thus did Man-Shepherd speak.

But tell me further, Mind of me, I cried, *how* shall *I* come to Life again . . . . for God doth say: "The man who hath Mind in him, let him learn to know that he himself [is deathless]."

22. Have not all men then Mind?

Thou sayest well, O thou, thus speaking. I, Mind, myself am present with holy men and good, the pure and merciful, men who live piously.

[To such] my presence doth become an aid, and straightway they gain gnosis of all things, and win the Father's love by their pure lives, and give Him thanks, invoking on Him blessings, and chanting hymns, intent on Him with ardent love.

And ere they give the body up unto its proper death, they turn them with disgust from its sensations, from knowledge of what things they

---

[43] Omitting the τά before ὄντα.
[44] πρόνοια, that is Nature as Sophia or Providence or Will.
[45] There is a word-play between πλάνης and πλανώμενος.
[46] *Sc.* Darkness.
[47] *Sc.* The Moist Nature.

operate. [48]Nay, it is I, the Mind, that will not let the operations which befall the body, work to their [natural] end. For being door-keeper I'll close up [all] the entrances, and cut the mental actions off which base and evil energies induce.

23. But to the Mind-less ones, the wicked and depraved, the envious and covetous, and those who murder do and love impiety, I am far off, yielding my place to the Avenging Daimon, who sharpening the fire, tormenteth him and addeth fire to fire upon him, and rusheth on him through his senses, thus rendering him the readier for transgressions of the law, so that he meets with greater torment; nor doth he ever cease to have desire for appetites inordinate, insatiately striving in the dark.[49]

24. Well hast thou taught me all, as I desired, O Mind. And now, pray, tell me further of the nature of the Way Above as now it is [for me]. [50]

To this Man-Shepherd said: When thy material body is to be dissolved, first thou surrenderest the body by itself unto the work of change, and thus the form thou hadst doth vanish, and thou surrenderest thy way of life, [51] void of its energy, unto the Daimon. [52] The body's senses next pass back into their sources, becoming separate, and resurrect as energies; and passion and desire [53]withdraw unto that nature which is void of reason.

25. And thus it is that man doth speed his way thereafter upwards through the Harmony.

To the first zone he gives the Energy of Growth and Waning; unto the second [zone], Device of Evils [now] de-energized [54]; unto the third, the Guile of the Desires de-energized; unto the fourth, his Domineering Arrogance, [also] de-energized; unto the fifth, unholy Daring and the Rashness of Audacity, de-energized; unto the sixth, Striving for Wealth by evil means, deprived of its aggrandisement; and to the seventh zone, Ensnaring Falsehood, de-energized. [55]

26. And then, with all the energizings of the Harmony stript from him, clothed in his proper Power, he cometh to that Nature which belongs unto the Eighth, [56] and there with those-that-are hymneth the Father.

They who are there welcome his coming there with joy; and he, made like to them that sojourn there, doth further hear the Powers who are above the

---

[48] εἰδότες αὐτῶν τὰ ἐνεργήματα.
[49] The text of this paragraph is hopelessly confused in the MSS.
[50] περὶ τῆς ἀνόδου τῆς γινομένης.
[51] τὸ ἦθος, the "habitual" part of man, presumably way of life impressed by habit on the body; or it may be "class" of life as in the Vision of Er.
[52] Cf. C. H., x. (xi.) 16.
[53] ὁ θυμὸς καὶ ἡ ἐπιθυμία,—the masculine and feminine as positive and negative aspects of the "animal soul."
[54] ἀνενέργητον.
[55] Cf. C. H., xiii. (xiv.) 7.
[56] Cf. C. H., xiii. (xiv.) 15.

Nature that belongs unto the Eighth, singing their songs of praise to God in language of their own.

And then they, in a band, [57] go to the Father home; of their own selves they make surrender of themselves to Powers, and [thus] becoming Powers they are in God. This the good end for those who have gained Gnosis—to be made one with God.

Why shouldst thou then delay? Must it not be, since thou hast all received, that thou shouldst to the worthy point the way, in order that through thee the race of mortal kind may by [thy] God be saved?

27. This when He'd said, Man-Shepherd mingled with the Powers. [58]

But I, with thanks and blessings unto the Father of the universal [Powers], was freed, full of the power He had poured into me, and full of what He'd taught me of the nature of the All and of the loftiest Vision.

And I began to preach to men the Beauty of Devotion and of Gnosis:

O ye people, earth-born folk, ye who have given yourselves to drunkenness and sleep and ignorance of God, be sober now, cease from your surfeit, cease to be glamoured by irrational sleep [59]!

28. And when they heard, they came with one accord. Whereon I say:

Ye earth-born folk, why have ye given up yourselves to Death, while yet ye have the power of sharing Deathlessness? Repent, O ye, who walk with Error arm in arm and make of Ignorance the sharer of your board; get ye from out the light of Darkness, and take your part in Deathlessness, forsake Destruction!

29. And some of them with jests upon their lips [60] departed [from me], abandoning themselves unto the Way of Death; others entreated to be taught, casting themselves before my feet.

But I made them arise, and I became a leader of the Race [61] towards home, teaching the words (*logoi*), how and in what way they shall be saved. I sowed in them the words (*logoi*) of wisdom [62]; of Deathless Water were they given to drink. [63]

---

[57] τάξει, order, group, *sc.* of the Nine;—the Father being the Ten, or consummation.
[58] *Cf. K. K.*, 25: "Thus speaking God became Imperishable Mind."
[59] *Cf.* the *logos*, "Jesus saith, I stood in the midst of the world, and in the flesh was I seen of them, and I found all men drunken, and none found I athirst among them, and my soul grieveth over the sons of men, because they are blind in heart." *Sayings of Our Lord from an Early Greek Papyrus*, Grenfell & Hunt (London; 1897).
[60] *Cf. P. S. A.*, xii. 2.
[61] The Race of the Logos, of all who were conscious of the Logos in their hearts, who had repented and were thus logoi.
[62] *Cf.* Mark iv. 4: "He who soweth soweth the Word (*Logos*)"
[63] *Cf. K. K.*, 1—the drink given by Isis to Horus.

And when even was come and all sun's beams began to set, I bade them all give thanks to God. And when they had brought to an end the giving of their thanks, each man returned to his own resting place.

30. But I recorded in my heart Man-Shepherd's benefaction, and with my every hope fulfilled more than rejoiced. For body's sleep became the soul's awakening, [64] and closing of the eyes—true vision, pregnant with Good my silence, and the utterance of my word (*logos*) begetting of good things.

All this befell me from my Mind, that is Man-Shepherd, Word (*Logos*) of all masterhood, [65] by whom being God-inspired I came unto the Plain of Truth. [66] Wherefore with all my soul and strength thanksgiving [67] give I unto Father-God.

31. Holy art Thou, O God, the universals' Father.

Holy art Thou, O God, whose Will perfects itself by means of its own Powers.

Holy art Thou, O God, who willeth to be known and art known by Thine own.

Holy art Thou, who didst by Word (*Logos*) make to consist the things that are.

Holy art Thou, of whom All-nature hath been made an Image.

Holy art Thou, whose Form Nature hath never made.

Holy art Thou, more powerful than all power.

Holy art Thou, transcending all pre-eminence.

Holy Thou art, Thou better than all praise.

Accept my reason's [68]offerings pure, from soul and heart for aye stretched up to Thee, O Thou unutterable, unspeakable, Whose Name naught but the Silence can express.

32. Give ear to me who pray that I may ne'er of Gnosis fail, [Gnosis] which is our common Being's nature[69]; and fill me with Thy Power, and with this Grace [of Thine], that I may give the Light to those in ignorance of the Race, my Brethren, and Thy Sons.

For this cause I believe, and I bear witness; I go to Life and Light. Blessed art Thou, O Father. Thy Man [70] would holy be as Thou art holy, e'en as Thou gavest him Thy full authority [71] [to be].

---

[64] νῆψις, lit. soberness, watchfulness, lucidity.
[65] See § 2 above.
[66] Cf. K. K. (Stob., Ec., i. 49; p. 459, 20, W.), and Damascius, in Phot., *Bibl.*, p. 337b, 23.
[67] εὐλογίαν,—a play on λόγος.
[68] λογικάς.
[69] τῆς γνώσεως τῆς κατ᾽ οὐσίαν ἡμῶν, "*our* being," that is, presumably, the "being" of man and God, the "being" which man shares with God.
[70] Cf. C. H., xiii. (xiv.) 20.
[71] ἐξουσίαν.

COMMENTARY

OF VISION AND APOCALYPSIS

The "Pœmandres" treatise not only belongs to the most important type of the Trismegistic literature, but is also the most important document within that type. It constitutes, so to speak, the Ground-Gospel of the Pœmandres Communities, in the form of a revelation or apocalypse received by the founder of the tradition, that founder, however, being not a historical personage but the personification of a teaching-power or grade of spiritual illumination—in other words, of one who had reached the "Hermes," or rather "Thrice-greatest," state of consciousness or enlightenment.

This stage of enlightenment was characterized by a heightening of the spiritual intuition which made the mystic capable of receiving the first touch of cosmic consciousness, and of retaining it in his physical memory when he returned to the normal state.

The setting forth of the teaching is thus naturally in the form of apocalyptic, and of apocalyptic of an ordered and logical nature; for it purports to be a setting forth of the spiritual "Epopteia" of the Inner Mysteries, the Vision revealed by the Great Initiator or Master-Hierophant, Mind of all-masterhood.

This Vision, as we are told by many seers and prophets of the time, was incapable of being set forth by "tongue of flesh" in its own proper terms, seeing that it transcended the consciousness of normal humanity. Being in itself a living, potent, intelligible reality, apart from all forms either material or intellectual in any way known to man, it pervaded his very being and made his whole nature respond to a new key of truth, or rather, vibrate in a higher octave, so to say, where all things, while remaining the same, received a new interpretation and intensity.

The interpretation of this Vision, however, was conditioned by the "matter" of each seer; he it was who had to clothe the naked beauty of the Truth—as the Gnostic Marcus would have phrased it—with the fairest garment he himself possessed, the highest thoughts, the best science, the fairest traditions, the most grandiose imagination known to him. Thus it is that we have so many modes of expression among the mystics of the time, so many varieties of spiritual experience—not because the experience itself was "other," the experience was the "same" for all, but the speaking of it forth was conditioned by the religious and philosophical and scientific heredity of the seer.

This element, then, is the basic fact in all such apocalyptic. It is, however, seldom that we meet with a document that has come to us straight from the hand of a seer writing down his own immediate experience without admixture; for the delight of the Vision was not that it gave new facts or ideas of the same nature as those already in circulation, but that it threw light on existing traditions, and showed them forth as being parts of a whole. Once the man had come into touch with the Great Synthesis, there rushed into his mind innumerable passages of scripture, scraps of myths, fragments of cosmogenesis, logoi and logia, and symbols of all kinds that fitted naturally. These were not any special writer's monopoly, there was no copyright in them, they were all utterances of the same Logos, the Great Instructor of humanity.

Thus the literature that was produced was anonymous or pseudepigraphic. There was first of all a nucleus of personal vision and direct illumination, then a grouping of similar matter from various sources into a whole for didactic purposes. Nor was there any idea among these mystics and scripture-writers that the form once issued should become for ever stereotyped as inerrant; there were many recensions and additions and interpolations. It was left to those without the sense of illumination to stereotype the forms and claim for them the inerrancy of verbal dictation by the Deity. Those who wrote the apocalypses from personal knowledge of vision could not make such claim for their scriptures, for they *knew* how they were written, and what was the nature of hearing and sight.

We have accordingly to treat all such documents as natural human compositions, but while doing so, while on the one side analyzing them with microscopic attention as literary compositions, put together from other sources, over-written, redacted and interpolated, we have also, on the other, to bear in mind that this was not done by clever manipulators and literary charlatans, but by men who regarded such work as a holy and spiritual task, who endeavoured to arrange all under the inspiration of a sweet influence for good, who believed themselves under guidance in their selection of matter, and in recombining the best in other scriptures into a new whole that might prove still better for the purpose of further enlightenment suitable to their immediate environment.

The "Pœmandres" treatise is of this nature—that is to say, though we have not the original form before us, we have what was intended to be read as a single document. We shall accordingly endeavour in our comments not to allow the anomalies of its outer form to detract from our appreciation of its inner spirit, and yet, on the other hand, not to permit the beauty of much that is in it to blind us to the fact that the present form has evolved from simpler beginnings.

THE GREAT AND LITTLE MAN

1. In deep meditation the disciple reaches the consummation of his efforts, and receives initiation from the Master of the masters, who is to confer upon him authority (ἐξουσίαν—see § 32) to teach, that is, to be a master or a Hermes.

2. That this Grand Master of the Inner Mysteries was Man and Shepherd of men, the Very Self of men, has been amply shown in the Prolegomena, but the striking parallelism with the very wording of our text, the Great Man, the "Being more than vast," who tells the little man, that though for the first time he now knows his Greater Self, that Self has ever been "everywhere with thee," is best shown by the beautiful *logos* from the *Gospel of Eve* (presumably an Egyptian gospel), which we have already quoted elsewhere [72]:

"I stood on a lofty mountain, [73] and saw a gigantic Man and another, a dwarf; and I heard, as it were, a voice of thunder, and drew nigh for to hear; and He spake unto me and said: I am thou, and thou art I; and wheresoever thou mayest be, I am there. [74] In all am I scattered, and whencesoever thou willest, thou gatherest Me; and gathering Me, thou gatherest Thyself."

THE PRESENCE

3. The conditions of the seeing of the Holy Sight had been fulfilled by the disciple; he had weaned himself from all lower desires. No longer, like the theurgist in the Hermes-invocations of the popular cult, does he pray for wealth and fame and cheerful countenance, and the rest; his one desire, his only will, is now to "learn the things that are, and comprehend their nature and know God." He craves for Gnosis,—Gnosis of Cosmos and its mysteries, Gnosis of Nature, the Great Mother, and, finally, Gnosis of God, the Father of the worlds. This is the one question he "holds in his mind," his whole nature is concentrated into this one point of interrogation.

It is to be noticed that we are not told, as in the *Gospel of Eve*, that the seer stood, as it were, apart from himself, and saw his little self and Greater Self simultaneously. He is conscious of a Presence, of a Persona in the highest theological meaning of the word, who is not seen so much as felt, speaking to him Mind to mind; he *hears* this Presence rather than *sees* it.

THE VISION OF CREATION

4. The first part of his mental question is: How came this cosmos into being? The answer is the changing of the Boundless Presence into "Light, sweet joyous Light." He loses all sight of "all things" in his mind, the mental image he had formed of cosmos, and is plunged into the infinitude of Limitless Light and Joy, which transports him out of himself in highest ecstasy.

---

[72] From Epiphanius, *Hæres.*, xxvi. 3; see note to the first Hermes-Prayer (i. 11).

[73] Symbolical of a high state of consciousness, the Mount of Perfection.

[74] *Cf.* the Oxyrhynchus *logion* 5: "Jesus saith: Wherever there are [two], they are not without God, and wherever there is one alone, I say, I am with him."

But he has craved for Gnosis, not Joy and Light, but Wisdom, the understanding and reconciliation of the great Opposites, the Cross of all Manifestation.

Therefore must he know the Mystery of Ignorance as well as that of Knowledge. Within the Infinitude of Light appears the Shadow of the Unknown, which translates itself to his consciousness as Darkness,—the Shadow of the Thrice-unknown Darkness, which, as Damascius tells us,[75] was the First Principle of the Egyptians, the Ineffable Mystery, of which they "said nothing," and of which our author says nothing.

This Darkness comes forth from within outwards to the disciple's consciousness, it spreads "downwards" in sinuous folds like a Great Snake, symbolizing, presumably, the unknown, and to him unknowable, mysteries of the differentiation of the root of matter of the cosmos that was to be; its motion was spiral, sinuous, unending vibrations, not yet confined into a sphere; not yet ordered, but chaotic, in unceasing turmoil, a terrible contrast to the sweet peace of the Light, gradually changing from Dark Space or Spirit into a Fluid or Flowing Matter, or Moist Nature; that is, presumably, what the Greek mystics would have called Rhea, the Primal Mother or Matter of the future universe.

It wails and groans—that is, its motion is as yet unharmonized. In the terminology of the Sophia-mythus, it is the inchoate birth from the Sophia Above, in the Fullness, brought forth by herself alone, without her syzygy or consort. On account of its imperfection she wails and groans to the Father of All and His Perfections, that her Perfection may be sent to fashion her child, who is herself in manifestation, into a world of order, and eventually into a Perfection in its turn. [76]

The Primal Undifferentiated or Chaotic Sound, from the Darkness of its first state, gradually manifests itself under the brooding power of the Boundless Light, into less confused thunderings and murmurings, and finally reaches a stage symbolized by a "Cry," a "Voice of Fire," of Fire, not Light, expressing a need and want, longing for union with the Articulate Power or Cosmic Word.

The three most primal stages thus seem to be symbolized by Darkness, Moist Essence, Fire. These were not our differentiated elements, but the Primal Pre-cosmic Elements.

The same idea, though in different forms, is met with in a system of the Gnosis preserved for us by the Old Latin translator of Irenæus, [77] and also by Theodoret, [78] who ascribes it to the Sēthians, whom he says are also called Ophianæ or Ophitæ. Now Sēth was Typhon or Darkness, Dark Light, and

---

[75] See note to the fifth Hermes-Prayer (v. 2).
[76] Cf. *F. F. F.*, 340, 341.
[77] *Hær.*, I. xxx. (Stieren, i. 363 ff.).
[78] *Hær., Fabb.*, i. 14. See *F. F. F.*, pp. 188 ff.

this Sēth may very well have been symbolized as the Great Serpent of Darkness, as it is in our text; hence the name "Those of the Serpent," perhaps given them by their theological adversaries (orthodox Jews and Christians). In this system the Primal Elements are given as Water, Darkness, Abyss, and Chaos. The Light was the Child of the supreme Trinity—the First Man, the Second Man, and the Holy Spirit or First Woman. This Light the Jewish and Christian over-working of the original tradition called the Cosmic Christ.

Thus the Fire of Desire, or Cry of the Darkness, was to be satisfied or checked or quenched by the Light's fashioning its inchoate substance into the cosmos; and so in another Vision, preserved in a treatise of the same type, Hermes sees, by gazing "through the Master," the cosmos in its finished beauty, when all things in it are full of Light and nowhere is there Fire. [79]

THE DESCENT OF THE LOGOS

5. Upon this Cry for Light, into the Heart of the Dark-Moist-Fiery-Nature is dropped a Holy Word, the Seed of the future Cosmos. This Word is Articulate (its Limbs are perfect), Seasonable and Ordering. The Cosmic Animal Nature is impregnated with the Light of the Supernal Reason, which pervades its whole being.[80]

This pervading immediately effects an ordering of the Chaotic Elements into Pure Fire, Pure Air, and Pure Water-Earth. Moreover, it is to be gathered from the sequel that Nature *saw* the Word and all his Beauty in her Fire and Air, but as yet only *heard* him in her Water-Earth.

6. The Shepherd thus explains that Light [81]is really Mind, and Mind is God,—God prior to Nature, but not prior to Darkness. The Unity of Light and Darkness is a still higher Mystery. Light and Mind is the highest concept the disciple can yet form of God. The Light-Word, or emanation of Supernal Reason, is Son of God, Son of Great Mind.

THE REVELATION OF THE PLĒRŌMA

With the words "What then?" Reitzenstein (p. 37) perceives that the sequence of the narrative is broken by a second vision, and is only resumed with § 9. This he regards as an interpolation of another form of cosmogenesis, into the one which is being described.

It seems to me, however, that the breaking of the main narrative may be regarded as a necessary digression rather than as an interpolation of foreign material—necessary in order to bring on to the scene the hitherto invisible

---

[79] "The Mind to Hermes," *C. H.*, xi. (xii.) 6, 7.
[80] That is, the condition "seeing."
[81] That is, the condition "seeing."

Greatnesses, "within" the Veil of Light, which constitute the Economy of the Plērōma. More had to be seen by the disciple before he was in a position to understand what he had so far seen. He must now unite with the Light, his previous seeing being that of its reflection, the logos within him. Not that this logos and Light (or Mind) are separate. They are in reality one, the Son is one with the Father in the state that transcends the opposites. The Logos apparently comes forth, yet it remains ever with the Father, and this coming forth and yet remaining constitutes its Life—in other words, it is an emanation. Thus Hermes is bidden to understand the Light as Life, and so make friends with it.

7. Hitherto the Light had been one for him a sameness which his highest vision could not pierce, the Veil of Light that shut the Beauties, Perfections and Greatnesses of the Intelligible from the eyes of his mind. To pierce this veil a still more expanded power of sight had to be given him by the Master. The little word or light-spark within him is intensified by the Great Word of the Master, this Word being an Intelligible Utterance of the Mind, an intensification of being.

He now sees and understands the countless Powers within the Light, which constitute the Intelligible Archetypal Form or Idea of all worlds. Between the special sensible cosmos of his prior vision and this Immensity was a Mighty Power, or Great Boundary (Horos),[82] that encircled the elements of the sensible cosmos and held its Fire in check.

8. In amazement he asks whence come these apparently disorderly and untamed elements of the new world in process that have to be subdued and separated from the Concord of the Perfection of the Powers? And the answer is that Chaos, too, has its being from God's Will. Discord and Concord, Chaos and Cosmos, are both of God. The Primal Elements are, as it were, the Passions of God's Will desiring Himself. It is Himself as Mother or Spouse desiring Himself as Father. In other of the Trismegistic tractates [83] this "Feminine Aspect" of Deity is called Wisdom and Nature and Generation and Isis. He is Wisdom as desiring Himself,—that Desire being the Primal Cause as Mother of the whole world-process, which is consummated by His Fullness uniting with His Desire or Wisdom, and so perfecting it.

This is the whole burden of the Gnostic Sophia-mythus, which I have given very good reasons for believing derived its main element from Egypt. [84] Curiously enough, Reitzenstein (pp. 39, 40) quotes the two chapters (liii. and liv.) from Plutarch on which I base my conclusions, but he does not notice that in this respect the Christianized Gnosis is distinctly dependent on Egypt.

---

[82] Not Hōrus.
[83] For references, see R. 39, n. 1; also 44.
[84] *Cf.* my note on Plut., *De Is. et Os.*, liv. 6, in the Prolegg.

And so Philo[85] also tells us that the Mother of All is Gnosis (ἐπιστήμη), the very same name that Plutarch gives to Isis.

The Mother, when thought of as without the Plērōma, is impregnated by the Word, which Basilides would have called the All-seed Potency of the Plērōma, endowed with all Powers, and sent forth as the seed of the sensible cosmos that is to be. The Mother in her higher Nature contemplates the Eternal Cosmos or Order of the Plērōma, and in her lower Nature copies its Beauties by means of the permutations and combinations of her elements and the generations and transformations of her lives or souls.

This form of cosmogenesis Reitzenstein (p. 46) regards as of a pantheistic nature, while the general narrative he holds to set forth a world-representation of a dualistic tendency. It is true, as he himself admits, that this blend of contradictory conceptions meets us frequently in Gnostic systems of a more or less contemporary date; nevertheless he lays great stress upon this difference, and so insists upon an interpolation.

In this he is confirmed (p. 39) by the fact that whereas § 9 speaks of God the Mind being male-female, we are in the second vision face to face with "*eine weibliche Allgottheit*" who stands next to the Highest God.

I must, however, confess that these contradictions do not make so great an impression upon my mind as they seem to have done on the critical faculty of Professor Reitzenstein. There is no system known to me, even of the most exclusive monotheism, into which dualism does not creep somehow or other at some stage; it cannot be avoided, for it is in the nature of things.

The dualism of our text is, however, by no means so very marked, for though it is not distinctly stated in § 4, it leaves it clearly to be inferred that the Darkness comes from the Light itself, for previously there was nothing but Light; "all things" had become Light to the eye of the seer. It is the mystery of the sad-eyed Serpent of Darkness wrapping itself round the lower limbs of the Light.

It was, in my opinion, precisely for the sake of removing the thought of dualism that the seer is shown a still more intimate vision within the Light Veil, where all ideas of monotheism, dualism, tritheism, polytheism, and pantheism lose their formal distinctions in a Formless State, or, at any rate, in a State of Being where all are interblended with all. In describing it, the "tongue of flesh" has to use the familiar language of form, but every word employed has a new significance; for even the "tongue of angels" cannot describe it, or any of the "tongues" of heaven; He alone who speaks forth the Words of the One Tongue can express it.

Whence this sublime conception of the Plērōma came, I do not know; it seems to me impossible to find a geographical origin for such things, as, indeed, it seems vain to seek a geographical origin for dualism and the rest.

---

[85] *De Ebriet.*, § 30.

For the writer or writers of our tractate these ideas came from the nature of things, from the immediate experience of sight.

The form of expression, of course, may be susceptible of a geographical treatment, but as yet I am not satisfied that any clear heredity has been made out for this supposed interpolation. The Feminine Divinity, next the Highest God, is not set over against that God, but is His own Will. He is in the Plērōma Vision as much and as little male and female as in the general narrative. He transcends all opposites and contains all opposites in Himself.

What is clear, however, is that in the combination of both visions we have before us a simple and early form of the Gnosis which we meet with later in Christian over-workings, and especially in the very elaborate expositions of the Basilidian and Valentinian schools, the systems of which can, in their main elements, be paralleled and compared point by point with our treatise; but this would be too lengthy a proceeding in our present study, for it would require a volume to itself in any way adequately to treat of it. [86]

THE SECOND EMANATION

9. We now return to the main narrative. Within the World-Egg, which was encircled by the Mighty Power (the Gnostic Horos), there had already been developed three Cosmic Elements (not our mixed elements)—Fire, Air, and Water-Earth. This had been effected by the descent of the Cosmic Logos into the Primal Elements of Disorder. As the Logos descended, Fire and Air ascended, and the Logos remained in Water-Earth. This was the result of the First Outpouring from the Potency of the Plērōma, the First Word uttered by Mind.

The Second Outpouring of Mind was of Mind no longer regarded as Light only, but as Light and Life, Male-Female. This emanation appeared as Enforming Mind—that is, the Fashioner or Former, Artificer or Demiurge of lives or souls; it was the ensouling of the Ordered Elements of Nature with lives, whereby these Elements were drawn together into forms.

The Great Mind, as Light and Life, reflected itself in the "pure formation" of Nature—that is to say, in Fire and Spirit (Air), Fire for Light and Spirit for Life, to further enform things.

The Mighty Power or Self-limitation of Mind, the Boundary that no mortal can pass, marks off the formative area of the whole cosmos. This area, however, was by no means only the mixed sensible world (cosmos) which we perceive with our present physical senses. On the contrary, there are within it various orders (cosmoi) of the main cosmos. For the Ordering Mind, as the Enformer or Soul-fashioner, differentiates itself into seven Ruling Forms or

---

[86] The reader, however, may be referred to the chapters on "The Basilidian Gnosis," "The Valentinian Movement," "Some Outlines of Æonology," and "The Sophia-Mythus," in F. F. F., pp. 253-357.

Spheres which "enclose" the mixed sensible cosmos; these spheres, therefore, must be of a psychic nature—that is to say, of a pure or subtle substance; they are Forms of subtle matter endowed with reason. They constitute the Cosmic Engine of the fashioning of souls, or psychic natures, and of their perpetual transforming. Their energies and activities are those of Fate, or the ordered sequence of cause and effect, symbolized by spheres perpetually entering into themselves.

10. In all the main phases there is to be observed the idea of a downward tendency followed by an upward. The Darkness descends; it then transmutes itself and aspires above in a Cry or Yearning for Light. The Word descends; immediately the Fire and Air ascend. The Formative Mind descends; immediately the Word ascends from the mixed Water-Earth—and at-ones itself with its co-essential emanation from the Father—to a space about the Seven, and thus leaves the still down-tending elements in the Element Water-Earth deprived of its immediate presence, after giving physical matter the initial impulse to order. This physical matter our author calls "pure matter," meaning thereby matter deprived of the immediate presence of Reason.

11. Hereupon from the impulse she has received Nature begins her physical enformation, develops her physical elements and bodies of irrational lives. Water-Earth divides into water and earth, and also air, for this air is clearly something different from the Spirit-Air that ascended; the lower air is one of the downward elements.

THE DESCENT OF MAN

12. When this had been accomplished, there followed a Third Outpouring—the descent of Man, the consummation of the whole Enformation of things, a still more transcendent manifestation of Mind, the One Form that contains all forms, His Very Image coequal with Himself. He finally comes Himself to consummate and save the cosmos in the Form of Man—that is, to gather it to Himself and take it back into the Plērōma.

Nevertheless the Word and the Formative Mind and Man are not three different Persons; they are all co-essential with each other and one with the Father. For the Word is co-essential with the Demiurgic Mind (§ 10), and the latter is Brother of Man (§ 13), and Man is co-equal with God (§ 12).

13. And so Man, the Beloved, descends; and in his descent he is clothed with all the powers of his Brother's creative energy, the creative energy of Life conjoined with rational Light.

Having learned the lesson of the conformations and of the limitations of the Spheres, he desires to break right through the Great Boundary itself; but to do this he must descend still further into matter. Before he can burst through upwards he must break through downwards.

14. Accordingly he breaks through the Spheres downwards, seeking his consort Nature below, and shows her his Divine Form radiant with all the energies bestowed on him by all the Powers above.

And she in her great love wound herself round the image of this Form mirrored upon her water, and the shadow of it thrown upon her earth; just as the Darkness wound itself, like a Great Serpent, round the lower parts of the Light, so does Nature coil herself round the shadow and reflection of Man. Man is above, yet is he below; man is free, yet is he bound—bound willingly in love for her who is himself.

Reitzenstein (pp. 47-49) is greatly puzzled with all this, and seeks to distinguish several contradictory elements, presumably supposing that these elements are woven together into a literary patchwork from distinct traditions. I cannot myself follow him here with any clearness. Of course the writer or writers of our treatise did not discover new ideas or invent new terms; they used what was in their minds and the minds of their circle. It was, however, the weaving of it into a whole, not as a literary exercise, but as a setting forth in the most understandable terms with which they were acquainted of the "things seen," that was their main interest. Those who had the "sight" would understand and appreciate their labours, those who had not would never understand, no matter what terms or what language were used.

When, then, Reitzenstein (p. 47) says that in § 11, in the bringing forth by Nature of irrational lives, there is a confusion of contradictory conceptions, he fails to see that Nature is ever the World-Soul, the spouse of Mind; though Darkness she is spouse of Light. Unaided she brings forth things irrational, a phase of that birth of Nature by herself that is incomplete.

So also in § 13, Reitzenstein detects contradictory elements, which he ascribes to two different regions of ideas. He does not, however, perceive that though in one sentence the "formations" are said to be those of the Father, and in the next those of the Brother, this is no real confusion, because the Formative Mind is the Father, enforming Himself in Himself; this self-energizing, when regarded by itself, may be spoken of as other than the Father, but is not really so.

Nor can I see that there is any real contradiction in the breaking through of the Spheres as though they were the product of an opposing Power to that of the Son. The Fate was certainly so regarded by men who were under its sway; but our treatise is endeavouring precisely to give an insight into the state of things beyond the Fate. The burden of its teaching is that all these oppositions are really illusory; man can transcend these limitations and come into the freedom of the Sons of God. Even the most terrible and fundamental oppositions are not really so, but all are Self-limitations of God's Will; and man is Son of God co-equal with Him.

THE FIRST MEN

16. Our treatise then describes the first appearance of man on earth, which it regards as a great mystery never before revealed, "the mystery kept hid until this day." This I take to mean that it had hitherto never been written about, but had been kept as a great secret.

This secret was the doctrine that the first men, of which there were seven types, were hermaphrodites, and not only so, but lived in the air; their frames were of fire and spirit, and not of the earth-water elements. The Celestial Man, or type of humanity, was gradually differentiating himself from his proper nature of Light and Life, and taking on bodies of fire and air, was changing into mind (Light-fire) and soul (Life-spirit).

This presumably lasted for long periods of time, the lower animal forms gradually evolving to greater complexity as Nature strove to copy the "Form" of Man, and Man devolving gradually until there was a union, and the human subtle form could find vehicles among the highest animal shapes.

The first incarnate men appear to have been at first also hermaphrodite; and it must have been a time when everything was in a far greater state of flux than things are now.

"INCREASE AND MULTIPLY"

18. This period of pre-sexual or bi-sexual development having come to an end, the separation of the sexes took place. The commandment is given by the Word: "Increase ye in increasing and multiply in multitude" (αὐξάνεσθε ἐν αὐξήσει καὶ πληθύνεσθε ἐν πλήθει).

It is true that this is reminiscent of the oft-repeated formula in the Greek Targum of Genesis,—αὐξάνεσθε καὶ πληθύνεσθε, [87]—but it is only slightly reminiscent, the main injunction being strengthened, and the rest of the *logos* being quite different from anything found in Genesis. As nothing else in the whole treatise can be referred to direct Hebrew influence, we must conclude that the formula was, so to speak, in the air, and has so crept into our treatise. [88]

It has, however, given rise to a diatribe copied on to the margin of one MS.—B. (Par. 1220)—by a later hand, and incorporated into the text of M. (Vat. 951). It is in B. ascribed to Psellus,[89] who goes out of his way to stigmatize Hermes as a sorcerer and a plagiarist throughout of Moses; in brief,

---

[87] *Cf.* Gen. i. 22 and 28, viii. 17, ix. 7, and xxxv. 11 (in the singular).
[88] See, however, Frag. XX., and R. 126, n. 1. *Cf.* the same formula in *C. H.*, iii. (iv.) 3 (P. 32, 11), and R. 116, n. 2.
[89] And is printed in Boissonade's (V. C.) edition of Michael Psellus, *De Operatione Dæmonum* (Nürnberg, 1838), pp. 153, 154.

the Devil is a thief of the Truth to lead men astray. In this we learn more about the limitation of the so-called "Prince of Philosophers" [90] than of aught else.

19. This increasing and multiplying, the perpetual coupling of bodies, and the birth of new ones, is effected by the Fate, or Harmony of the Formative Spheres, the Engine of Birth, set under Forethought or Providence (πρόνοια). This Pronoia can be none else than Nature herself as the Wisdom or Knowledge of God—in other words, His Will.

LOVE

The motive power of all is Love. If this Love manifests itself as Desire for things of Matter, the Lover stays in Darkness wandering; if it becomes the Will to know Light, the Lover becomes the Knower of himself, and so eventually at-one with Good.

20. But why should love of body merit Death—that is to say, make man mortal? The disciple attempts an explanation from what he has seen. Although his answer is approved, the meaning is by no means clear.

The physical body, or body in the sense-world, is composed of the Moist Nature, which in a subsequent phase remains as Water-Earth, and in a still subsequent phase divides itself into the elements of physical earth, water, and air. The dissolution of the combination of these elements is effected by Death—that is, Darkness, the Drainer of the Water, the Typhonean Power. Water must thus here symbolize the Osirian Power of fructification and holding together. The Moist Nature then seems to be differentiated from the Darkness by the energizing of Light in its most primitive brooding. But seeing that the Light is also Life, the Darkness, which is posited as the ultimate opposite, is Death.

THE WAY OF DEATHLESSNESS

21. The Way of Deathlessness is then considered. The disciple repeats his lesson, and the Master commends him; the Way Up is the Path of Self-knowledge.

Still the disciple cannot believe that this is for him; he cannot understand that Mind is in him, or rather is himself, in so much as Mind as Teacher seems to be without him. The play is on Mind and mind; the one gives the certitude of Immortality, the other is still bound by the illusion of Death. The disciple has not this certitude; Mind, then, is not his.

---

[90] If, indeed, the Psellus of our scholion is the Younger Psellus (eleventh century); the *De Op. Dæm.*, however, is ascribed by many to the Elder Psellus (ninth century). See, however, the section "The Original MS. of our Corpus" in ch. i. of the "Prolegomena."

22. The Master then further explains the mystery. Gnosis must be preceded by moral purification; there must be a turning-away before the Return can be accomplished. The whole nature must be changed. Yet every effort that the little man seems to make of his own striving is really the energizing of the Great Man.

23. Those, however, who yield themselves to lower desires, drive the Mind away, and their appetites are only the more strengthened by the mind.

The text of this paragraph is very corrupt, so that the exact sense of the original is not recoverable; and this makes it all the more difficult to understand what is meant by the Avenging Daimon, the Counterpart of the Mind. This difficulty is increased by § 24, where we are told that the "way of life" (τὸ ἦθος) is at death surrendered to the Daimon.

If, however, the reader will refer to the section on "The Vision of Er" (in the Miscellanea of the "Prolegomena"), which in my original MS. followed as a Digression on this passage, he will be put in contact with the Platonic view of the Daimon and "way of life"; in our treatise, however, the teaching is of a more intimate character, and must be taken in conjunction with *C. H.*, x. (xi.) 16 and 21, where we shall comment on it at further length.

THE ASCENT OF THE SOUL

24. The subject of instruction is now the Way Above (ἄνοδος), or ascent of the soul out of the body at death.

The physical body is left to the work of change and dissolution. The life of integration and conservation ceases, and the life of disintegration begins.

The form (εἶδος) thus vanishes, apparently from the man's consciousness; that is to say, presumably, he is no longer clothed in the form of his physical body, but is apparently in some other vehicle; the particular fixed form, or "way of life," or "habit," he wore on earth being handed over to the Daimon deprived of all energy, so that apparently it becomes an empty shell.

The next sentence is a great puzzle, and I can only guess at the meaning. The senses which had previously been united by the mind become separate—that is, instead of a whole they become parts (μέρη), they return to the natural animal state of sensation, and the animal part of man, or his vehicle of passion and desire, begins in its turn to disintegrate, the mind or reason (*logos*) being gradually separated from it, or, rather, its true nature showing forth in the man as he gradually strips off the irrational tendencies of the energies.

25. Those irrational tendencies have their sources in the Harmony of the Fate-Sphere of seven subordinate spheres or zones; and in these zones he leaves his inharmonious propensities, deprived of their energy. For the Harmony is only evil apparently; it is really the Engine of Justice and Necessity to readjust the foolish choice of the soul—that is, to purify its irrational

desires, or those propensities in it that are not under the sway of right reason and philosophy. For a better understanding of the characteristics ascribed to the "seven spheres," we must "run off" into another Digression, which the reader will find relegated to ch. xii. of the "Prolegomena," under the title "Concerning the Seven Zones and their Characteristics." This, then, having been taken as a direct commentary on § 25, we continue with the text of our treatise.

THE EIGHTH SPHERE

26. The soul of the initiated strips itself naked of the "garment of shame," the selfish energizings, and stands "clothed in its own power." This refers probably to the stripping off of the "carapace of selfhood," the garments woven by its vices, and the putting on of the "wedding garment" of its virtues.

This state of existence is called the Eighth,[91] a state of comparative "sameness" as transcending the zones of "difference." It is the Ogdoad of the Gnostics, the Jerusalem Above, the plane of the Ego in its own form, the natural state of "those-that-are."

In another sense it may perhaps mean that the man, after passing through the phases of the lower mind, now enters within into the region of the pure mind, the Higher Ego, and there is at-oned with all the experiences of his past lives that are worthy of immortality, his virtuous energizings,—the "those-that-are," that perhaps constitute the "crown of mighty lives" sung of by the Pythian Oracle when celebrating the death of Plotinus.[92]

In this state the man, who has freed himself from the necessity of reincarnation, hears the Song of the Powers above the Ogdoad—that is to say, in Gnostic terms, the Hymn of the Æons of the Plērōma. Such a man would have reached the consummation of his earthly pilgrimage, and be ready to pass on into the Christ-state, or, at any rate, the state of super-man. He would be the Victor who had won the right of investiture with the Robe of Glory, and the dignity of the crowning with the Kingship of the Heavens. This Final Initiation is most beautifully set forth in the opening pages of the *Pistis Sophia*, and especially in the Song of the Powers (pp. 17 ff.) beginning with the words: "Come unto us, for we are thy fellow-members. We are all one with thee."

The consummation of the mystery is that the alter-egos of the Individual Ego, or the sum total of purified personalities which in that state constitute its membership, or *taxis*, of their own selves surrender themselves to a fullness of union or a transcendency of separation, in which they become the powers or energies of a New Man, the true Son of Man; they pass into a state

---

[91] *Cf.* Com. on *C. H.*, xiii. (xiv.) 14.
[92] *Cf.* Porphyry, *Plotini Vita*, xxii., ed. Creuzer (Oxford, 1835); also *Theosoph. Rev.* (July 1898), p. 403.

where they each blend with all, and yet lose nothing of themselves, but rather find in this new union the consummation of all their powers. In this state of Sonship of the Divine they are no longer limited by bodies, nor even by partial souls or individual minds; but, becoming Powers, they are not only *in* God, but one with the Divine Will—nay, in final consummation, God Himself.

27. Of such a nature was the Shepherd; He, too, was the Christ of God, the Son of the Father, who could take all forms to carry out the Divine Will. When the form,—even though that form might for the disciple take on the appearance of the cosmos itself, as he conceived it,—had served its purpose, the Shepherd once more "mingled with the Powers."

THE THREE "BODIES" OF THE BUDDHA

The Shepherd was a Christ for those who prefer the name of Christian Tradition, a Buddha for those who are more familiar with Eastern terms. And that this is so may be clearly seen by considering the so-called "three bodies" (*trikāyam*) of *a* or *the* Buddha, for Buddhahood is a state beyond individuality in the separated sense in which we understand the term.

In the Chinese Version of Ashvaghosha's now lost Sanskrit treatise, *Mahāyāna-shraddhotpāda-shāstra*,[93] we read:

"It is characteristic of all the Buddhas that they consider all sentient beings as their own self, and do not cling to their individual forms. How is this? Because they know truthfully that all sentient beings as well as their own self come from one and the same Suchness, and no distinction can be established among them."

"All Tathāgatas are the Dharinakāya [94]itself, are the highest truth (*paramārthasatya*) itself, and have nothing to do with conditionality (*samvrittisatya*) and compulsory actions; *whereas the seeing, hearing, etc., of the sentient being diversify the Activity* [95] of Tathāgatas.

"Now this Activity has a twofold aspect.

"The first depends on the phenomena-particularizing consciousness *by means of which the Activity is conceived* by the minds of all who fall short of the state of a Bodhisattva in their various degrees. This aspect is called the Body of Transformation (Nirmānakāya).

"But as the beings of this class do not know that the Body of Transformation is merely *the shadow [or reflection] of their own evolving consciousness, they imagine it comes from some external sources, and so they give it a corporeal limitation.* But the Body of Transformation [or what

---

[93] *Ashvaghosha's Discourse on the Awakening of Faith in the Mahāyāna.* Translated for the first time from the Chinese Version by Teitaro Suzuki (Chicago, 1900). Mahāyāna means the "Great Vehicle" of Buddhism.
[94] Lit. Body of the Law.
[95] The italics are mine throughout.

amounts to the same thing, the Dharmakāya] has nothing to do with Limitation or measurement."

That is to say, a Buddha can only communicate with such minds by means of a form, that form being really that of their own most highly evolved consciousness. There are, however, others who have the consciousness of the "formless" state, but have not yet reached the Nirvāṇic Consciousness. These in this system are called Bodhisattvas.

"The second aspect [of the Dharmakāya] depends on the activity-consciousness (*karmavijñāna*), by means of which the Activity is conceived by the minds of the Bodhisattvas while passing from their first aspiration (*chittotpāda*) stage up to the height of Bodhisattva-hood. This is called the Body of Bliss (Sambhogakāya)" (pp. 100, 101).

We have used the term "formless state" in the penultimate paragraph to signify the states of consciousness in "worlds" called Arūpa; but these are only "formless" for consciousness which has not reached the Bodhisattva level—presumably the Buddhic plane of Neo-theosophical nomenclature.

For "this Body has infinite forms. The form has infinite attributes. The Attribute has infinite excellencies. And the accompanying reward of Bodhisattvas—that is, the region where they are predestined to be born—also has infinite merits and ornamentations. Manifesting itself everywhere, the Body of Bliss is infinite, boundless, limitless, unintermittent, directly coming forth from the Mind" (p. 101).

The older Chinese Version says: "It is boundless, cannot be exhausted, is free from the signs of limitation. Manifesting itself wherever it should manifest itself, it always exists by itself and is never destroyed" (p. 101, n. 2).

In other words, one who has reached the Nirvāṇic Consciousness—that is to say, a Master—can teach or be active on "planes" that are as yet unmanifest to us ordinary folk; these "planes," however, even when the disciple is conscious of them, are conditioned by the self-limitation of his own imperfection. The Vehicles of this Activity are called Dharmakāya, Sambhogakāya and Nirmānakāya; and the limitation of their Activity is determined on the side of the disciple by the degree of his ability to function consciously in those states which are known in Neo-theosophical nomenclature respectively as those of Ātman, Buddhi and Higher Manas, or, in more general terms, those of the divine, spiritual and human aspects of the self.

In the first degree of conscious discipleship, then, the Master communicates with His disciples and teaches them by means of the Nirmānakāya; that is to say, He quickens the highest form of consciousness or conception of masterhood they have so far attained to—taking the form of their greatest love, perhaps, as they have known Him in the flesh, or as He has been told of as existing in the flesh, but not His own-form, which would transcend their consciousness.

The next stage is when the disciple learns to transcend his own "egoity," in the ordinary sense of the word; this does not mean to say that his true individuality is destroyed, but instead of being tied down to one ego-vehicle, he has gained the power of manifesting himself wherever and however he will, at any moment of time; in brief, the power of self-generation on the plane of egoity, in that he has reached a higher state which is free from the limitations of a single line of egoity.

He now begins to *realise* in the very nature of his being that the "Self is in all and all in the Self." Such a disciple, or Bodhisattva, is taught by the Master in this state of being, and the Kāya which he supplies for the energizing of his beloved Father is perfectly unintelligible to us, and can only be described as an expanded consciousness of utmost sympathy and compassion, which not only strives to blend with the Life of all beings, but also with the One Being in the world for him, the Beloved. Such a sensing of the Master's Presence is called the Sambhogakāya of the Master, His Body of Bliss.

There is a still higher Perfection, the Dharmakāya, or Own-Nature of Masterhood. But how should the dim mind of one who is Without imagine the condition of One who is not only Within, but who combines both the Without and the Within in the Transcendent Unity of the Perfect Fullness?

THE PREACHING OF THE GNOSIS

27. With the exposition of the Consummation of the Teaching and the return to earth of the consciousness of the Seer, our treatise breaks off into a graphic instruction of how the Gnosis is to be utilized. The Wisdom is no man's property; he who receives it holds it in trust for the benefit of the world-folk.

I am, however, inclined to believe that §§ 27 to 29 are a later interpolation, and that the treatise originally ran straight on after the conclusion of the Shepherd's Instruction with the words: "But I recorded in my heart the Shepherd's benefaction" (§ 30).

Until the end of § 26 we have moved in the atmosphere of an inner intimate personal instruction, set forth in a form evidently intended only for the few; indeed, as we find in other treatises emphatic injunctions to keep the teaching secret, we cannot but conclude that the oldest and most authoritative document of the school was guarded with the same secrecy. The general impression created by the instruction is not only that it itself is the consummation and reward of a strict and stern probation, and not a sermon to be preached on the house-tops, but also that those who followed that way were not propagandists, but rather members of a select philosophic community.

With § 27, however, all is changed; we are introduced to the picture of a man burning with enthusiasm to communicate, if not the direct teaching itself, at any rate the knowledge of its existence and saving power to all without distinction. In a few graphic sentences the history of the fortunes of this propagandist endeavour is sketched. An appeal is made of the most uncompromising nature; it is a clarion call to repentance, and we seem to be moving in an atmosphere that is Hebrew rather than Greek, prophetical rather than philosophical.

It would seem almost that this propagandist phase had been forced upon the community rather than that it was natural to it; something seems to have occurred which obliged it to enter the arena of general life and proclaim its existence publicly. What this compulsion was we have no means of determining with any exactitude, for the historical indications are very obscure. If we were to conjecture that it was the vigorous preaching of nascent Christianity which wrought this change, we should, I think, be taking part for whole, for prior to Christianity there was the most energetic propaganda made by the Jews, the intensity of which may be estimated by the phrase "Ye compass sea and land to make one proselyte," and the nature of which may be most clearly seen in the propaganda of the Sibylline writers, with whose diction the appeals to the "earth-born folk" in our text may be aptly compared, while the prayer at sunset may be paralleled with the prayers of the Essenes and Therapeuts.

On the other hand, the tradition of the Gnosis and Saving Faith preached by our Pœmandrists is distinctly not Hebrew; it is a philosophizing of other materials—materials which, as we have seen, were also partly used by Jewish and Christian mystics, and adapted to their own special traditions.

We thus see that at the time when Christianity came to birth there were many rival traditions contending for general recognition, all of them offering instruction in the Gnosis and hopes of Salvation, and I myself believe that all of them were partial manifestations of the impartial Quickening of the Spiritual Life which was at that time more abundantly poured forth than ever before or after in the Western world.

With § 30, if my conjecture of an interpolation is correct, the original treatise is continued, and we are told the nature of the awakening of the spiritual consciousness which has come to the new-born disciple.

Henceforth all things are new for him, they all have new meanings. He has become a *man*, instead of a "procession of fate"; he has reached the "Plain of Truth." In Christian terms the Christ has been born in his heart consciously.

A HYMN OF PRAISE AND PRAYER FOR THE GNOSIS

31. The treatise is concluded with a most noble hymn, in which the further growth and effort of the *man* in spirit is set forth. Henceforth his effort will be to become like unto the Father Himself, to pass from Sonship into the Perfection of perfection, Identity or At-one-ment with the Father.

The sentence, "That I may give the Light to those in ignorance of the Race, my Brethren and Thy Sons," seems to me to be either an interpolation, showing the same tendency as that of the propagandist section, or an indication that the whole hymn was added at the same time as the propagandist paragraphs, for the treatise proper seems to end naturally and consistently in the Hellenistic form of the tradition with the words, "I reached the Plain of Truth." [96]

THE NAME "POIMANDRES"

Many have already remarked that the name "Poimandres" is formed irregularly in Greek, and this has led to an interesting speculation by Granger, who writes:

"While, however, the name Poimandres does not answer to any Greek original, it is a close transliteration of a Coptic phrase. In the dialect of Upper Egypt $p^e m^e n^e tre$ means 'the witness.' That the Coptic article [p^e] should be treated as part of the name itself is not unusual; compare the name *Pior.* [97] Such a title corresponds very closely in style with the titles of other works of this same period—for example, the *True Word* of Celsus, or the *Perfect Word*, which is an alternative title of the *Asclepius*. The term Poemandres, therefore, on this supposition, contains an allusion to the widely spread legend of Hermes as witness, [98] a legend which is verified for us from several sources. But the writer has adapted the details to his purpose. Hermes is not himself the witness, but the herald of the witness." [99]

Granger then propounds the very strange theory, contradicted by all the phenomena and opposed to every authority, that the Coptic Gnostic works of the Askew and Bruce Codices were originally composed in Coptic with the adoption of Greek technical terms, whereas they are manifestly translations from the Greek. He, however, continues:

"There seems no adequate reason why such works may not have been composed in Coptic. The Egyptian Gnostic writings of the third century exhibit the same qualities of style as the Coptic biographies and apocalypses of the fourth and following centuries. And so I am prepared to believe that the *Poemandres* may have been first composed in Coptic. Or shall we say that the work was current from the first in both languages?" [100]

We should say that the last guess is most highly improbable, and only denotes the indecision of the writer. The *original* "Pœmandres" may very

---

[96] It is to be noticed that the Hymn is a Song of Holiness. "Holy art thou" is nine times repeated—most probably intentionally. This was noticed long ago by Casaubon. See R. 58, n. 3.
[97] Palladius, *Hist. Laus.*, 89.
[98] G. has just referred to the story of Hermes being witness for Horus when indicted on a charge of bastardy by Typhon, as related in Plutarch.
[99] Granger (F.), "The Poemandres of Hermes Trismegistus," *J. Th. Stud.*, vol. v., no. 191, p. 400.
[100] *Ibid.*, p. 401.

well have been composed not in Coptic but in Demotic; but the reasons given by Granger, as based on the phenomena of the Gnostic Coptic writings, are not to be seriously considered. Nevertheless, the *name* "Poimandres" may be a Greek transliteration of an Egyptian name, though we hardly think that "The Witness" will suit the theme. In any case "Man-Shepherd" was certainly the *idea* conveyed to the Non-Egyptian by the name, however philologically unsound its form may be in Greek.

THE GOOD SHEPHERD

It has been no part of our task to attempt to trace the Hermes-idea along the line of pure Greek descent, for this would have led us too far from our immediate subject. There is, however, one element of that tradition which is of great interest, and to which we may draw the attention of the reader in passing. The beautiful idea of the Christ as the "Good Shepherd" is familiar to every Christian child. Why the Christ is the Shepherd of all men is shown us by this first of our marvellous treatises. In it we have the universal doctrine apart from any historical dogma, the eternal truth of an ever-recurring fact, and not the exaggeration of one instance of it.

The representation of Christ as the Good Shepherd was one of the earliest efforts of Christian art; but the prototype was far earlier than Christianity—in fact, it was exceedingly archaic. Statues of Hermes Kriophoros, or Hermes with a ram or lamb standing beside him, or in his arms, or on his shoulder, were one of the most favourite subjects for the chisel in Greece. We have specimens dating to the archaic period of Greek art.[101] Hermes in these archaic statues has a pointed cap, and not the winged head-dress and sandals of later art. This type in all probability goes back to Chaldæan symbolic art, to the bearers of the twelve "signs of the zodiac," the "sacred animals." These were, in one human correspondence, the twelve septs or classes of priests. Here we see that the Greek tradition itself was not pure Āryan even in its so-called archaic period. Chaldæa had given of her wisdom to post-diluvian Greece, even as she had perchance been in relation with Greece before the "flood." Here, then, we have another element in the Hermes-idea. In fact, nowhere do we find a pure line of tradition; in every religion there are blendings and have been blendings. There was unconscious syncretism (and conscious also) long before the days of Alexandria, for unconscious syncretism is as old as race-blendings. Even as all men are kin, so are popular cults related; and even as the religion of nobler souls is of one paternity, so are the theosophies of all religions from one source.

One of the greatest secrets of the innermost initiated circles was the grand fact that all the great religions had their roots in one mother soil. And it

---

[101] See Reseller's *Lexikon*, art. "Hermes." "Hermes in der Kunst"—"Periode des Archaïsmus."

was the spreading of the consciousness of this stupendous truth which subsequently—after the initial period of scepticism of the Alexandrian schools—gave rise to the many conscious attempts to synthesise the various phases of religion, and make "symphonies" of apparently contradictory philosophical tenets. Modern research, which is essentially critical and analytical, and rarely synthetical, classifies all these attempts under the term "syncretism," a word which it invariably uses in a depreciatory sense, as characterising the blending of absolutely incompatible elements in the most uncritical fashion. But when the pendulum swings once more towards the side of synthesis, as it must do in the coming years—for we are but repeating to-day in greater detail what happened in the early centuries—then scholarship will once more recognise the unity of religion under the diversity of creeds and return to the old doctrine of the mysteries.

In connection with the "Good Shepherd" glyph, it will be useful to quote from Granger's instructive exposition on the subject, [102] where he writes:

"Since the identification of Jesus with Hermes took place in circles which formed part of the Christian community, [103] we shall not be surprised to find that one of the leading types of Christian art, the Good Shepherd, was immediately adopted from a current representation of the Greek Hermes. [104] As we see from Hippolytus (*Refut.*, v. 7), the Gnostics were especially interested in Hermes as Hermes Logius, a type which was increasingly frequent in later Greek art. And this epithet was connected by them with the conception of Jesus as the Logos. Now another type of Hermes, the Kriophoros, seemed to bring together Jesus as the Logos and Jesus as the Good Shepherd. These representations of Jesus begin in the second century; and so they correspond in order of time with the appearance of the *Gospel according to the Egyptians*, and of those Gnostic compositions which largely depend upon it. [105]

"Another fact leads us to think that the figure of the Good Shepherd had its roots in a previous tradition. 'It is probable that there were no statues before the age of Constantine, except the Good Shepherd.' [106] We must therefore add Hermes to the list of pagan types which were taken over for its own purpose by the rising Christian art.

---

[102] *Op. cit.*, pp. 408 ff.
[103] G. seems here to be referring to the Naassene Document, but without any suspicion apparently of its composite character.
[104] See Sittl, *Klassische Kunstarchäologie*, 777, 809, 819.
[105] G. here again refers apparently to the Naassene Documents, which, however, did *not* depend on the *Gospel according to the Egyptians*, as we have shown; nor have we any sure ground for dating this widespread mystic gospel of Egypt as being of the second century rather than of the first. G. (p. 411) suggests that the scene of the *Gospel of the Egyptians* was on top of the Mount of Olives after the resurrection, which may very well be the case, and that the title of *C. H.*, xiii. (xiv.), "The Secret Sermon on the Mountain," has reference to this gospel, which is by no means probable, for our sermon keeps entirely within its own tradition in its setting.
[106] Lowrie, *Christian Art and Archæology*, p. 290.

"Moreover, we are enabled to advance one step further the long-standing controversy as to the portraits of Jesus. Since the figure of the Good Shepherd is borrowed from Greek sculpture, it cannot be used as evidence for the earliest conceptions about the appearance of Jesus. And so the arguments of Farrar and others fall to the ground, in so far as they take the presence of this type to show that there was no genuine tradition of Christ's appearance.[107]

"We are now in a position to throw a little further light upon the famous inscription of Abercius. The inscription speaks of a Shepherd—'Who feedeth on the plains His flock of sheep, and hath great eyes that gaze forth every way. For He did teach me [how to understand and] scriptures worthy to believe.'[108]

"The Shepherd, whose great eyes look in every direction, is no other than Hermes treated as a symbol of Christ. And so some of the arguments which may be directed against the Christian character of this inscription, and to which Harnack [109] attaches an exaggerated weight, are turned aside."

With all of this may be compared what we have already written in the Prolegomena on "The Popular Symbolic Representation of the Shepherd" in the chapter on "'Hermas' and 'Hermes.'"

Compare also the Hymn to Attis in the Naassene tradition, where he is invoked "as Pan, as Bacchus, as Shepherd of bright stars." This is the macrocosmic side of the microcosmic mystery.

We should also not forget the interesting grouping on a Christian lamp [110] and gem, [111] which goes back very probably to the third century. [112] It represents the Christ as the Good Shepherd, after the Hermes type, with a lamb on his shoulder. Above his head are the Seven "Planets," the Lords of the Fate, and in addition the Sun and Moon on either side, as is frequently the case in Mithraic representations. Round his feet seven lambs [113] crowd, symbolical of the "seven peoples," one under each "planet." Moreover, on the right is Noah's dove and ark, and Jonah being swallowed by the whale, while on the left is Jonah again, vomited on to the land and peacefully resting beneath the shade of the miraculous gourd-tree.

This seems to me to be a symbol of the mysteries, a glyph of rebirth. The lambs are the purified lower nature of the man, the purest essence of which is exalted to the head of the Great Man. This purified "little man" is swallowed by the Cosmic Fish, the Great Mother, the Womb of the Almighty,

---

[107] Taken in connection with the above quotation from Lowrie, we should say that it disposes of the whole contention. And for further corroboration of this view we would refer the reader to the *Acts of John*.

[108] G. gives the Greek text only, omitting the first line, which runs: "The disciple of the Pure Shepherd." Cf. R. 115.

[109] Cf. *Class. Rev.*, ix. 297.

[110] Garucci, *Storia della Arte christiana*, vi. tav. 474; Perret, *Catacombes de Rome*, tab. 17, no. 5.

[111] Perret, *ibid.*, tab. 16, no. 80

[112] R. 113.

[113] The gem has only six.

and the man is born again to rest under his own tree in the Paradise of the Further Shore.

It is also of interest to note that the Hermetic colonies already planted in Mesopotamia, in the earliest Islāmic times of which the Arabian writers tell us, called their head the "Shepherd." [114]

From all of which we conclude that the Good Shepherd was one of the leading ideas of Hellenistic theology.

---

[114] *Cf.* Chwolsohn (D.), *Die Ssabier und der Ssabismus*, ii. 628. *Cf.* R. 166 ff.

CORPUS HERMETICUM (II.)

THE GENERAL SERMON

(THE title only is preserved in our Corpus, the text having disappeared with the loss of a quire or quires before the parent copy came into the hands of Psellus.)

CORPUS HERMETICUM II. (III.)

TO ASCLEPIUS

(Text: P. 19-30; Pat. 18b-20.)

✻   ✻   ✻   ✻   ✻

1. *Hermes.* [115] All that is moved, Asclepius, is it not moved *in* something and *by* something?

Asclepius. Assuredly.

Her. And must not that in which it's moved be greater than the moved?

Asc. It must.

Her. Mover, again, has greater power than moved?

Asc. It has, of course.

Her. The nature, furthermore, of that in which it's moved must be quite other from the nature of the moved?

Asc. It must completely.

2. *Her.* Is not, again, this cosmos vast, [so vast] that than it there exists no body greater?

Asc. Assuredly.

Her. And massive too, for it is crammed with multitudes of other mighty frames, nay rather all the other bodies that there are?

Asc. It is.

Her. And yet the cosmos is a body?

Asc. It is a body.

Her. And one that's moved?

3. *Asc.* Assuredly.

Her. Of what size, then, must be the space in which it's moved; and of what kind [must be] the nature [of that space]? Must it not be far vaster [than the cosmos], in order that it may be able to find room for its continued course, so that the moved may not be cramped for want of room and lose its motion?

Asc. Something, Thrice-greatest one, it needs must be, immensely vast.

4. *Her.* And of what nature? Must it not be, Asclepius, of just the contrary? And is not contrary to body bodiless?

---

[115] From here till the end of § 4 is quoted by Stobæus, *Phys.*, xviii. 2; G. pp. 147-149; W. 157, 6 ff.

Asc. Agreed.

Her. Space, then, is bodiless. But bodiless must either be some godlike thing or God [Himself]. And by "some godlike thing" I mean no more the generable but the ingenerable. [116]

5. If, then, space be some godlike thing, it is substantial [117]; but if 'tis God [Himself], it transcends substance. But it is to be thought of otherwise [than God], and in this way.

God is first "thinkable" [118] for us, not for Himself, for that the thing that's thought doth fall beneath the thinker's sense. God then can not be "thinkable" unto Himself, in that He's thought of by Himself as being nothing else than what He thinks. But He is "something else" for us, and so He's thought of by us.

6. If space is, therefore, to be thought, [it should] not, [then, be thought as] God, but space. If God is also to be thought, [He should] not [be conceived] as space, but energy that can contain [all space].

Further, [119] all that is moved is moved not in the moved but in the stable. And that which moves [another] is of course stationary, for 'tis impossible that it should move with it.

Asc. How is it, then, that things down here, Thrice-greatest one, are moved *with* those that are [already] moved? For thou hast said [120] the errant spheres were moved by the inerrant one.

Her. This is not, O Asclepius, a moving *with*, but one *against*; they are not moved *with* one another, but one *against* the other. It is this contrariety which turneth the resistance of their motion into rest. For that resistance is the rest of motion.

7. Hence, too, the errant spheres, being moved contrarily to the inerrant one, are moved by one another by mutual contrariety, [and also] by the stable one through contrariety itself. And this can otherwise not be.

The Bears [121] up there, which neither set nor rise, think'st thou they rest or move?

Asc. They move, Thrice-greatest one.

Her. And what their motion, my Asclepius?

Asc. Motion that turns for ever round the same.

Her. But revolution—motion round same—is fixed by rest. For "round-the-same" doth stop "beyond-same." "Beyond-same" then, being stopped, if it be steadied in "round-same"—the contrary stands firm, being rendered ever stable by its contrariety.

---

[116] That is, beyond genesis, the universe of becoming, or the sensible universe.
[117] οὐσιωδές.
[118] Or intelligible.
[119] From here till the end of § 9 (exclusive of the last sentence) is quoted by Stobæus, *Phys.*, xix. 2; G. pp. 154-157; W. 163, 14 ff.
[120] *Sc.* in some previous sermon.
[121] *Sc.* Ursa Major and Ursa Minor.

8. Of this I'll give thee here on earth an instance, which the eye can see. Regard the animals down here,—a man, for instance, swimming! The water moves, yet the resistance of his hands and feet give him stability, so that he is not borne along with it, nor sunk thereby.

Asc. Thou hast, Thrice-greatest one, adduced a most clear instance.

Her. All motion, then, is caused in station and by station.

The motion, therefore, of the cosmos (and of every other hylic animal[122]) will not be caused by things exterior to the cosmos, but by things interior [outward] to the exterior—such [things] as soul, or spirit, or some such other thing incorporal.

'Tis not its body that doth move the living thing in it; nay, not even the whole [body of the universe a lesser] body e'en though there be no life in it. [123]

9. *Asc.* What meanest thou by this, Thrice-greatest one? Is it not bodies, then, that move the stock and stone and all the other things inanimate?

Her. By no means, O Asclepius. The something-in-the-body, the that-which-moves the thing inanimate, this surely's not a body, for that it moves the two of them—both body of the lifter and the lifted? So that a thing that's lifeless will not move a lifeless thing. That which doth move [another thing] is animate, in that it is the mover.

Thou seest, then, how heavy laden is the soul, for it alone doth lift two bodies. That things, moreover, moved are moved *in* something as well as moved *by* something is clear.

10. *Asc.* Yea, [124] O Thrice-greatest one, things moved must needs be moved in something void. [125]

Her. Thou sayest well, O [my] Asclepius! [126] For naught of things that are is void. Alone the "is-not" 's void [and] stranger to subsistence. For that which is subsistent can never change to void.

Asc. Are there, then, O Thrice-greatest one, no such things as an empty cask, for instance, and an empty jar, a cup and vat, and other things like unto them?

Her. Alack, Asclepius, for thy far-wandering from the truth! Think'st thou that things most full and most replete are void?

11. *Asc.* How meanest thou, Thrice-greatest one?

Her. Is not air body?

---

[122] That is, living material organism.

[123] The variant in Stobæus reads: "No single thing of things that are is void by reason of the [very nature of] subsistence. The 'is' could not be 'is' were it not *full* of subsistence [itself]." The rest of the variants need not be noted in translation.

[124] For a criticism of Parthey's text of the following three paragraphs, see R., pp. 209, 300. Parthey had uncritically conflated the text of our Corpus and the readings of Stobæus, in ignorance that he had before him two different recensions of the same text. I follow Reitzenstein.

[125] *Cf. P. S. A.*, xxxiii. 1.

[126] From here to the end of § 12 is quoted by Stobæus, *Phys.*, xviii. 3; G. pp. 149-150; W. 158, 13 ff.

Asc. It is.

Her. And doth this body not pervade all things, and so, pervading, fill them? And "body"; doth body not consist from blending of the "four"? Full, then, of air are all thou callest void; and if of air, then of the "four." [127]

Further, of this the converse follows, that all thou callest full are void—of air; for that they have their space filled out with other bodies, and, therefore, are not able to receive the air therein. These, then, which thou dost say are void, they should be hollow named, not void; for they not only are, but they are full of air and spirit.

12. *Asc.* Thy argument (*logos*), Thrice-greatest one, is not to be gainsaid; air is a body. Further, it is this body which doth pervade all things, and so, pervading, fill them. What are we, then, to call that space in which the all doth move?

Her. The Bodiless, Asclepius.

Asc. What, then, is Bodiless?

Her. 'Tis Mind and Reason (*Logos*), whole out of whole, all self-embracing, free from all body, from all error free, unsensible to body and untouchable, self stayed in self, containing all, preserving those that are, whose rays, to use a likeness, are Good, Truth, Light beyond light, the Archetype of soul.

Asc. What, then, is God?

13. *Her.* Not any one of these is He; for He it is that causeth them to *be*, both all and each and every thing of all that are. Nor hath He left a thing beside that is-not; but they are all from things-that-are and not from things-that-are-not. For that the things-that-are-not have naturally no power of being anything, but rather have the nature of the inability-to-be. And, conversely, the things-that-are have not the nature of some time not-being.

14. *Asc.* What say'st thou ever, then, God is?

Her. God, therefore, is not Mind, but Cause that the Mind is; God is not Spirit, but Cause that Spirit is; God is not Light, but Cause that the Light is. Hence should one honour God with these two names [the Good and Father]—names which pertain to Him alone and no one else.

For no one of the other so-called gods, no one of men, or daimones, can be in any measure Good, but God alone; and *He* is Good alone and nothing else. The rest of things are separable all from the Good's nature; for [all the rest] are soul and body, which have no space that can contain [128] the Good.

---

[127] The physical elements—earth, air, water and fire—were supposed to be severally combinations of the Primal Elements, Earth, Air, Water and Fire, one Element dominating in each. Thus our air would consist of a proportion of all four Great Elements, but would have Air predominant in it; and so for the rest.

[128] In the original there is a word-play—χωριστά (separable) and χωρῆσαι (contain)—which is impossible to reproduce in translation.

15. For that as mighty is the Greatness of the Good as is the Being of all things that are—both bodies and things bodiless, things sensible and intelligible things. Call not thou, therefore, aught else Good, for thou would'st impious be; nor anything at all at any time call God but Good alone, for so thou would'st again be impious.

16. Though, then, the Good is spoken of by all, it is not understood by all, what thing it is. Not only, then, is God not understood by all, but both unto the gods and some of men they out of ignorance do give the name of Good, though they can never either be or become Good. For they are very different from God, while Good can never be distinguished from Him, for that God is the same as Good.

The rest of the immortal ones are natheless honoured with the name of God, and spoken of as gods; but God is Good not out of courtesy but out of nature. For that God's nature and the Good is one; one is the kind of both, from which all other kinds [proceed].

The Good is He who gives all things and naught receives. [129] God, then, doth give all things and receive naught. God, then, is Good, and Good is God.

17. The other name of God is Father, again because He is the that-which-maketh all. The part of father is to make.

Wherefore child-making is a very great and a most pious thing in life for them who think aright, and to leave life on earth without a child a very great misfortune and impiety; and he who hath no child is punished by the daimons after death.

And this the punishment: that that man's soul who hath no child, shall be condemned unto a body with neither man's nor woman's nature, a thing accurst beneath the sun.

Wherefore, Asclepius, let not your sympathies be with the man who hath no child, but rather pity his mishap, knowing what punishment abides for him.

Let all that has been said, then, be to thee, Asclepius, an introduction to the gnosis of the nature of all things.

---

[129] *Cf. C. H.*, x. (xi.) 3: 'Tis "He alone who taketh naught."

COMMENTARY

"AN INTRODUCTION TO THE GNOSIS OF THE NATURE OF ALL THINGS"

This treatise has no precise title, for, as we have already seen in treating of the make-up of the Corpus, the traditional title, "Of Hermes to Tat, the General Sermon," found in all the MSS., cannot apply to our tractate, which is addressed to Asclepius, and from which Stobæus quotes under the general title, "Of Hermes, from the [Sermons] to Asclepius."

The supposition, however, that Sermon (II.) has dropped out from the parent copy of our Corpus, owing to the loss of one or more quires or quaternions, explains those phenomena so admirably, that it has only to be brought forward, as it has been by Reitzenstein, to carry conviction.

It is a curious fact, however, that Stobæus starts his quotations from this treatise precisely with the same words with which our text begins; nevertheless these words plunge us so immediately into a secondary subject, that Reitzenstein thinks there may have been a more general introduction which Johannes may very well have omitted.

That, however, the lost pages of our Corpus should have contained such an introduction, broken at precisely the very same point to a word, would seem to be a coincidence the reverse of probable; nevertheless the treatise itself purports to be a very formal one, for we learn from the concluding words (§ 17) that it was intended to be "An Introduction to the Gnosis (πρoγνωσία) of the Nature of All Things."

We are, therefore, driven to conclude that, in spite of a most improbable coincidence, the beginning may have been lost, and that we have therefore to regret the loss not only of the whole of the "General Sermon" to Tat, but also of the introduction to the "Introduction to the Gnosis" addressed to Asclepius, and therewith, in all probability, some precious indications of how "Tat" and "Asclepius" are to be precisely defined.

Parthey's conflated title (p. 19) from the MSS., and Stobæus, "Of Hermes the Thrice-greatest, the General Sermon to Asclepius," must therefore be definitely abandoned, and, in lieu of the lost general title, we must be content with the simple heading, "To Asclepius."

SPACE IS A PLENUM

The subject is that of the Fullness of Being or the Plenum of things. Space is a Plenum,—the fundamental concept of modern scientific speculation.

Asclepius, however, must guard himself against the confusion of Space with God; for God is not Space, but Cause thereof,—the True Transcendency of "that which can contain all things" (§ 6).

"In Him we move." "All that is moved is moved in what is stable," or "in Him who stands" (ἐν ἑστῶτι); where it is to be noticed that the term, "He who stands," is found in Philo, and is made much of in Gnostic tradition, especially in the so-called Simonian Gnosis, for in *The Great Announcement*, from which Hippolytus has preserved some passages, the Logos is called "He who stands" or "He who has stood, stands and will stand." [130] This is the aspect of the Reason of things that holds and compacts all together, the Stock or Pillar of Immobility, the opposite aspect being that of the Separator or Divider; the two together forming the Cross of Manifestation, the resolution of the Sphere of Sameness.

The World-Soul is in perpetual motion; this perpetual motion is ordered and reduced to a cosmos and harmony of motion by the introduction into it, by means of the Reason, of the root-forms of motion (mentioned in the *Timæus* and elsewhere);—up, down; right, left; front, back; in, out; round,—and no-motion.

All bodies are essentially inert; it is the soul that moves them, either immediately or mediately (§ 9).

What the precise meaning of § 10 may be I cannot say; the tradition of the original text was variable, showing that the copyists had difficulty with it. As, however, the doctrine throughout is that of a Plenum (as, indeed, it is elsewhere in the Trismegistic writings), I can only suppose that the instructor of "Asclepius" was endeavouring to clinch his point by arguing that the only Void was the "is-not" or non-being; now as nonbeing cannot possibly "exist," there can *be* no such thing as Void.

THE SPOUSE OF DEITY

That, then, in which "the All doth move," in which all things "live and move and have their being," is the Bodiless; in other words, the Mind or Reason of God, the Logos,—who, as Philo tells us, is the Place of God,—that is, Infinite Space itself, the Container of all things, the very Spouse of Deity. Spouse or Son, it matters not; that in which all moves and lives and breathes is Wisdom, Good and Truth, the Æon of æons, Light of light, Life of life, the Archetype of Soul itself (§ 12).

GOD IS CAUSE THAT SPIRIT IS

"God, then, is not Spirit," [131] much less "a spirit," [132] "but Cause that Spirit is"; for God is "Good alone." Therefore: "Call not thou aught else Good."

---

[130] R., p. 305, also makes a brief reference to this.
[131] *Cf.* Joh. iv. 24: "πνεῦμα ὁ Θεός."

And now let us turn to F. C. Conybeare's important criticism of Matt. xix. 17 = Mk. x. 18 = Lk. xviii. 19, in the first number of *The Hibbert Journal*, [133] where he brings forward very strong evidence that the original reading was: "Call thou me not Good; One only is Good, God the Father,"—a reading known to Marcion, the *Clementine Homilies*, Athanasius, Didymus, Tatian, and Origen (the two last inferentially).

If we compare this with our text, "Call not thou, therefore, aught else Good, for thou would'st impious be; nor any thing at all at any time call Good but God alone," and "He is Good alone and nothing else,"—we cannot fail to be struck with the precise similarity of the phrasing and blend of ideas.

If, further, we take this in connection with the still more striking contrast, "God is not Spirit," with the Johannine "God is Spirit," we might at first sight almost persuade ourselves that our treatise had these Christian declarations immediately in mind. But the general phenomena of similarity of diction and idea of the Trismegistic literature with those of the New Testament documents is so much more satisfactorily explained by the fact that both literatures use mainly the common Hellenistic theological phrases of the time, that we need not distress ourselves with any suggestions either of plagiarism or of direct controversy.

Doubtless the declaration, "God is Spirit," was a commonplace among the religio-philosophical circles of the time, and Hermes is here simply refining on a common idea. The reading, "Call thou not me Good," which appears to have been preserved mainly in Gnostic tradition, may also as easily have come from a similar general idea that the One and Only One was Good alone.

It is, moreover, of special interest to notice that the second clause of the Marcionite reading runs: "There is one [only] Good, God the Father," while in our treatise the two names of God are given as Good and Father; and so we read (§ 16): "God, then, is Good, and Good is God"; and immediately after (§ 17): "The other name of God is Father." [134]

Striking however, as are those coincidences, we are nevertheless wholly unpersuaded that there was any immediate literary contact between those two sets of Scripture. All that can be said is that their literary similarities are due to a common theological language and their many points of contact in ideas to a generally common atmosphere of theological conceptions.

---

[132] As the A.V. has it erroneously.
[133] See his article, "Three Early Doctrinal Modifications of the Text of the Gospels," in *The Hibbert Journal* (Oct. 1902), pp. 98-113. J. R. Wilkinson's few remarks (*H. J.*, Ap. 1903, pp. 575, 576) on Conybeare's criticism of this synoptic passage do not seem to me to be of any weight.
[134] *Cf.* the expression, "God, Father and the Good," *C. H.*, x. (xi.) 1.

HE WHO IS WITHOUT A WIFE IS HALF A MAN

Again, the doctrine of the duty to beget children (§ 17) seems at first sight to be an interpolation by a Jewish editor, the Jews holding that "he who is without a wife is half a man." We must, however, remember that the Egyptian priests were married, and that the rule with them, as with the Pythagoreans, was that a man should first of all discharge his duty to society and live the "practical," "political" or "social" life, before retiring into the life of contemplation. He must first beget children, not only that the race might be continued, but also that bodies might be supplied by parents devoted to the ideal of the religious or philosophic life, so that advanced souls might find birth in favourable conditions, and so the Order be continued.

This also is the ancient rule laid down by the Manu of the Āryan Hindus in the *Mānava Dharma Shāstra*. The duties of the householder station of life (Gṛihastha āshrama) must first be performed, before the parents can retire to the contemplative life (Vānaprastha āshrama). In special cases, however, exceptions could be made.

It may then be that Asclepius stands for those pupils who were still living the married life.

The scribe of the thirteenth century, Codex B. (Parisinus, 1220), has laconically written on the margin of this paragraph the single word "nonsense" (φλυαρία); he was presumably a monk.

CORPUS HERMETICUM III. (IV.)

THE SACRED SERMON
OF HERMES

(Text: P. 31-33; Pat. 8b-9.)

1. THE Glory of all things is God, Godhead and Godly Nature. Source of the things that are is God, who is both Mind and Nature,—yea Matter, the Wisdom that reveals all things. Source [too] is Godhead,—yea Nature, Energy, Necessity, and End, and Making-new-again. [135]

Darkness that knew no bounds was in Abyss, and Water [too] and subtle Breath intelligent; these were by Power of God in Chaos.

Then Holy Light arose; and there collected 'neath Dry Space [136] from out Moist Essence Elements; and all the Gods do separate things out from fecund Nature.

2. All things being undefined and yet unwrought, the light things were assigned unto the height, the heavy ones had their foundations laid down underneath the moist part of Dry Space, [137] the universal things being bounded off by Fire and hanged in Breath to keep them up.

And [138] Heaven was seen in seven circles; its Gods were visible in forms of stars with all their signs; while Nature had her members made articulate together with the Gods in her. And [Heaven's] periphery revolved in cyclic course, borne on by Breath of God.

3. And every God by his own proper power brought forth what was appointed him. Thus there arose four-footed beasts, and creeping things, and those that in the water dwell, and things with wings, and everything that beareth seed, and grass, and shoot of every flower, all having in themselves seed of again-becoming. [139]

And they selected out [140] the births [141] of men for gnosis of the works of God and attestation of the energy of Nature; the multitude of men for

---

[135] Cf. P. S. A., xxvi 2.
[136] Lit. "Sand"; this presumably refers to the Light, and would thus mean "within the area or sphere of Light"—that is to say, manifestation. The "Moist Essence" is apparently the Water of Chaos, or primal substance.
[137] ὑφ' ὑγρᾷ ἄμμῳ; presumably the "Water" of space. The heavy things are apparently primæval or cosmic "Earth."
[138] The emended text from here to the end of the first sentence of § 3 is given by R. 47, n. 1.
[139] Or "reincarnation" (παλιγγενεσίας).
[140] ἐσπερμολόγουν.
[141] τὰς γενέσεις.

lordship over all beneath the Heaven and gnosis of its blessings, that they might increase in increasing and multiply in multitude, and every soul infleshed by revolution of the Cyclic Gods, for observation of the marvels of the Heaven and Heaven's Gods' revolution, and of the works of God and energy of Nature, for tokens of its blessings, for gnosis of the power of God, that they might know the fates that follow good and evil [deeds] and learn the cunning work of all good arts.

4. [Thus] there begins their living and their growing wise, according to the fate appointed by the revolution of the Cyclic Gods, and their deceasing for this end.

And there shall be memorials mighty of their handiworks upon the earth, leaving dim trace behind when cycles are renewed.

For every birth of flesh ensouled, and of the fruit of seed, and every handiwork, though it decay, shall of necessity renew itself, both by the renovation of the Gods and by the turning-round of Nature's rhythmic wheel.

For that whereas the Godhead is Nature's ever-making-new-again the cosmic mixture, Nature herself is also co-established in that Godhead.

COMMENTARY

TEXT AND TITLE

The text seems to be very corrupt, and at one time I thought it incomplete; but it may very well end with the reference to the mighty deeds of the men of old.

The title "Sacred Sermon" would lead us to expect something of a special nature, something that would constitute a basis of doctrine. For we hear of the "Sacred Sermon" of Orpheus, and of the "Sacred Sermon" of Pythagoras, and are told that they formed the most sacred deposits of these two mystic schools respectively, and were regarded with special reverence; they thus seem to have been looked upon in some fashion as containing the groundwork of these systems.

And this is precisely what we find with our treatise; it is to a large extent a summary of the general ideas of the "Shepherd" cosmogony adapted to the needs of a simpler formularization.

When, however, Reitzenstein (p. 193) refers to this treatise cursorily as the preaching of some prophet or other which has been transferred to Hermes by the Redactor of our Corpus, he suggests that we are dealing with a doctrine foreign to the cosmogonical ideas of the "Shepherd." It is, indeed, true that if we compare the *data* of the two treatises together, detail by detail, we shall find strong contradictions; but the general "feel" of both is the same, the general atmosphere is identical.

THE TRINITY

Prefixed to the cosmogenesis is a formal theological proœm, the precise meaning of which escapes me because of its almost mnemonic nature; it is, indeed quite in *sūtra* style. There appears, however, to be a distinct trinitarian [142] idea lurking in the first sentence, the trinity consisting of God (ὁ Θεός) and Godhead (τὸ θεῖον) and Nature (ἡ φύσις). The Glory or Power of all things is this Divine Trinity. The Source (or Beginning), the End and the Ever-renewing of all things are owing to this Triad. All three seem to be almost interchangeable terms. The Godhead is the Mind of God, Godly Nature is the Wisdom of God. Again, at the end of the sermon (§ 4) we are told that the Godhead (or that which is Divine) is "Nature's ever-making-new-again the cosmic mixture." Godhead in operation is Nature, while at the same time Nature is co-established in Godhead, and both are one in God, the Source of all.

---

[142] Not, of course, in a technical Christian sense.

The cosmogenesis begins with the grandiose image: "Darkness that knew no bounds was in Abyss."

We have already, in commenting on "Darkness" in the "Pœmandres" treatise, referred, in explanation, to a Gnostic tradition in which the Primal Elements appear as Water, Darkness, Abyss, and Chaos, and have given some reason for ascribing the form of this tradition to Egypt—that is, Archaic Egypt, a parallel tradition to the Sumerian, both derived from a still more Archaic source.

FROM THE SYSTEM OF THE NICOLAÏTANS

If, now, we turn to Epiphanius (remembering that he picked up what he knew or thought he knew about the Gnostics in Egypt), we shall find that he has preserved from another Gnostic system an even more striking parallel with our text.

The Bishop of Salamis is denouncing the Nicolaïtans,[143] who for him were the earliest Christian Gnostics, there being very numerous and various sects of them, all deriving from a certain Nicolaus, whom Epiphanius would have us believe to have been one of the first seven deacons of the Church.

If, in reality, however, the Nicolaïtans = the Balaamites of early Talmudic Rabbinism,[144] then the original Nicolaïtans were the earliest Christians, for "Balaamites" was the Rabbinical by-name of the followers of Balaam (Bileam) = Jeschu, and Balaam = Nicolaos, in Hebrew and Greek respectively.

Curiously enough, moreover, in the paragraph (§ 4) before the one from which we are going to quote, Epiphanius ascribes the use of the mystic words, "Kaulakau Kaulakau," to the Nicolaïtans, words which we have, with high probability, shown in the chapter "Myth of Man in the Mysteries" (§ 16 J., end) to have been used by a Jewish Gnostic of the time of Philo, writing in an Egyptian environment, and dealing with the Man-tradition, which is one of the main elements of the "Pœmandres" doctrine. All of which carries us back to the dawn of Christianity.

Speaking, then, of these Nicolaïtans, Epiphanius writes (xxv. 5):

"Others of them, again, plaster together empty names, saying: There was Darkness and Abyss (βυθός) and Water; and Spirit in the midst of them made separation of them."[145]

Here we have precisely the same elements as in our text for the foundation of a cosmogonical representation. What precise relationship these various traditions may have had to one another we cannot say with any

---

[143] *Adv. Hær.*, xxv. 1-5.
[144] See *D. J. L.*, p. 188, where this identification is worked out with some probability.
[145] Ed. Dindorf (Leipzig, 1859), ii. 35, 36.

certainty; but what we can say is that the writer or writers of our treatise are dealing with a material common to themselves, to pre-Christian Jewish Gnosticism and the earliest forms of the Christian Gnosis.

THE "BOOKS OF THE CHALDÆANS"

The sentence (in § 2), "All things being undefined and yet unwrought (ἀκατασκευάστων)" is also to be noticed, and, together with the opening sentence of the cosmogony, compared with the LXX. version of Gen. i. 2:

"And the earth was invisible and as yet unwrought (ἀκατασκεύαστος), and Darkness was upon the Abyss, and the Spirit of God was borne upon the Water."

Are we, then, to suppose that our Trismegistic writer based himself directly upon this famous "oracle" of Jewish Scripture?

The Jewish Gnostics would doubtless do so in their commentaries; but the phenomena of the Christianized Jewish Gnostic systems persuade us rather that these Gnostic Jews did not derive their ideas directly from the text of their national Scripture, but from what we may call parallel traditions of an esoteric nature. We shall see later on, when treating of Zosimus, that there were translations of the Chaldæan sacred books in the Alexandrian Library, and we cannot but believe that the general ideas of Chaldæan cosmogony were familiar to all the learned of the time. For Chaldæa and Egypt were regarded as the two most wisdom-loving nations of antiquity, the two most sacred lands. What wonder, then, that Chaldæan and Egyptian ideas should be blended together, and turned out into a "scientific" whole, by the spirit of Greek "philosophizing," in our treatises?

I would therefore conclude that both here, and in the repetition of the formula, "increase in increasing and multiply in multitude" (§ 3), from the "Pœmandres" treatise (§ 18), the similarities are not due to direct plagiarism, but to the fact that such *logoi* were "in the air." I would also suggest that the somewhat peculiar term ἀκατασκεύαστος was not original with the Greek Targum of Genesis, first made at Alexandria some 250 years B.C., but that it was rather taken from the theological and philosophical language of the day and used by the Hebrew translators; that, in brief, in the LXX. translation already we have to take into account the strong influence of the technology of Hellenistic theology.

With regard to the whole of our treatise, I would suggest that we have the heads of topics which were to be subsequently explained and commented upon, rather than a didactic treatise setting forth a clear teaching. Like the proem, the cosmogenesis itself is straitly condensed, so condensed that the indications are too vague for us to form any clear mental picture of the process that is suggested. We have nothing but a series of headings that may have meant something very definite to the writer—may, in fact, have summed up for him a whole body of doctrine—but which for us, in our ignorance of detail, can have but little precise meaning.

To add to our difficulties, the text, as we have already said, appears to be very faulty. It is very probable that owing to its original brevity, copyists and readers would be tempted to gloss it in the interests of what would appear to them greater clearness; these glosses creeping into the text later on would, since the gloss-makers did not know the original scheme, blur rather than elucidate the mother-text—and hence our tears.

The most striking doctrine in the exposition is that of Renewal or Making-new-again (ἀνανέωσις). All animal and vegetable forms contain in themselves "the seed of again-becoming" (τὸ σπέρμα τῆς παλιγγενεσίας). I do not think that this is intended simply to mean that the individual is continued in the species; for we read that "every birth of flesh ensouled . . . shall of necessity renew itself (ἀνανεωθήσεται)." The doctrine that is preached is, therefore, that of *palingenesis* or "re-incarnation"; the renewal on the kārmic wheel of birth-and-death (φύσεως κύκλου ἐναριθμίου δρόμημα).

THE "FLOOD"

The last point to which we need call the reader's attention is the sentence: "And there shall be memorials mighty of their handiworks upon the earth, leaving dim trace behind when cycles are renewed."

The thought of the writer is evidently turned back towards the past, to a time when a mighty race, devoted to growth in wisdom, lived on earth and left great monuments of their wisdom in the work of their hands, dim traces of which were to be seen "in the renewal of the times." This seems to me to be a clear reference to the general belief of the time (commonly, though erroneously, called Stoic) that there were alternate periods of destruction, by fire and water, and of renewal. In Egypt the common belief, as we have pointed out elsewhere, was that the last destruction had been by water and flood. Before this Flood our author believed there had been a mighty race of Egyptians, the race of the First Hermes, and that some dim traces of the mighty works of this bygone wisdom-loving civilization were still to be seen.

I am, myself, strongly inclined to believe in this tradition; and I have sometimes speculated as to the possibility of there being buried beneath one or more of the pyramids the remains of some prehistoric buildings (perhaps also of pyramid-shape) that have survived the "Flood."

CORPUS HERMETICUM IV. (V.)

THE CUP OR MONAD

OF HERMES TO TAT

(Text: P. 34-40; Pat. 26b-27.)

1. *Hermes.* With Reason (*Logos*), not with hands, did the World-maker [146] make the universal World [147]; so that thou thus shouldst think of Him as everywhere and ever-being, the Author of all things, and One and Only, who by His Will [148] all beings hath created.

This Body of Him is a thing no man can touch, or see, or measure, a Body inextensible, like to no other frame. 'Tis neither Fire nor Water, Air nor Breath [149]; yet all of them come from it. [150] Now being Good He willed to consecrate this [Body] to Himself alone, and set its Earth in order and adorn it. [151]

2. So down [to Earth] He sent the Cosmos [152] of this Frame Divine,[153]—man, a life that cannot die, and yet a life that dies. And o'er [all other] lives and over Cosmos [too], did man excel by reason of the Reason (*Logos*) and the Mind. For contemplator of God's works did man become; he marvelled and did strive to know their Author.

3. Reason (*Logos*) indeed, O Tat, among all men hath He distributed, but Mind not yet; not that He grudgeth any, for grudging cometh not from Him, [154] but hath its place below, within the souls of men who have no Mind.

Tat. Why then did God, O father, not on all bestow a share of Mind?

Her. He willed, my son, to have it set up in the midst for souls, just as it were a prize.

---

[146] ὁ δημιουργός.
[147] τὸν πάντα κόσμον.
[148] θέλησις.
[149] Perhaps meaning Æther.
[150] Cf. *C. H.*, xiii. (xiv.) 6.
[151] κοσμῆσαι, the whole is a play on the word κόσμος (*kosmos*) which means "order," "ornament," and "world." I have tried to retain it in English by using both meanings. The three preceding sentences, from "This Body" onwards, are quoted by Stobæus, *Phys.*, I. ii. 30; G. i. 26; W. 38, 10 ff., under the heading "Of Hermes."
[152] That is, "Order."
[153] That is, the Body of God; the One Element.
[154] Cf. *C. H.*, v. (vi.) 2.

4. *Tat.* And where hath He had it set up?

Her. [155] He filled a mighty Cup [156] with it, and sent it down, joining a Herald [to it], to whom He gave command to make this proclamation to the hearts of men:

Baptize [157] thyself with this Cup's baptism, what heart can do so, thou that hast faith thou canst ascend to Him that hath sent down the Cup, thou that dost know for what thou didst come into being!

As many then as understood the Herald's tidings and doused themselves in Mind, became partakers in the Gnosis; and when they had "received the Mind" they were made "perfect men."

But they who do not understand the tidings, these, since they possess the aid of Reason [only] and not Mind, are ignorant wherefor they have come into being and whereby.

5. The senses of such men are like irrational creatures'; and as their [whole] make-up is in their feelings and their impulses, [158] they fail in all appreciation of [159] those things which really are worth contemplation. These centre all their thought upon the pleasures of the body and its appetites, in the belief that for its sake man hath come into being.

But they who have received some portion of God's gift, [160] these, Tat, if we judge by their deeds, have from Death's bonds won their release; for they embrace in their own Mind all things, things on the earth, things in the heaven, and things above the heaven,—if there be aught. [161] And having raised themselves so far they sight the Good; and having sighted It, they look upon their sojourn here as a mischance; and in disdain of all, both things in body and the bodiless, they speed their way unto that One and Only One.

6. This is, O Tat, the Gnosis of the Mind, Vision of things Divine; God-knowledge is it, for the Cup is God's.

Tat. Father, I, too, would be baptized.

Her. Unless thou first shalt hate thy Body, son, thou canst not love thy Self. But if thou lov'st thy Self thou shalt have Mind, and having Mind thou shalt share in the Gnosis.

Tat. Father, what dost thou mean?

Her. It is not possible, my son, to give thyself to both,—I mean to things that perish and to things divine. For seeing that existing things are twain, Body and Bodiless, in which the perishing and the divine are understood,

---

[155] A critical text of most of these two paragraphs is given, R. 214, n. 1.

[156] κρατῆρα, lit. a cratēr or mixing-bowl.

[157] The meaning of this term is not to "sprinkle" with water, but to "plunge the whole body" into water.

[158] καὶ ἐν θυμῷ καὶ ἐν ὀργῇ τὴν κρᾶσιν ἔχοντες.

[159] Lit. "they do not wonder at."

[160] *Sc.* the Mind.

[161] *Cf. C. H.* xi. (xii.) 19: "And contemplate what is beyond—if there be aught beyond the Cosmos."a

the man who hath the will to choose is left the choice of one or other; for it can never be the twain should meet. And in those souls to whom the choice is left, the waning of the one causes the other's growth to show itself.

7. Now the choosing of the Better not only proves a lot most fair for him who makes the choice, seeing it makes the man a God, but also shows his piety to God. Whereas the [choosing] of the Worse, although it doth destroy the "man," it only doth disturb God's harmony to this extent, that as processions pass by in the middle of the way, without being able to do anything but take the road from others, so do such men move in procession through the world led by their bodies' pleasures.[162]

8. This being so, O Tat, what comes from God hath been and will be ours; but that which is dependent on ourselves, let this press onward and have no delay; for 'tis not God, 'tis we who are the cause of evil things, preferring them to good.

Thou see'st, son, how many are the bodies through which we have to pass, how many are the choirs of daimones, how vast the system of the star-courses [163] [through which our Path doth lie], to hasten to the One and Only God.

For to the Good there is no other shore [164]; It hath no bounds; It is without an end; and for Itself It is without beginning, too, though unto us it *seemeth* to have one—the Gnosis.

9. Therefore to It Gnosis is no beginning; rather is it [that Gnosis doth afford] to *us* the first beginning of *Its being known.*

Let us lay hold, therefore, of the beginning, and quickly speed through all [we have to pass].

'Tis very hard, to leave the things we have grown used to, which meet our gaze on every side, and turn ourselves back to the Old Old [Path].

Appearances delight us, whereas things which appear not make their believing hard.

Now evils are the more apparent things, whereas the Good can never show Itself unto the eyes, for It hath neither form nor figure.

Therefore the Good is like Itself alone, and unlike all things else; for 'tis impossible that That which hath no body should make Itself apparent to a body.

10. The "Like's" superiority to the "Unlike "and the "Unlike's" [165] inferiority unto the "Like" consists in this:

---

[162] Critical text of simile is also given by R. 102, n. 2. Quoted by Zosimus in § "On the Anthropos Doctrine."

[163] καὶ συνέχειαν καὶ δρόμους ἀστέρων, the Septenary Spheres or "Cyclic Gods"; for the συνέχεια (lit. continuity) is evidently the same as the ἁρμονία, Harmony, Concord, System.

[164] ἀδιάβατον,—lit. not to be crossed, not to be forded.

[165] Reading with B., τοῦ ἀνομοίου.

The Oneness [166]being Source [167]and Root of all, is in all things as Root and Source. Without [this] Source is naught; whereas the Source [Itself] is from naught but Itself, since It is Source of all the rest. It is Itself Its Source, since It may have no other Source.

The Oneness then being Source, containeth every number, but is contained by none; engendereth every number, but is engendered by no other one.

11. Now all that is engendered is imperfect, it is divisible, to increase subject and to decrease; but with the Perfect [One] none of these things doth hold. Now that which is increasable increases from the Oneness, but succumbs through its own feebleness when it no longer can contain the One.

And now, O Tat, God's Image [168]hath been sketched for thee, as far as it can be [169]; and if thou wilt attentively dwell on it and observe it with thy heart's eyes, believe me, son, thou'lt find the Path that leads above; nay, that Image shall become thy Guide [170] itself, because the Sight [Divine] hath this peculiar [charm], it holdeth fast and draweth unto it those who succeed in opening their eyes, just as, they say, the magnet [draweth] iron. [171]

---

[166] μονάς,—the Monad, that is the Good.
[167] Or, Beginning.
[168] The Universal Cosmos or Monad.
[169] The above sentences, beginning with "The Oneness," second paragraph of § 10, are quoted by Stobæus, *Phys.*, I. x. 15; G. pp. 116, 117; W. 127, 6 ff .; under the heading, "Of Hermes."
[170] Cf. *C. H.*, vii. (viii.) 2; ix. (x.) 10; x. (xi.) 21; R. 23, n. 5.
[171] This simile is also used in the Naassene Document, and in Plutarch, *On Isis and Osiris*, where I have noticed it.

COMMENTARY

THE TITLE

This beautiful little treatise, in which the great principles of the Gnosis are set forth so clearly and lucidly by the philosopher-mystic who penned it so many centuries ago, bears a double, or rather a triple, title: "Of Hermes to Tat: The Cup or Monad [or Oneness]." [172] The double title, however, is but a choice of names, for The Cup is The Oneness,—The One Element,[173] the "Body" of God, which is the Cause of all bodies and yet itself is bodiless; in other words, the Monad is the Intelligible Cosmos itself, God's Image, elsewhere called His Alone-begotten Son.

That this idea of a Cup or Mixing-bowl (Cratēr), in the symbolic sense of an all-containing receptacle, in which all the elements were blended together, and in the metaphysical sense of a transcendent Unity, the source of all things measurable and numberable, was one of the main doctrines of the Trismegistic tradition, is plain from the Pœmandrist Zosimus, who refers especially to this Cup as the symbol of Spiritual Baptism—that is, the plunging of the whole nature into the Great Ocean of Spirit or Mind, so that the man becomes irradiate with Life and illumined with Light.

For a consideration of this Crater or Cup symbolism I must refer the reader to the chapter so entitled in the "Prolegomena"; it there being shown that in all probability it was transmitted along the Orphic line of tradition, though doubtless the Egyptian had some similar ideas.

Our treatise should be read in the closest connection with C. H., xi. (xii.), "The Mind to Hermes," which is its "esoteric" counterpart. What is here set forth for Tat by Hermes is there imparted to Hermes by the Mind; what is here set forth for the probationer or "hearer" is there set forth for the advanced disciple or "seer"; or, to use Mystery terms, what is here told to the Mystes is there revealed to the Epopt. Thus, then, the Tat-instruction begins.

THE BAPTISM OF THE MIND

1. All things are made by Reason, the Formative Energy of the Mind. The Ideal Cosmos, or World-Order, is the Divine Body.

2. Earth is the sensible Cosmos; on Earth man, the image of the Image, or Reason, of God rules. The purpose of man is thus to become the contemplator (θεατής) of the works of God; it is by the "wonder" aroused in him by the sight of these marvels that he will rise eventually into a knowledge

---

[172] See R. 193. Unfortunately, though he twice quotes from our treatise, Stobæus adds nothing to our knowledge of the title, since he prefixes his extracts with the simple heading, "Of Hermes."
[173] Which is to be equated, I believe, "meta-physically" with the Quintessence or Æther.

of God Himself. This "wonder" is, then, the beginning of the True Philosophy or God-knowledge (ἡ τοῦ θεοῦ κατανόησις).

3. All men have in them "reason" (the ray of the Reason or Logos), but as yet few have "Mind." This "mind" is the true Son of Mind, it is the real *man*, the perfect man, self-conscious of his Self. This true Self-consciousness is the prize set up for souls to win: the crown of humanity, the Christ-state (or, at any rate, the super-man or true man state).

The Christ-Baptism is the plunging of the whole nature into the Mind-filled Cup,—the Plērōma of the Divine Being whose Body and Mind are one,—for is not the Cup the Body of God, "consecrated unto Himself alone" (§ I), the Universal Body of all things?

THE HOLY GRAIL

It would be fascinating to speculate on what connection this Cup of Initiation may have had with the Mystic Eucharist, and the Original of the later Grail-tradition, which a great master of music and song has in our days made to live again in undying melody, and so restored it to its more universal significance. How Wagner sensed the marvel of the wondrous Vision with a poet's intuition may be seen from his own words:

"To the enraptured gaze of one longing for celestial love, the clear blue atmosphere of heaven seems at first to condense itself into a wonderful, scarcely perceptible, but dazzlingly beautiful Vision. Then with gradually increasing precision the wonder-working angelic host is delineated in infinitely delicate outlines, as, conveying the holy vessel in its midst, it insensibly descends from the blazing heights of heaven. As the vision grows more and more distinct, . . . the heart throbs with the pain of ecstasy; . . . and when at last the Grail shows itself in the marvel of undraped reality, . . . the beholder's brain reels—he falls down in a state of adoring annihilation. . . . With chaste rejoicing the angelic host then returns to the heavenly height, fading away into the nothingness whence it first emanated."

But for the Seers of the Gnosis there was a more intimate realization, for they were bidden to cast aside all hesitation and fearlessly to plunge themselves into the very Cup Itself, the Ocean of Divine Love and Wisdom.

This was the Proclamation or Preaching (κήρυγμα), or Good Tidings, of the Herald of God to men, to those who had the Living Faith they could "ascend to Him who had sent down the Cup," God's Greatest Gift.

By such a Baptism as this, not by a symbolic sprinkling with water, is it that man is to be redeemed. This is the consummation of man's earthly pilgrimage, the realization of the "Gnosis of the Mind, Vision of things Divine; God-knowledge is it; for the Cup is God's."

THE "HATING OF THE BODY"

6. In § 6 we have given us a discipline of the mystic way, the "hating of the body," which is by no means to be taken literally.

A misunderstanding of this discipline led many of the mystics of the time (and, for a matter of that, has led most of the mystics of all time) to the false belief that the body (or matter generally) was the source of evil. Hence we have all the mortifications and chastisements of the flesh which the monkish spirit introduced into Christendom, and which persist in some quarters even to our own day. Against this the Common Sense of Christianity as a general religion, basing itself on the general utterances of the Christ, has ever protested.

Our mystic philosopher, in urging his disciples to hate the body, apparently does so because they are in the first stages of awakening, and so far have not got the "Mind" active in them.

In taking the first steps there must be developed a consciousness of the strong antithesis of good and evil, of love and hate, in order that the will of the disciple may be strengthened towards the good and weakened towards the bad.

When, however, his will is *balanced* between the two, when he as easily wills good as evil, then, and not till then, is he prepared to learn the further great lesson: that real wisdom consists in balance, in the Middle Way; that nothing is evil in itself—the Body is as honourable in its own sphere, as absolutely necessary and indispensable, as is the Mind in its.

He learns the great secret that to have one's thoughts always in heaven is as erroneous as to have them always on earth; that there is a higher mode of existence, when the things of heaven and earth are within each other, and not apart.

As the Introduction to *The Book of the Great Logos according to the Mystery* has it:

"Jesus saith: Blessed is the man who knoweth this Word (*Logos*), and hath brought down the Heaven and borne up the Earth and raised it Heavenwards." [174]

Heaven and Earth must kiss each other for this consummation, this truly Sacred Marriage.

And yet in the third Synoptic (xvi. 25, 26) we read:

"Jesus saith: If any man come unto Me, and hate not his father, and mother, and wife, and children, and brethren and sisters, yea, and his own soul also, he cannot be My disciple."

Here we have precisely the same word "hate" ($\mu\iota\sigma\epsilon\hat{\iota}$) as in our text. That, however, this "dark saying" was interpreted in a mystical sense by

---

[174] Codex Brucianus; see *F. F. F.*, p. 520.

Gnostic tradition, as by no means referring to physical parents but to the past causes of our imperfections, [175] I have already pointed out on several occasions [176]; we may therefore conclude that in a gnostic teaching, such as is our treatise, the terms "hate" and "body" are not to be literally interpreted.

8. And that this is so may be seen from the declaration in § 8: "For 'tis not God, 'tis *we* who are the cause of evil things, *preferring* them to good";—where the cause of evil is not assigned to the body but to man's own choice. And finally, to clinch our contention, we would refer the reader to the Sermon to Asclepius, *C. H.*, vi. (vii.) 6:

"Such are the things that men call good and beautiful, Asclepius—things which we cannot flee *or hate.*"

THE GNOSIS AND ITS BLESSINGS

9. In § 9 we have to notice the phrase: "Therefore *to It* Gnosis is no beginning; rather is it that Gnosis doth afford *to us* the first beginning of *Its being known*"; and compare it with the *logos* quoted by the Jewish commentator in the Naassene Document (§ 25): "The Beginning of Perfection is Gnosis of Man, but Gnosis of God is Perfect Perfection."

The claim for the Gnosis is therefore a modest one. The Gnosis is not an end in itself; it is but the beginning of the True Knowledge of God. They who receive the Baptism of the Mind are made "perfect men," not Perfect; not until they have received this touch of the Christ-consciousness have they reached true manhood.

Those who have received this Baptism know why they have come into being,—the purpose of life. They become consciously immortal; they *know* they are deathless, they do not only *believe* it; their immortality is no longer a *belief,* it is a *fact of knowledge.*

They have won their freedom from Death and Fate, and know the real constitution of the cosmos up to the Threshold of the Good, the Plain of Truth—that is to say, presumably in Buddhist terms, as far as the Nirvāṇic state of consciousness. Not yet, however, have they entered Nirvāṇa—that is to say, become one with the Logos. They have seen the Sight or Vision of Nirvāṇa, but not entered into the Promised Land, that "Blessed Space," which, as Basilides tells us, "can neither be conceived of nor characterized by any word." [177]

The Vision is an earnest of what they may be. They have become Gods, it is true, already, or, in other words, enjoy the same freedom and

---

[175] *Cf.* the *Pistis Sophia,* 341-343, where the text is given as: "He who shall not leave father and mother to follow after Me is not worthy of Me," and explained by the Saviour to mean: "Ye shall leave your Parents the Rulers, that ye may be Children of the First Everlasting Mystery."
[176] See, for instance, *Extracts from the "Vâhan"* (London, 1904), pp. 374-376.
[177] See *F. F. F.,* p. 261.

consciousness as the Gods or Angels, but there is a still more transcendent state, when they will be at-oned with Deity Himself.

THE ANCIENT PATH

Hard as it is to leave the "things we have grown used to," the things habitual, it must be done if we are to enter into the Way of the Gnosis. But no new Path is this, no going forth into new lands (though it may have all the appearance of being so). The entrance on the Path of the Gnosis is a Going-Home, it is a Return—a Turning-Back (a True Repentance). "We must turn ourselves back unto the Old Old Way" (τὰ παλαιὰ καὶ ἀρχαῖα).

And for the followers of the Doctrine of Thrice-greatest Hermes, this Old Old Path could have meant nothing but the Archaic Wisdom of Ancient Egypt. The Wisdom of Egypt was thus the Gnosis.

CORPUS HERMETICUM V. (VI.)

THOUGH UNMANIFEST GOD IS MOST MANIFEST

OF HERMES TO HIS SON TAT

(Text: P. 41-48; Pat. 12b-13b.)

1. I WILL recount for thee this sermon (*logos*) too, O Tat, that thou may'st cease to be without the mysteries of the God beyond all name. [178] And mark thou well how That which to the many seems unmanifest, will grow most manifest for thee.

Now were It manifest, It would not *be*. For all that is made manifest is subject to *becoming*, for it hath been *made* manifest. But the Unmanifest for ever *is*, for It doth not desire to be made manifest. It ever is, and maketh manifest all other things.

Being Himself unmanifest, as ever being and ever making-manifest, Himself is not made manifest. God is not made Himself; by thinking-manifest, [179] He thinketh all things manifest.

Now "thinking-manifest" deals with things made alone, for thinking-manifest is nothing else than making.

2. He, then, alone who is not made, 'tis clear, is both beyond all power of thinking-manifest, and is unmanifest.

And as He thinketh all things manifest, He manifests through all things and in all, and most of all in whatsoever things He wills to manifest.

Do thou, then, Tat, my son, pray first unto our Lord and Father, the One-and-Only One, from whom the One [180] doth come, to show His mercy unto thee, in order that thou mayest have the power to catch a thought of this so mighty God, one single beam of Him to shine into thy thinking. For thought alone "sees" the Unmanifest, in that it is itself unmanifest.

If, then, thou hast the power, He will, Tat, manifest to thy mind's eyes. The Lord begrudgeth not Himself to anything, but manifests Himself through the whole world.

Thou hast the power of taking thought, of seeing it and grasping it in thy own "hands," and gazing face to face upon God's Image. [181] But if what

---

[178] *Cf.* § 8 end, and § 9 beginning.

[179] ἐν φαντασίᾳ—that is to say, by thinking into manifestation.

[180] Presumably the Manifested God; the One-and-Only One being the Unmanifested, the God beyond all name.

[181] The Intelligible Cosmos.

is within thee even is unmanifest to thee, how, then, shall He Himself who is within thy self be manifest for thee by means of [outer] eyes?

3. But if thou wouldst "see" Him, bethink thee of the sun, bethink thee of moon's course, bethink thee of the order of the stars. Who is the One who watcheth o'er that order? For every order hath its boundaries marked out by place and number.

The sun's the greatest god of gods in heaven; to whom all of the heavenly gods give place as unto king and master. And he, this so-great one, he greater than the earth and sea, endures to have above him circling smaller stars than him. Out of respect to Whom, or out of fear of Whom, my son, [doth he do this]?

Nor like nor equal is the course each of these stars describes in heaven. Who [then] is He who marketh out the manner of their course and its extent?

4. The Bear up there that turneth round itself, and carries round the whole cosmos with it—Who is the owner of this instrument? Who He who hath set round the sea its bounds? Who He who hath set on its seat the earth?

For, Tat, there *is* someone who is the Maker and the Lord of all these things. It could not be that number, place and measure could be kept without someone to make them. No order whatsoever could be made by that which lacketh place and lacketh measure; nay, even this [182] is not without a lord, my son. For if the orderless lacks something, in that it is not lord of order's path, it also is beneath a lord—the one who hath not yet ordained it order.

5. Would it were possible for thee to get thee wings, and soar into the air, and, poised midway 'tween earth and heaven, behold the earth's solidity, the sea's fluidity (the flowings of its streams), the spaciousness of air, fire's swiftness, [and] the coursing of the stars, the swiftness of heaven's circuit round them [all]!

Most blessed sight were it, my son, to see all these beneath one sway—the motionless in motion, and the unmanifest made manifest; whereby is made this order of the cosmos and the cosmos which we see of order.

6. If thou would'st see Him too through things that suffer death, [183] both on the earth and in the deep, [184] think of a man's being fashioned in the womb, my son, and strictly scrutinize the art of Him who fashions him, and learn who fashioneth this fair and godly image of the Man. [185]

Who [then] is He who traceth out the circles of the eyes; who He who boreth out the nostrils and the ears; who He who openeth [the portal of] the mouth; who He who doth stretch out and tie the nerves; who He who

---

[182] Namely, that which lacketh place, number, and order; that is, disorder, chaos.
[183] As opposed to the immortal world-order.
[184] *Cf.* § 9 below, where it almost seems to mean "water."
[185] The Heavenly Man of "The Shepherd" treatise; man is the image of The Man, the Logos or Image of God. This and the following passage is referred to by Lactantius, *D. Institt.*, ii. 10.

channels out the veins; who He who hardeneth the bones; who He who covereth the flesh with skin; who He who separates the fingers and the joints; who He who widens out a treading for the feet; who He who diggeth out the ducts; who He who spreadeth out the spleen; who He who shapeth heart like to a pyramid; who He who setteth ribs together; who He who wideneth the liver out; who He who maketh lungs like to a sponge; who He who maketh belly stretch so much; who He who doth make prominent the parts most honourable, so that they may be seen, while hiding out of sight those of least honour?

7. Behold how many arts [employed] on one material, how many labours on one single sketch; and all exceeding fair, and all in perfect measure, yet all diversified! Who made them all? What mother, or what sire, save God alone, unmanifest, who hath made all things by His Will?

8. And no one saith a statue or a picture comes to be without a sculptor or [without] a painter; doth [then] such workmanship as this exist without a Worker? What depth of blindness, what deep impiety, what depth of ignorance! See, [then] thou ne'er, son Tat, deprivest works of Worker!

Nay, rather is He greater than all names, so great is He, the Father of them all. [186] For verily He is the Only One; and this His work, to be a father.

9. So, if thou forcest me somewhat too bold, to speak, His being is conceiving of all things and making [them]. [187]

And as without its maker it is impossible that anything should be, so ever is He not unless He ever makes all things, in heaven, in air, in earth, in deep, in all of cosmos, in every part that is and that is not of everything. For there is naught in all the world that is not He.

He is Himself, both things that are and things that are not. The things that are He hath made manifest, He keepeth things that are not in Himself.

10. He is the God beyond all name; He the unmanifest, He the most manifest; He whom the mind [alone] can contemplate, He visible unto the eyes [as well]; He is the one of no body, the one of many bodies, nay, rather He of every body.

Naught is there which He is not. For all are He and He is all. [188] And for this cause hath He all names, in that they are one Father's. And for this cause hath He Himself no name, in that He's Father of [them] all. [189]

Who, then, may sing Thee praise of Thee, or [praise] to Thee?

Whither, again, am I to turn my eyes to sing Thy praise; above, below, within, without?

---

[186] The translation of this sentence is conjectural; for the text is not only corrupt, but there appears to be a lacuna in it.

[187] The male and female energies of the Divine Parent.

[188] For emended reading, see R. 244.

[189] That is, of all names. For the following, cf. *P. S. A.*, xxxi. 3.

There is no way, no place [is there] about Thee, nor any other thing of things that are.

All [are] in Thee; all [are] from Thee, O Thou who givest all and takest naught, for Thou hast all and naught is there Thou hast not.

11. And *when*, O Father, shall I hymn Thee? For none can seize Thy hour or time.

For what, again, shall I sing hymn? For things that Thou hast made, or things Thou hast not? For things Thou hast made manifest, or things Thou hast concealed?

How, [190] further, shall I hymn Thee? As being of myself? As having something of mine own? As being other?

For that Thou art whatever I may be; Thou art whatever I may do; Thou art whatever I may speak.

For Thou art all, and there is nothing else which Thou art not. Thou art all that which doth exist, and Thou art what doth not exist,—Mind when Thou thinkest, and Father when Thou makest, and God when Thou dost energize, and Good and Maker of all things.

(For that the subtler part of matter is the air, of air the soul, of soul the mind, and of mind God.)

---

[190] Text from here on given in R. 68, n. 4.

COMMENTARY

THE TITLE

The redactor of our Corpus must have taken this sermon from some collection of "Those to Tat," for it begins "καὶ τόνδε σοι τὸν λόγον." One other sermon at least, then, must have preceded it; but whether it was our *C. H.*, iv. (v.), "The Cup," or the lost *C. H.* (ii.), "The General Sermon," it is impossible to say.

The sermon bears no title proper, and the enunciation of the subject, which stands in its place, is derived from the second sentence of the treatise itself, and has plainly been superscribed by some later Byzantine editor.

MĀYĀ

The opening paragraphs of this fine tractate are very difficult to render into English in any way that can preserve the subtle shades of meaning of the Greek. As this subtle word-play has been entirely missed by all previous translators, I have made a rough attempt to preserve it by using the somewhat clumsy term "manifest." The word-play in Greek may be seen from the following list of the original terms taken in the order of their occurrence: ἀφανές, φανερώτατον, ἐμφανές, φαινόμενον, ἐφάνη, ἀφανές, φανῆναι, φανερά, ἀφανής, φανερῶν, φανεροῦται, φαντασία, φαντασιῶν, φαντασία, ἀφαντασίαστος καὶ ἀφανής, φαντασιῶν, φαίνεται, φανῆναι. These all occur in § 1 and the first two lines of § 2.

I have translated **φαντασία** by "thinking-manifest," seeing that it is the power by which an object is made apparent or manifest. The doctrine is the same as that of the Vedānta philosophy, the Māyā of the Vedāntavādins. Māyā is generally translated "illusion," but this is not a good equivalent, for it comes from the root *ma*, to make or measure. The Logos is called in the Vedānta, Māyin (masc.), the Maker, Measurer, or Creator, and His Power, or Shakti, is Māyā (fem.). It is the Power of the Divine Thought, and so far from being illusion in any ordinary sense of the word, is very real for us, and is only non-real as compared to the Logos Himself, the One Reality in the highest philosophical sense of the term.

The idea is magnificently summed up for us in a *logos* of Phōsilampēs,[191] quoted by the redactor of the *Untitled Apocalypse* of the Codex Brucianus, which runs as follows:

---

[191] Perhaps a by-name of Basilides; see *F. F. F.*, p. 554.

"Through Him is that-which-really-is and that-which-really-is-not, through which the Hidden-which-really-is and the Manifest-which-really-is-not exists."

Also compare Hippolytus' summary of the "Simonian" Gnosis:

"Of this Twofold Nature he calls the one side the Hidden and the other the Manifest, saying that the concealed [parts] of the Fire are hidden in the manifest, and the manifest produced by the concealed. . . .

"And the manifest side of the Fire has all things in itself which a man can perceive of things visible, or which he unconsciously fails to perceive. Whereas the hidden side is everything that we can conceive as intelligible, . . . or which a man fails to conceive."[192]

2. "The Lord begrudgeth not Himself to any thing." Compare this with *C. H.,* iv. (v.) 3: "Not that He grudgeth any, for grudging cometh not from Him"; and compare both with the saying of Plato in the *Timæus* (29 E):

"He was Good, and to the Good there can never at any time be any grudging of aught."

THE HIGHER PANTHEISM OR PANMONISM

10. With the soul-satisfying pantheism of § 10 we may with interest compare the address to the Logos in *The Martyrdom of Peter,* which still retains many Gnostic elements.

"Thou that art to be understood by spirit alone! Thou art my father, Thou my mother, Thou my brother, Thou my friend, Thou my servant, Thou my master. Thou art the all, and all is in Thee. Yea, all that is, is Thou; and there is nothing else that is but Thee alone!"[193]

HYMN TO ALL-GOD

The treatise ends with one of the most magnificent Hymns to God ever written in any language—a hymn which some foolish copyist has spoilt by tagging on to it the gloss of a reader noted on the margin of the MS. from which our scribe copied.

With the sentence: "All are in Thee, all are from Thee," compare the Naassene Hymn (quoted in Hippolytus' Introduction, in "The Myth of Man"):

"'From Thee' is Father, and 'Through Thee,' Mother,—the two Immortal Names, Parents of Æons, O Thou who hast the Heaven for Thy City, O Man of Mighty Names!"

---

[192] Hipp., *Philos.,* vi. 9; see my *Simon Magus* (London, 1892), p. 13.
[193] Lipsius (R. A.) and Bonnet (M.), *Acta Apostolorum Apocrypha* (Leipzig, 1891), i. 98.

CORPUS HERMETICUM VI. (VII.)

IN GOD ALONE IS GOOD AND ELSEWHERE NOWHERE

(Text: P. 48-53; Pat. 14a-15a.)

1. GOOD, O Asclepius, is in none else save God alone; nay, rather, Good is God Himself eternally.

If it be so, [Good] must be essence, from every kind of motion and becoming free (though naught is free from It), possessed of stable energy around Itself, never too little, nor too much, an ever-full supply. [Though] one, yet [is It] source of all; for what supplieth all is Good. When I, moreover, say [supplieth] *altogether* [all], it is *for ever* Good. But this belongs to no one else save God alone.

For He stands not in need of any thing, so that desiring it He should be bad; nor can a single thing of things that are be lost to Him, on losing which He should be pained; for pain is part of bad.

Nor is there aught superior to Him, that He should be subdued by it; nor any peer to Him to do Him wrong, or [so that] He should fall in love on its account; nor aught that gives no ear to Him, whereat He should grow angry; nor wiser aught, for Him to envy.

2. Now as all these are non-existent in His being, what is there left but Good alone?

For just as naught of bad is to be found in such transcendent Being, so too in no one of the rest will Good be found.

For in them all are all the other things [194]—both in the little and the great, both in each severally and in this living one [195] that's greater than them all and mightiest [of them].

For things subject to birth [196] abound in passions, birth in itself being passible. But where there's passion, nowhere is there Good; and where is Good, nowhere a single passion. For where is day, nowhere is night; and where is night, day is nowhere.

Wherefore in genesis the Good can never *be*, but only be in the ingenerate.

But seeing that the sharing in all things hath been bestowed on matter, so doth it share in Good.

---

[194] That is, things not Good.
[195] Or animal; that is, cosmos as a single life or living creature. Or animal; that is, cosmos as a single life or living creature.
[196] Or genesis.

In this way is the Cosmos good; that, in so far as it doth make all things, as far as making goes it's Good, but in all other things it is not Good. For it's both passible and subject unto motion, and maker of things passible.

3. Whereas in man by greater or by less of bad is good determined. For what is not too bad down here, is good; and good down here is the least part of bad.

It cannot, therefore, be that good down here should be quite clean of bad, for down here good is fouled with bad; and being fouled, it stays no longer good, and staying not it changes into bad.

In God alone, is, therefore, Good, or rather Good is God Himself.

So then, Asclepius, the *name* alone of Good is found in men, the thing itself nowhere [in them], for this can never be.

For no material body doth contain It,—a thing [197] bound on all sides by bad, by labours, pains, desires and passions, by error and by foolish thoughts.

And greatest ill of all, Asclepius, is that each of these things that have been said above, is thought down here to be the greatest good.

And what is still an even greater ill, is belly-lust, the error that doth lead the band of all the other ills—the thing that makes us turn down here from Good.

4. And I, for my own part, give thanks to God, that He hath cast it in my mind about the Gnosis of the Good, that it can never be It [198] should be in the world. [199] For that the world is "fullness" [200] of the bad, but God of Good, and Good of God.

The excellencies of the Beautiful are round the very essence [of the Good]; nay, they do seem too pure, too unalloyed; perchance 'tis they that are themselves Its essences.

For one may dare to say, Asclepius,—if essence, sooth, He have—God's essence is the Beautiful; the Beautiful is further also Good.

There is no Good that can be got from objects in the world. For all the things that fall beneath the eye are image-things and pictures as it were; while those that do not meet [the eye are the realities [201]], especially the [essence] of the Beautiful and Good.

Just as the eye cannot see God, so can it not behold the Beautiful and Good. For that they are integral parts of God, wedded to Him alone, inseparate familiars, most beloved, with whom God is Himself in love, or they with God.

---

[197] *Sc.* the body.
[198] *Sc.* the Good.
[199] Cosmos.
[200] Or plērōma. The "world" is the plērōma of evil, but 'God" the plērōma of good.
[201] A lacuna unfortunately occurs here in the text.

5. If thou canst God conceive, thou shalt conceive the Beautiful and Good, transcending Light, made lighter than the Light by God. That Beauty is beyond compare, inimitate that Good, e'en as God is Himself.

As, then, thou dost conceive of God, conceive the Beautiful and Good. For they cannot be joined with aught of other things that live, since they can never be divorced from God.

Seek'st thou for God, thou seekest for the Beautiful. One is the Path that leadeth unto It—Devotion joined with Gnosis.

6. And thus it is that they who do not know and do not tread Devotion's Path, do dare to call man beautiful and good, though he have ne'er e'en in his visions seen a whit that's Good, but is enwrapped with every kind of bad, and thinks the bad is good, and thus doth make unceasing use of it, and even feareth that it should be ta'en from him, so straining every nerve not only to preserve but even to increase it.

Such are the things that men call good and beautiful, Asclepius,—things which we cannot flee or hate; for hardest thing of all is that we've need of them and cannot live without them.

COMMENTARY

THE TITLE

This sermon, which bears no proper title, but has been headed by some editor with the enunciation of the subject taken from the opening sentence of the treatise itself, belongs to the Asclepius-group.

Reitzenstein (p. 194) thinks that this tractate and the previous Asclepius-Dialogue—*C. H.*, ii. (iii.)—may very well have formed part of the same collection of Asclepiana.

DUALISM?

The teaching of our sermon is apparently dualistic; but is it not only formally so, and as an exercise to raise the thought of the pupil away from the "things he has grown used to"? For at the end Hermes declares:

"Such are the things that men call good and beautiful, Asclepius—*things which we cannot flee or hate*; for hardest thing of all is that we've need of them and cannot live without them."

This is a clear advance on the formal Tat-teaching as to "hating" the body given in *C. H.*, iv. (v.) 6, and points clearly to an instruction in which the cosmos was not regarded as the plērōma of bad, in spite of the formal and emphatic statement in § 4:

"ὁ γὰρ κόσμος πλήρωμά ἐστι τῆς κακίας."

Moreover, if we turn to *C. H.*, ix. (x.), 4—another treatise of Hermes to Asclepius, and curiously enough having as superscription almost the same proposition as heads our present treatise we read:

"χωρίον γὰρ αὐτῆς [κακίας] ἡ γῆ, οὐχ ὁ κόσμος, ὡς ἔνιοι ποτὲ ἐροῦσι βλασφημοῦντες."

"Bad's place is earth, and not the world, as some will sometimes say with impious tongue."

Here we have a formal denial in an Asclepius-tractate of the formal proposition in our Asclepius-sermon.

The cosmos is not evil; it is the beautiful world-order. Evil is a thing connected with the earth; there is no such thing as a πλήρωμα of evil; evil has at best only a χωρίον. They who say such things blaspheme.

This is strong language, and there seems no other conclusion to be drawn from it but that there were various schools within the Trismegistic tradition, and that they wrangled theologically together.

Is it, however, possible that the Hermes of our treatise is only speaking metaphorically, so that he may intensify the ideal of the Good, and that he was subsequently taken as speaking literally? For he must have known that the Cosmos was regarded as the Son of God, *par excellence*, the fairest and best-beloved of all, God's Very Image.

On the other hand, we know that in the Trismegistic doctrine the "cosmic man" was opposed to the "essential man," that, in fact, the term "cosmic" was used in the nomenclature of the time in a theological as well as in a philosophical sense. This was especially the case in Christianity. Many instances could be cited from the New Testament documents; and we have also a striking example of the use of "cosmos" in this sense in the second *logion* of the First Oxyrhynchus Fragment:

"Jesus saith: Except ye fast to the world (τὸν κόσμον), ye shall in no wise find the Kingdom of God."

As, moreover, we nowhere else find mention of a "pleroma of evil," we may permissibly conclude that it is here not intended to be taken literally, but only as a metaphorical expression.

GOD THE PLEROMA OF GOOD

"God is the Pleroma of Good, and Good is the Pleroma of God."

And so, speaking of the Triumphant Christ as the Cosmic Logos, Paul writes:

"And Him hath He (God) given as Head over all things unto the Church, [202] which is His Body—the Fullness (Plērōma) of Him who doth fulfil all things in all." [203]

The thought-atmosphere in which the idea of the "Church" as the Pleroma arose may be sampled from Philo, *De Prœm. et Pœn.*, § xi. (M. ii. 418, p. 920; Ri. v. 232):

"And thus the soul, becoming a Pleroma of virtues by means of the three best [blessings]—nature, instruction (*mathēsis*) and practice (*askēsis*),—leaving no vacant spot in her for entrance of aught else, brings unto birth a perfect number,—her two hexads of sons, a miniature and copy of the circle of the types of life, [204] for the improvement of the things down here.

"This is the House [205] that naught can harm, the perfect and continual in the public scriptures, and also in the secret meanings of the mystic ones,—the House that won the prize, as I have said, of lordship o'er the tribes of its [own] race."

"It was thus from this House in course of time, as it increased and became populous, that well-regulated cities were established, yea, disciplines of wisdom and of righteousness and holiness, in which the transmutation

---

[202] τῇ ἐκκλησίᾳ, that is, the Spiritual Body of the "Elect."
[203] Eph. i. 23. *Cf.* Col. ii. 19: "In Him dwelleth the whole Fullness of the Godhead as in a body."
[204] *Sc.* the Zodiac.
[205] *Sc.* of God.

(μεταποίησις) of the rest of virtue was sought out in manner worthy of so high a work."

In the Trismegistic tradition, however, the idea is simpler, as we learn from "The Definitions of Asclepius," *C. H.* (xvi.) 3:

"For that the Fullness of all things is One and is in One,—this latter One not coming as a second One, but both being One. . . .

"For should one try to separate what *seems* to be both All and One and Same from One,—he will be found to take his epithet of 'All' from the idea of multitude and not from that of fullness (plērōma),—which is impossible; for if he put All for the One, he will destroy the All."

Nevertheless, the Pleroma [206] of Life is more specially the Cosmos as the Son of God—that is, as the Logos. Thus in *C. H.*, xii. (xiii.) 15, we read:

"Matter is one; and the World-order (Cosmos), as a whole,—the Mighty God and Image of the Mightier One, both with Him unified, and the Conserver of the Will and Order of the Father,—is Life's Fullness (Plērōma). . . .

"How then, O son, could there be in the God,—the Image of the Father, the Plenitude (Plērōma) of Life, [207]—dead things?"

And again in *C. H.*, ix. (x.) 7:

"For [Cosmos] being a most wise Breath, bestows their qualities on bodies together with the one Pleroma—that of Life."

5. This Pleroma of God is the Good and Beautiful. The Path to this True Good is one of balance,—for it is the Way of Devotion united unto Gnosis—in Sanskrit terms, the Bhakti-Mārga and Jñāna-Mārga combined. [208]

6. Finally we learn, though inferentially, that things are not bad in themselves; the evil is that men are content with the little goods they have and cling desperately to these, in ignorance of the greater blessings to which they could attain, did they but open their spiritual eyes for the True Vision of the Good. For even the psychic visions of the soul, in spite of their beauty, give man no hint of that Most Blessed Sight of All.

---

[206] *Cf.* John i. 16: "Of His Fullness we have all received, and grace on grace."
[207] *Cf.* John i. 4: "In Him was Life and the Life was the Light of men."
[208] Compare *C. H.*, i. 27: "And I began to preach to men the beauty of Devotion and of Gnosis."

CORPUS HERMETICUM VII. (VIII.)

THE GREATEST ILL AMONG MEN IS IGNORANCE OF GOD

(Text: P. 54, 55; Pat. 18a.)

1. WHITHER stumble ye, sots, who have sopped up the wine of ignorance unmixed, and can so far not carry it that ye already even spew it forth?

Stay ye, be sober, gaze upwards with the [true] eyes of the heart! And if ye cannot all, yet ye at least who can!

For that the ill of ignorance doth pour o'er all the earth and overwhelm the soul that's battened down within the body, preventing it from fetching port within Salvation's harbours.

2. Be then not carried off by the fierce flood, but using the shore-current, [209] ye who can, make for Salvation's port, and, harbouring there, seek ye for one to take you by the hand and lead you [210] unto Gnosis' gates.

Where shines clear Light, of every darkness clean; where not a single soul is drunk, but sober all they gaze with their hearts' eyes on Him who willeth to be seen.

No ear can hear Him, nor can eye see Him, nor tongue speak of Him, but [only] mind and heart.

But first thou must tear off from thee the cloak which thou dost wear,—the web of ignorance, the ground of bad, corruption's chain, the carapace of darkness, the living death, sensation's corpse, the tomb thou carriest with thee, the robber in thy house, who through the things he loveth, hateth thee, and through the things he hateth, bears thee malice.

3. Such is the hateful cloak thou wearest,—that throttles thee [and holds thee] down to it, in order that thou may'st not gaze above, and, having seen the Beauty of the Truth, and Good that dwells therein, detest the bad of it; having found out the plot that it hath schemed against thee, by making void of sense those seeming things which men think senses.

For that it hath with mass of matter blocked them up and crammed them full of loathsome lust, so that thou may'st not hear about the things that thou should'st hear, nor see the things that thou should'st see.

---

[209] Lit. back or up-current.
[210] Cf. C. H., iv. (v.) 11; ix. (x.) 10; x (xi.) 2; R. 23, n. 5.

COMMENTARY

A PREACHING

THERE is little to be said about this powerful appeal to cease from the drunkenness of physical sensations and to awaken to the Light.

Reitzenstein (p. 194) calls it a "*Prophetenpredigt*" and says that nowhere in the MSS. is it ascribed to Hermes; by which he can only mean that it bears no other superscription than the descriptive sentence which heads it.

The style and spirit remind us not so much of *C. H.*, iii. (iv.), as Reitzenstein (p. 206, 1) suggests, as of the interpolated or superadded passages in the "Pœmandres" treatise (§ 27):

"O ye people, earthborn folk, ye who have given yourselves to drunkenness, and sleep, and ignorance, be sober now, cease from your surfeit, cease to be glamoured by irrational sleep!"

Did this sentence give rise to our little sermon; or is the sentence a summary of the preaching? Or do both sentence and sermon come from a common stock?

THE PROBABLE COMPLETION OF AN OXYRHYNCHUS LOGION

The last hypothesis seems to be the most satisfactory choice; and we may compare what would appear to be a familiar figure of speech among such communities with *logion* 3 of the First Oxyrhynchus Fragment:

"Jesus saith: I stood in the midst of the world (τοῦ κόσμου), and in the flesh did I appear unto them; and I found all men drunken, and none found I athirst among them; and my soul grieveth over the souls of men, because they are blind in their heart and see not . . ."

Can we fill up the missing word from our sermon?

"But sober all they gaze with their hearts' eyes on Him who willeth to be seen."

The missing word seems, therefore, to be "God."

The Gospel that is preached is the Beauty of the Gnosis,—"the Beauty of the Truth and Good that dwells therein"; just as in *C. H.*, i. 27:

"And I began to preach to men the Beauty of Devotion and of the Gnosis."

The tempest-tossed on the Sea of Ignorance are to make for the Harbour of Salvation—evidently some great organization devoted to the holy life; therein they must seek for one who knows, who can take them by the hand and lead them unto the Gates of the Gnosis.

This suggests that the organization consisted of a general body, within which were grades of instruction; the many were striving for illumination, some few had reached it.

CORPUS HERMETICUM VIII. (IX.)

THAT NO ONE OF EXISTING THINGS DOTH PERISH, BUT MEN IN ERROR SPEAK OF THEIR CHANGES AS DESTRUCTIONS AND AS DEATHS

[OF HERMES TO TAT]

(Text: P. 56-59; Pat. 48a, 48b.)

1. [*Hermes.*] Concerning Soul and Body, son, we now must speak; in what way Soul is deathless, and whence comes the activity [211] in composing and dissolving Body.

For there's no *death* for aught of things [that are]; the thought [this] word conveys, is either void of fact, or [simply] by the knocking off a syllable what is called "death," doth stand for "deathless." [212]

For death is of destruction, and nothing in the Cosmos is destroyed. For if Cosmos is second God, a life [213] that cannot die, it cannot be that any part of this immortal life should die. All things in Cosmos are parts of Cosmos, and most of all is man, the rational animal.

2. For truly first of all, eternal and transcending birth, is God the universals' Maker. Second is he "after His image," Cosmos, brought into being by Him, sustained and fed by Him, made deathless, as by his own Sire, living for aye, as ever free from death.

Now that which ever-liveth, differs from the Eternal; for He [214] hath not been brought to being *by another*, and even if He have been *brought to being*, He hath not *been* brought into being by Himself, but ever *is* brought into being.

For the Eternal, in that It is eternal, is the all. The Father is Himself eternal *of* Himself, but Cosmos hath become eternal and immortal *by* the Father.

3. And of the matter stored beneath it, [215] the Father made of it a universal body, and packing it together made it spherical—wrapping it round

---

[211] ἐνέργεια.
[212] The text is obscure, and the translations without exception make nonsense of it. Some words seem to be missing.
[213] Living thing, "animal."
[214] *Sc.* the Eternal.
[215] *Sc.* beneath the cosmos, world-order or universe.

the life [216]—[a sphere] which is immortal in itself, and that doth make materiality eternal.

But He, the Father, full-filled with His ideas, did sow the lives [217] into the sphere, and shut them in as in a cave, willing to order forth [218] the life with every kind of living.

So He with deathlessness enclosed the universal body, that matter might not wish to separate itself from body's composition, and so dissolve into its own [original] unorder.

For matter, son, when it was yet incorporate, was in unorder. And it doth still retain down here this [nature of unorder] enveloping the rest of the small lives [219]—that increase-and-decrease which men call death.

4. It is round earthly lives that this unorder doth exist. For that the bodies of the heavenly ones preserve one order allotted to them from the Father as their rule [220]; and it is by the restoration [221] of each one [of them] this order is preserved indissoluble. [222]

The "restoration" then of bodies on the earth is [thus their] composition, whereas their dissolution restores them to those bodies which can never be dissolved, that is to say, which know no death. Privation, thus, of sense is brought about, not loss of bodies.

5. Now the third life—Man, after the image of the Cosmos made, [and] having mind, after the Father's will, beyond all earthly lives—not only doth have feeling with the second God, but also hath conception of the first; for of the one 'tis sensible as of a body, while of the other it conceives as bodiless and the Good Mind.

Tat. Doth then *this* life not perish?

Her. Hush, son! and understand what God, what Cosmos [is], what is a life that cannot die, and what a life subject to dissolution.

Yea, understand the Cosmos is by God and in God; but Man by Cosmos and in Cosmos.

The source and limit and the constitution of all things is God.

---

[216] The text here seems to me to be very faulty; for ποιόν, ποιά, I read ζῷον, ζῷα. In such unintelligible phrases as αὐτῷ τὸ ποιόν, and τὸ μετ' αὐτοῦ ποιόν, the writer is evidently dealing with the Cosmos as the one life, the αὐτόζωον, from which all other lives are derived; and if he did not write αὐτόζωον, he assuredly wrote ζῶν. He wrote sense and not the nonsense of the present text.

[217] *Sc.* the great lives or so-called heavenly "bodies."

[218] Or beautify.

[219] As distinguished from the great lives or animals, the so-called heavenly "bodies."

[220] τὴν ἀρχήν,—or source or principle.

[221] ἀποκατάστασις, a term used of the cyclic return of stars to their original positions.

[222] If we may be permitted to coin a neologism.

COMMENTARY

THE COSMOS AS "SECOND GOD"

The superscription enunciates the nature of the treatise. It is evidently taken from the Dialogues to Tat, and originally formed part of some General Dissertation or of a collection of Dissertations.

It formed part of an instruction in which the Cosmos was treated of as "Second God," as we find it also in Philo [223]; but just as Philo guards against any idea of duality, so does our treatise when it ends with the words (§ 5):

"The source and limit and the constitution of all things is God."

The Great Body of the Cosmos, the Sphere or Perfect Form, the root of all forms, seems to be bounded by the idea of the Æon or Eternity, or Deathlessness. It is, as it were, the Cave or Womb of all things in genesis, centred in the Pleroma of ideas, the Intelligible Cosmos, which is full-filled with the ideas of God (§ 3).

THE LAW OF APOKATASTASIS

The eternal order and life of Cosmos is preserved by the law of *apokatastasis* or restoration (§ 4), the law of ever-becoming, and cyclic renewal, the making-new-again (ἀνανέωσις) of *C. H.*, iii. (iv.) 1.

There is no question of loss of body,—this is an illusion; there is a privation of sense, a going into latency of some particular phase of consciousness.

There are then Great Lives—God, Cosmos, Man. Cosmos is made in the image of God, Man in the image of Cosmos. Therefore has Man sense and mind; by the former he is "in sympathy with" the Cosmos, as Body by the latter he is conscious of God as Mind,—that is the Bodiless. Or as we might phrase it, by sense Man knows the Sensible Cosmos, by mind the Intelligible Cosmos, the Good Mind; for God is Source and Limit and the Constitution of all things—the Cosmos, both Intelligible and Sensible, included.

---

[223] *Leg. Alleg.*, § 21; M. i. 82; P. 1103 (Ri. i. 113); *Quæst. Sol.*, i. (quoted by Euseb., *Præp. Evang.*, vii. 13). See in the "Prolegomena," "Philo Concerning the Logos."

CORPUS HERMETICUM IX. (X.)

ON THOUGHT AND SENSE

THAT THE BEAUTIFUL AND GOOD IS IN GOD ONLY AND ELSEWHERE NOWHERE

(Text: P. 60-67; Pat. 14, 15.)

1. I GAVE the Perfect Sermon (*Logos*) yesterday, Asclepius; to-day I think it right, as sequel thereunto, to go through point by point the Sermon about Sense.

Now sense and thought do seem to differ, in that the former has to do with matter, the latter has to do with substance. But unto me both seem to be at-one and not to differ—in men I mean. In other lives [224]sense is at-oned with nature, but in men thought.

Now mind doth differ just as much from thought as God doth from divinity. For that divinity by God doth come to be, and by mind thought, the sister of the word (*logos*) [225] and instruments of one another. For neither doth the word (*logos*) find utterance without thought, nor is thought manifested without word.

2. So sense and thought both flow together into man, as though they were entwined with one another. For neither without sensing can one think, nor without thinking sense.

But it is possible [they say] to think a thing apart from sense, as those who fancy sights in dreams. But unto me it seems that both of these activities occur in dream-sight, and sense doth pass out of the sleeping to the waking state.

For man is separated into soul and body, and only when the two sides of his sense agree together, does utterance of its thought conceived by mind take place.

3. For it is mind that doth conceive all thoughts good thoughts—when it receives the seeds from God, their contraries when [it receiveth them] from one of the daimonials; no part of Cosmos being free of daimon, who stealthily doth creep into the daimon who's illumined by God's Light,[226] and sow in him the seed of its own energy.

---

[224] Or animals.
[225] There is here the usual play on the meanings, reason, word, sermon or sacred discourse.
[226] That is to say man, or rather the ego in man. The translators seem to make nonsense of this passage through rejecting the original reading.

And mind conceives the seed thus sown, adultery, murder, parricide, [and] sacrilege, impiety, [and] strangling, casting down precipices, and all such other deeds as are the work of evil daimones.

4. The seeds of God, 'tis true, are few, but vast and fair, and good—virtue and self-control, devotion. Devotion is God-gnosis; and he who knoweth God, being filled with all good things, thinks godly thoughts and not thoughts like the many [think].

For this cause they who Gnostic are, [227] please not the many, nor the many them. They are thought mad and laughed at [228]; they're hated and despised, and sometimes even put to death.

For we did say [229] that bad must needs dwell here on earth, where 'tis in its own place. Its place is earth, and not Cosmos, as some will sometimes say with impious tongue.

But he who is a devotee of God, will bear with all—once he has sensed the Gnosis. For such an one all things, e'en though they be for others bad, are for him good; deliberately he doth refer them all unto the Gnosis. And, thing most marvellous, 'tis he alone who maketh bad things good.

5. But I return once more to the Discourse (*Logos*) on Sense. That sense doth share with thought in man, doth constitute him man. But 'tis not [every] man, as I have said, who benefits by thought; for this man is material, that other one substantial.

For the material man, as I have said, [consorting] with the bad, doth have his seed of thought from daimons; while the substantial men [consorting] with the Good, are saved by God.

Now God is Maker of all things, and in His making, He maketh all [at last] like to Himself; but they, while they're becoming [230] good by exercise of their activity, are unproductive things.

It is the working of the Cosmic Course [231] that maketh their becomings what they are, befouling some of them with bad and others of them making clean with good.

For Cosmos, too, Asclepius, possesseth sense-and-thought peculiar to itself, not like to that of man; 'tis not so manifold, but as it were a better and a simpler one.

---

[227] **οἱ ἐν γνώσει ὄντες**, lit. they who are in Gnosis.
[228] *Cf.* Plat., *Phædr.*, 249 D: The wisdom-lover "is admonished, by the many as though he were beside himself."
[229] *Sc.* in some other sermon.
[230] Or being made.
[231] It is difficult to bring out the full delicacy of wording of the original in translation. First God's ultimate intention is stated to be the making all things like (**ὅμοια**) Himself; this is the great sameness of union with Him. But meantime while this making, creating or becoming, is going on, these imperfections cannot produce—that is, become creators in their turn; they are unproductive (**ἄφορα**). That which is the instrument of God's making is the cosmic course (**φορά**). We are finally (§ 7) told that it is bodies which are the cause of difference or diversity (**ἐν διαφορᾷ**), the opposite pole, so to speak, to the likeness (**ὅμοια**) with God.

6. The single sense-and-thought of Cosmos is to make all things, and make them back into itself again, as Organ of the Will of God, so organised that it, receiving all the seeds into itself from God, and keeping them within itself, may make all manifest, and [then] dissolving them, make them all new again; and thus, like a Good Gardener of Life, things that have been dissolved, it taketh to itself, and giveth them renewal once again.

There is no thing to which it gives not life; but taking all unto itself it makes them live, and is at the same time the Place of Life and its Creator.

7. Now bodies matter [-made] are in diversity. Some are of earth, of water some, some are of air, and some of fire.

But they are all composed; some are more [composite], and some are simpler. The heavier ones are more [composed], the lighter less so.

It is the speed of Cosmos' Course that works the manifoldness of the kinds of births. For being a most swift Breath, it doth bestow their qualities on bodies together with the One Pleroma—that of Life.

8. God, then, is Sire of Cosmos; Cosmos, of [all] in Cosmos. And Cosmos is God's Son; but things in Cosmos are by Cosmos.

And properly hath it been called Cosmos [Order]; for that it orders [232] all with their diversity of birth, with its not leaving aught without its life, with the unweariedness of its activity, the speed of its necessity, the composition of its elements, and order of its creatures.

The same, then, of necessity and of propriety should have the name of Order.

The sense-and-thought, then, of all lives doth come into them from without, inbreathed by what contains [them all]; whereas Cosmos receives them once for all together with its coming into being, and keeps them as a gift from God.

9. But God is not, as some suppose, beyond the reach of sense-and-thought. It is through superstition men thus impiously speak.

For all the things that are, Asclepius, all are in God, are brought by God to be, and do depend on Him—both things that act through bodies, and things that through soul-substance make [other things] to move, and things that make things live by means of spirit, and things that take unto themselves the things that are worn out.

And rightly so; nay, I would rather say, He doth not *have* these things; but I speak forth the truth, He *is* them all Himself. He doth not *get* them from without, but *gives* them out [from Him].

This is God's sense-and-thought, ever to move all things. And never time shall be when e'en a whit of things that are shall cease; and when I say "a whit of things that are," I mean a whit of God. For things that are, God hath; nor aught [is there] without Him, nor [is] He without aught.

---

[232] Or adorns.

10. These things should seem to thee, Asclepius, if thou dost understand them, true; but if thou dost not understand, things not to be believed.

To understand is to believe, to not believe is not to understand.

My word (*logos*) doth go before [thee] [233] to the truth. But mighty is the mind, and when it hath been led by word up to a certain point, it hath the power to come before [thee [234]] to the truth.

And having thought o'er all these things, and found them consonant with those which have already been translated by the reason, it [235] hath [e'en now] believed, and found its rest in that Fair Faith.

To those, then, who by God['s good aid] do understand the things that have been said [by us] above, they're credible; but unto those who understand them not, incredible.

Let so much, then, suffice on thought-and-sense.

---

[233] *Cf. C. H.,* iv. (v.) 11; vii. (viii.) 2; x. (xi.) 21; R. 23, n. 5.
[234] That is, presumably, before the pupil of the Gnosis is conscious of it in his physical brain.
[235] *Sc.* the mind.

COMMENTARY

TITLE AND ORDERING

This treatise bears a double title:—"On Thought and Sense," and "That the Beautiful and Good is in God only." The former heading is clearly taken from the concluding words: "Let so much then suffice on thought-and-sense"; whereas the introductory sentence speaks of the Sermon on Sense only. The latter heading seems to be a thoughtless repetition of the title of C. H., vi. (vii.).

The opening words: "I gave the Perfect Sermon yesterday, Asclepius," inform us not only that we have to do with an Asclepius Dialogue, but also that our sermon followed directly on the "Perfect Sermon," a Latin version of which has fortunately been preserved to us. [236]

It is, therefore, of very great interest to find that Lactantius, [237] in quoting a sentence from our treatise (§ 4)—"Devotion is God-gnosis"—continues with the words: "Asclepius, his hearer, has also explained the same idea at greater length in the Perfect Sermon."

Lactantius had, therefore, a collection before him in which these two sermons stood in close connection.

Reitzenstein (p. 195) thinks that our sermon must be an extract from a longer one, because he cannot bring himself to believe that so short a treatise could have been found in immediate connection (as the opening words suggest) with so lengthy and detailed a tractate as the "Perfect Sermon." This may be so; and yet the formal beginning and ending of our sermon would seem to suggest that we are dealing with a complete tractate and not with an extract.

"SENSE-AND-THOUGHT"

The doctrine that in men "sense-and-thought" together constitutes human "sense" throws some light on the meaning of the term "sense" as used elsewhere in the Trismegistic literature, where we should expect to find "mind" employed, and that, too, in the sense of the higher mind.

Normal human "thought," then, is, so to say, sensible, entirely bound up in sense-impressions; it is the mind alone that can soar beyond the senses, for it alone can be "illumined by God's Light" (§ 3).

The mind is, as it were, a womb or woman, that can be impregnated either by the "Seeds of God" or by the "Daimonial Energy"; she thus conceives and brings forth virtues or vices.

---

[236] For it would, of course, be absurd to suppose that the "Perfect Sermon" could in any way be thought to indicate C. H., vi. (vii.), the last Asclepius Dialogue in our Corpus; especially when our sermon (§ 4) directly combats the teaching of C. H., vi.
[237] *Div. Institt.*, ii. 15 (Ed. Fritz., i. 106); cf. also v. 14.

All of this is precisely the same doctrine as Philo preaches, as may be seen by the passages we have quoted in the "Prolegomena" on the subject of the "Sacred Marriage."

THOSE IN GNOSIS

The Seeds of God are Virtue and Self-control and Devotion or Piety; and Devotion in its true sense is God-gnosis, or Knowledge of God. The Gnostics, then, "they who are in Gnosis"—a curious expression—because of their natural divorcement from the "world," "please not the many, nor the many them."

"They are thought mad and laughed at; they're hated and despised, and sometimes even put to death."

Mark the impersonal note, the calm laying down of the causes of misunderstanding between the "many" and the "few"; and compare this with the more personal note of the saying underlying the following Synoptic accommodations:

"Blessed are ye when men hate you and excommunicate you, and revile and expel your Name as evil, for the Son of Man's sake" (Luke vi. 22).

"Blessed are ye when men revile you and persecute you and say all evil against you, lying, for My sake" (Matt. v. 11).

It is clear, at least it seems so to me, that "Luke" has kept closer to the original, and that that original was addressed not only to the members of a community, but to those who had been cast forth from some other community "for the sake of the Son of Man"—that is, because of the immediate inspiration of the Logos, which doubtless did not pay sufficient attention to the prejudices of the "many" of that community.

"Matthew," on the contrary, seems to have adapted the Saying for general purposes and the necessities of the Cult of Jesus. [238]

THE TRUE GNOSTIC

Excellent also is the doctrine that the true "Gnostic," the man who is consciously growing into the stature of the Christ, the true "Devotee of God," "will bear with all," for he is beginning to know the Reason of things.

"For such an one all things, e'en though they be for others bad, are for him good; deliberately he doth refer them all unto the Gnosis."

He sees the Good, he sees God, in all things. He is the true Alchemist. For "thing most marvellous, 'tis he alone who maketh bad things good"; by spiritual alchemy he transmutes the evil of the world to good; he

---

[238] R. (p. 213, 1) brings this passage of our sermon into connection with some assumed persecution of the Pœmandres communities in the course of the fourth century; but I cannot myself see the slightest ground for such an assumption.

drains the "cup of bitterness" unto the dregs, and transmutes it into the pure Water of Life.

In every Man, then, there are two "men," the material (or hylic) and the substantial (or spiritual, οὐσιώδης).

Evil, however, is not a permanent thing; it is but the process of "becoming good," the productive side of things (§ 5).

THE GOAL OF THE GNOSIS

It is difficult to bring out the delicacy of the wording of the original in translation. First God's ultimate intention is stated to be the making of all things like unto (ὅμοια) Himself; the world-process is to be ultimately consummated in the Great Sameness of Union with Him. But meantime while this making, creating or becoming, or transformation, is going on, the imperfections cannot produce, that is, become creators in their turn; they are unproductive (ἄφορα). That which is the instrument or organ of God's making is the Cosmic Course (φορά). We are finally (§ 7) told that the differences of bodies are conditioned by the speed of this Cosmic Course; therefore the opposite poles, Other and Same, are both ultimately referable to Cosmos, the Likeness of God.

The end to be achieved is to develop the "sense-and-thought" of the Cosmos, the One Sense, not manifold, but simple. This is the deliberate working with the Will of God, the Cosmic Will, the perpetual renewing of all things (ἀνανέωσις).

The Cosmos, then, as the Logos of God, is the Good Gardener of Life; it is both the place of Life and its Creator—that is to say, both female and male, both Mother and Father.

THE POSSIBILITY OF KNOWING GOD

But the Cosmos is not apart from God, nor even *in* God; God does not *have* Cosmos as a possession, but *is* Cosmos and all therein (§ 9). Cosmos is Son of God, His Very Self (§ 8).

Therefore we can learn to know somewhat of the nature of God by sense and thought, for, "God is not, as some suppose, beyond the reach of sense and thought" (ἀναισθητὸς καὶ ἀνόητος); that is, God does not entirely transcend sense and thought, for God is all things.

"As some suppose" doubtless refers again to the "blasphemers" of § 4—that is, the apparently dualistic doctrine set forth in *C. H.*, vi. (vii.). [239]

---

[239] Reitzenstein (p. 171, 2) compares this doctrine of the insensibility and incognizability of God with the Sabæan Gnosis.

And so, finally, we learn that Faith, in the true sense, is a certitude of the mind, or of true manhood. "To understand is to believe" (§ 10). Gnosis and not belief is the Fair Faith.

Compare with this the "Perfect Sermon," x. 1:

"The reason for a thesis such as this, O my Asclepius, I would that thou should'st grasp, not only with the keen attention of thy soul, but also with its living power as well.

"For 'tis a reason that most men cannot believe; the Perfect and the True are to be grasped by the more holy minds."

CORPUS HERMETICUM X. (XI.)

THE KEY

OF THRICE-GREATEST HERMES

(Text: P. 67-84; Pat. 9b-12.)

1. *Hermes.* My yesterday's discourse (*logos*) I did devote to thee, Asclepius, and so 'tis [only] right I should devote to-day's to Tat; and this the more because 'tis the abridgment of the General Sermons (*Logoi*) which he has had addressed to him.

"God, Father and the Good," then, Tat, hath [240] the same nature, or more exactly, *energy.*

For *nature* is a predicate of growth, and used of things that change, both mobile and immobile, that is to say, both human and divine, each one of which He *willeth* into being.

But *energy* consists in something else, as we have shown in treating of the rest, both things divine and human things [241]; which thing we ought to have in mind when treating of the Good. [242]

2. God's energy is then His Will; further His essence is to will the being of all things. For what is "God and Father and the Good" but the *to be* of all that are not yet? Nay, subsistence [243] self of everything that is;—this, then, is God, this Father, this the Good; to Him is added naught of all the rest.

And though the Cosmos, that is to say the Sun, is also sire himself to them that share in him; yet so far is he not the cause of good unto the lives, he is not even of their living.

So that e'en if he be a sire, he is entirely so by the compulsion of the Good's Good-will, apart from which nor being nor becoming could e'er be.

3. Again, the parent is the children's cause, both on the father's and the mother's side, [244] only by *sharing in* [245] the Good's desire [that doth pour] through the Sun. It is the Good which doeth the creating.

---

[240] The three are only different names for one idea; the verb is in the singular in the Greek. *Cf. C. H.,* ii. (iii.) 16 and 17: "Good then is God and God is Good"; and "The other name of God is Father."

[241] That is to say, presumably, in the General Sermons.

[242] Lit. of this.

[243] ὕπαρξις. *Cf. C. H.,* xvi. 4.

[244] Lit. both with regard to seed and nourishment.

[245] Lit. *taking.*

And such a power can be possessed by no one else than Him alone who *taketh* naught, [246] but *wills* all things to be; I will not, Tat, say *makes*.

For that the *maker* is defective for long periods (in which he sometimes makes, and sometimes doth not make) both in the quality and in the quantity [of what he makes]; in that he sometimes maketh them so many and such like, and sometimes the reverse.

But "God and Father and the Good" is [cause] for all to be. So are at least these things for who can see.

4. For It doth will to be, and It is both Itself and most of all by reason of [247] Itself. Indeed all other things beside are just because of It; for the distinctive feature of the Good is "that it should be known." Such is the Good, O Tat.

Tat. Thou hast, O father, filled us so full [248] of this so good and fairest Sight, that thereby my mind's eye hath now become for me almost a thing to worship.

For that the Vision of the Good doth not, like the sun's beam, fire-like blaze on the eyes and make them close; nay, on the contrary, it shineth forth and maketh to increase the seeing [249] of the eye, as far as e'er a man hath the capacity to hold the inflow of the radiance that the mind alone can see.

Not only does it come more swiftly down to us, but it does us no harm, and is instinct with all immortal life.

5. They who are able to drink in a somewhat more than others of this Sight, ofttimes from out the body fall asleep into this fairest Spectacle, as was the case with Uranus and Cronus, our forebears. [250] May this be our lot too, O father mine!

Her. Yea, may it be, my son! But as it is, we are not yet strung to the Vision, and not as yet have we the power our mind's eye to unfold and gaze upon the Beauty of the Good—Beauty that naught can e'er corrupt or any comprehend.

For [only] then wilt thou upon It gaze when thou canst say no word concerning It. For Gnosis of the Good is holy silence and a giving holiday to every sense.

6. For neither can he who perceiveth It, perceive aught else; nor he who gazeth on It, gaze on aught else; nor hear aught else, nor stir his body any way. Staying his body's every sense and every motion he stayeth still.

And shining then all round his mind, It shines through his whole soul, and draws it out of body, transforming all of him to essence.

---

[246] *Cf. C. H.*, ii. (iii.) 16: "The Good is He who gives all things and naught receives."
[247] Lit. for.
[248] ἐπλήρωσας,—reminding us of πλήρωμα.
[249] Lit. light.
[250] See Lact, *D. Institt.*, i. 11; *P. S. A.*, xi. 4, xxxvii. 3; and Ex. i. 4.

For it is possible, my son, that a man's soul should be made like to God, e'en while it still is in a body, if it doth contemplate the Beauty of the Good.

7. *Tat.* Made like to God! What dost thou, father, mean?

Her. Of every soul apart are transformations, son.

Tat. What meanest thou? Apart!

Her. [251] Didst thou not, in the General Sermons, hear that from One Soul—the All-soul—come all these souls which are made to revolve in all the cosmos, as though divided off?

Of these souls, then, it is that there are many changes, some to a happier lot and some to [just] the contrary of this.

Thus some that were once creeping things change into things that in the water dwell, the souls of water things change to earth-dwellers, those that live on the earth change into things with wings, and souls that live in air change into men, while human souls reach the first step of deathlessness changed into daimones.

And so they circle to the choir of the Inerrant Gods; for of the Gods there are two choirs, the one Inerrant, and the other Errant. And this is the most perfect glory of the soul.

8. But if a soul on entering in the body of a man persisteth in its vice, [252] it neither tasteth deathlessness nor shareth in the Good; but speeding back again it turns into the path that leads to creeping things. This is the sentence of the vicious soul.

And the soul's vice is ignorance. [253] For that the soul who hath no knowledge of the things that are, or knowledge of their nature, or of Good, is blinded by the body's passions and tossed about.

This wretched soul, not knowing what she is, becomes the slave of bodies of strange form in sorry plight, bearing the body as a load; not as the ruler, but the ruled. This [ignorance] is the soul's vice.

9. But on the other hand the virtue of the soul is Gnosis. For he who knows, he good and pious is, and still while on the earth [254] divine.

Tat. But who is such an one, O father mine?

Her. He who doth not say much or lend his ear to much. For he who spendeth time in arguing and hearing arguments, doth shadow fight. For "God, the Father and the Good," is not to be obtained by speech or hearing.

And yet though this is so, there are in all the *beings* senses, in that they cannot without senses *be*.

---

[251] From here to end of § 8 is quoted by Stobæus, *Phys.*, I. xli. 48 (G. i. 429, 430; W. 416, 18 ff.).
[252] ἐὰν κακὴ μείνῃ.
[253] Cf. *C. H.*, xii. (xiii.) 3: "The great ill of the soul is Godlessness"; also below § 20: "What greater chastisement of any human soul can there be, son, than lack of piety?"
[254] Lit. already.

But Gnosis is far different from sense. For sense is brought about by that which hath the mastery o'er us, while Gnosis is the end of science, [255] and science is God's gift.

10. All science is incorporal, the instrument it uses being the mind, just as the mind employs the body.

Both then come into bodies, [I mean] both things that are cognizable by mind alone and things material. [256] For all things must consist out of antithesis and contrariety; and this can otherwise not be.

Tat. Who then is this material God of whom thou speakest?

Her. Cosmos is *beautiful*, but is not *good* [257]—for that it is material and freely passible [258]; and though it is the first of all things passible, yet is it in the second rank of being and wanting in itself.

And though it never hath itself its birth in time, but ever is, yet is its being in becoming, becoming for all time the genesis of qualities and quantities; for it is mobile and all material motion's genesis. [259]

11. It is intelligible [260] rest that moves material motion in this way, [261]since Cosmos is a sphere—that is to say, a head. And naught of head above's material, as naught of feet below's intelligible, [262] but all material.

And head itself moved in a sphere-like way—that is to say, as head should move, [263] is mind.

All then that are united to the "tissue" of this "head" (in which [264] is soul) are in their nature free from death,—just as when body hath been made in soul, are things that have more soul than body.

Whereas those things which are at greater distance from this "tissue"—there, where are things which have a greater share of body than of soul—are by their nature subject unto death.

The whole, however, is a life; so that the universe consists of both the hylic and of the intelligible. [265]

12. Again, the Cosmos is the first of living things, while man is second after it, though first of things subject to death.

Man hath the same ensouling power in him as all the rest of living things [266]; yet is he not only not good, but even evil, [267] for that he's subject unto death. [268]

---

[255] ἐπιστήμης.
[256] Or hylic.
[257] But *cf. P. S. A.*, xxvii. 1.
[258] That is capable of suffering, or impressionable by agencies other than itself.
[259] Genesis and becoming are both γένεσις in Greek.
[260] Noëtic as opposed to hylic—the antithesis and contrariety mentioned above.
[261] Namely the ever-becoming of genesis.
[262] Or mental, in the sense of being of the same nature as the mind.
[263] κεφαλικῶς.
[264] In which "tissue."
[265] §§ 12, 13 are quoted by Stobæus, *Phys.*, I. xxxix. 9 (G. i. 307; W. 350, 13 ff.).
[266] That is to say, the world-system itself and all the globes in it.

For though the Cosmos also is not good in that it suffers motion, it is not evil, in that it is not subject unto death. But man, in that he's subject both to motion and to death, is evil. [269]

13. Now then the principles [270] of man are this-wise vehicled: mind in the reason (*logos*), the reason in the soul, soul in the spirit, [271] [and] spirit in the body.

Spirit pervading [body] [272] by means of veins and arteries and blood, bestows upon the living creature motion, and as it were doth bear it in a way.

For this cause some do think the soul is blood, in that they do mistake its nature, not knowing that [at death] it is the spirit that must first withdraw into the soul, whereon the blood congeals and veins and arteries are emptied, and then the living creature is withdrawn; and this is body's death.

14. Now from One Source [273] all things depend; while Source [dependeth] from the One and Only [One]. Source is, moreover, moved to become Source again; whereas the One standeth perpetually and is not moved.

Three then are they: "God, the Father and the Good," Cosmos and man.

God doth contain Cosmos; Cosmos [containeth] man. Cosmos is e'er God's Son, man as it were Cosmos's child.

15. Not that, however, God ignoreth man; nay, right well doth He know him, and willeth to be known.

This is the sole salvation for a man—God's Gnosis. This is the Way Up to the Mount. [274]

By Him alone the soul becometh good, not whiles is good, whiles evil, but [good] out of necessity.

Tat. What dost thou mean, Thrice-greatest one?

Her. Behold an infant's soul, my son, that is not yet cut off,[275] because its body is still small and not as yet come unto its full bulk. [276]

Tat. How?

Her. A thing of beauty altogether is [such a soul] to see, not yet befouled by body's passions, still all but hanging from the Cosmic Soul!

But when the body grows in bulk and draweth down the soul into its mass, then doth the soul cut off itself and bring upon itself forgetfulness, and

---

[267] *Cf.* Ex. i. 11 and 15.
[268] Whereas the system and its globes are regarded as practically immortal.
[269] Reitzenstein (p. 40, 1) gives a revised text of the major part of this utterance of Hermes, from "Cosmos is beautiful" onwards, but unfortunately he omits just the most obscure sentences in it.
[270] Lit. a man's soul, where ψυχή is used in a general sense, and not in the particular sense applied to it in the category which immediately follows.
[271] πνεύματι.
[272] *Cf. P. S. A.*, vi. 4.
[273] ἀρχή.
[274] Lit. to Olympus.
[275] *Sc.* from the world-soul.
[276] *Cf.* the instructive exposition of Basilides in *F. F. F.*, pp. 274 f.

no more shareth in the Beautiful and Good. And this forgetfulness becometh vice.

16. It is the same for them who go out from the body.

For when the soul withdraws into itself, the spirit doth contract itself within the blood, and soul within the spirit. [277] And then the mind, stript of its wrappings, and naturally divine, taking unto itself a fiery body, doth traverse every space, after abandoning the soul unto its judgment and whatever chastisement it hath deserved.

Tat. [278] What dost thou, father, mean by this? The mind is parted from the soul and soul from spirit? Whereas thou said'st the soul was the mind's vesture, and the soul's the spirit.

17. *Her.* The hearer, son, should think with him who speaks and breathe with him [279]; nay, he should have a hearing subtler than the voice of him who speaks.

It is, son, in a body made of earth that this arrangement of the vestures comes to pass. For in a body made of earth it is impossible the mind should take its seat itself by its own self in nakedness.

For neither is it possible on the one hand the earthy body should contain such immortality, nor on the other that so great a virtue should endure a body passible in such close contact with it. It taketh, then, the soul for as it were an envelope.

And soul itself, being too a thing divine, doth use the spirit as *its* envelope, while spirit doth pervade the living creature.

18. When then the mind doth free itself from the earth-body, it straightway putteth on its proper robe of fire, with which it could not dwell in an earth-body.

For earth doth not bear fire; for it is all set in a blaze even by a small spark. And for this cause is water poured round earth, to be a guard and wall, to keep the blazing of the fire away.

But mind, the swiftest thing of all divine out-thinkings, and swifter than all elements, hath for its body fire.

For mind being builder [280] doth use the fire as tool for the construction of all things—the Mind of all [for the construction] of all things, but that of man only for things on earth.

Stript of its fire the mind on earth cannot make things divine, for it is human in its dispensation. [281]

---

[277] This is generally translated "the spirit is contracted *into* the blood, and the soul into the spirit," but such a translation contradicts § 13, where we are told that "the spirit withdraws *into* the soul" at death. It seems to mean that the spirit passes *within, out of* the blood, and the soul is then clothed in a spirit-vesture, or borne in a spirit-vehicle.

[278] From here to the end of § 18 is quoted by Stobæus, *Phys.*, xl. 3 (G. i. 312, 313; W. 310, 25 ff.); only the dialogue is ascribed in error to Asclepius and Tat and not to Hermes and Tat.

[279] Cf. *P. S. A.*, x. i.

[280] δημιουργός.

19. The soul in man, however,—not every soul, but one that pious is—is a daimonic something and divine.

And such a soul when from the body freed, if it have fought the fight of piety—the fight of piety is to know God and to do wrong to no man—such soul becomes entirely mind.

Whereas the impious soul remains in its own essence, chastised by its own self, and seeking for an earthy body where to enter, if only it be human.

For that no other body can contain a human soul; nor is it right that any human soul should fall into the body of a thing that doth possess no reason. For that the law of God is this: to guard the human soul from such tremendous outrage. [282]

20. *Tat.* How father, then, is a man's soul chastised?

Her. What greater chastisement of any human soul can there be, son, than lack of piety? What fire has so fierce flame as lack of piety? What ravenous beast so mauls the body as lack of piety the very soul?

Dost thou not see what hosts of ills the impious soul doth bear?

It shrieks and screams: I burn; I am ablaze; I know not what to cry or do; ah, wretched me, I am devoured by all the ills that compass me about; alack, poor me, I neither see nor hear!

Such are the cries wrung from a soul chastised; not, as the many think, and thou, son, dost suppose, that a [man's] soul, passing from body, is changed into a beast.

Such is a very grave mistake, for that the way a soul doth suffer chastisement is this:

21. When mind becomes a daimon, the law requires that it should take a fiery body to execute the services of God; and entering in the soul most impious it scourgeth it with whips made of its sins.

And then the impious soul, scourged with its sins, is plunged in murders, outrage, blasphemy, in violence of all kinds, and all the other things whereby mankind is wronged. [283]

But on the pious soul the mind doth mount and guide it [284] to the Gnosis' Light. And such a soul doth never tire in songs of praise [to God] and pouring blessing on all men, and doing good in word and deed to all, in imitation of its Sire. [285]

22. Wherefore, my son, thou shouldst give praise to God and pray that thou mayst have thy mind Good [Mind]. It is, then, to a better state the soul doth pass; it cannot to a worse.

---

[281] τῇ διοικήσει, *i.e.* in its economy.
[282] This paragraph is quoted by Stobæus, *Phys.*, xli. 49 (G. i. 430, 431; W. 417, 15 ff.). For the idea, *cf. P. S. A.*, xxxii. 2.
[283] *Cf. P. S. A.*, xxv. 4 and xxviii. 1.
[284] *Cf. C. H.*, iv. (v.) 11; vii. (viii.) 11; ix. (x.) 10; R. 23, n. 5.
[285] Namely, the Good.

Further [286] there is an intercourse [287] of souls; those of the gods have intercourse with those of men, and those of men with souls of creatures which possess no reason.

The higher, further, have in charge the lower; the gods look after men, men after animals irrational, [288] while God hath charge of all; for He is higher than them all and all are less than He.

Cosmos is subject, then, to God, man to the Cosmos, and irrationals to man. But God is o'er them all, and God contains them all.

God's rays, to use a figure, are His energies; the Cosmos's are natures; the arts and sciences are man's. [289]

The energies act through the Cosmos, thence through the nature-rays of Cosmos upon man; the nature-rays [act] through the elements; man [acteth] through the sciences and arts.

23. This is the dispensation [290] of the universe, depending from the nature of the One, pervading [all things] through the Mind, than which [291] is naught diviner or of greater energy; and naught a greater means for the at-oning men to gods and gods to men.

He, [Mind,] is the Good Daimon. Blessed the soul that is most filled with Him, and wretched [292] is the soul that's empty of the Mind.

Tat. Father, what dost thou mean, again?

Her. [293] Dost think then, son, that every soul hath the Good [Mind]? For 'tis of Him we speak, not of the mind in service [294] of which we just were speaking, the mind sent down for [the soul's] chastisement.

24. For soul without the mind "can neither speak nor act." [295] For oftentimes the mind doth leave the soul, and at that time the soul nor sees nor understands, but is just like a thing that hath no reason. Such is the power of mind.

Yet doth it not endure a sluggish [296] soul, but leaveth such a soul tied to the body and bound tight down by it. Such soul, my son, doth not have

---

[286] From here to the end is quoted by Stobæus, *Phys.*, I. xxxix. 8 (G. i. 305-307; W. 303, 14 ff.).
[287] κοινωνία. Cf. *P. S. A.*, xxiii. 1.
[288] Cf. *P. S. A.*, v. 1.
[289] Cf. Ex. viii. 1.
[290] διοίκησις, compare 19.
[291] *Sc.* the Mind.
[292] κακοδαίμων, as opposed to ὁ ἀγαθὸς δαίμων. It is impossible to reproduce the original word-play in translation.
[293] Stobæus (Gaisford) here reads "A."—that is, Asclepius.
[294] τοῦ ὑπηρετικοῦ, compare § 21, "the services of God" (τὰς τοῦ θεοῦ ὑπηρεσίας); that is to say, Hermes speaks of the Universal Mind and not of the mind in man.
[295] A quotation from the ancient gnomic poet Theognis (v. 177). Theognis lived *c.* 570-490 B.C.
[296] νωτρᾶς,—? νωθρᾶς. Everard translates "an idle or lazy soul," in his usual slipshod fashion of inserting doubles; Parthey gives "*inertem animam*"; Ménard, "*l'âme vicieuse*"; Chambers, "inert." Several of the old editors omit the entire sentence.

Mind; and therefore such an one should not be called a *man*. [297] For that man is a thing-of-life [298] divine; man is not measured with the rest of lives of things upon the earth, but with the lives above in heaven, who are called gods.

Nay more, if we must boldly speak the truth, the true "man" is e'en higher than the gods, or at the [very] least the gods and men are every whit in power each with the other equal.

25. For no one of the gods in heaven shall come down on the earth, o'er-stepping heaven's limit; whereas man doth mount up to heaven and measure it; he knows what things of it are high, what things are low, and learns precisely all things else besides. And greater thing than all; without e'en quitting earth, he doth ascend above. So vast a sweep doth he possess of ecstasy. [299]

For this cause can a man dare say that man on earth is god subject to death, while god in heaven is man from death immune.

Wherefore the dispensation of all things is brought about *by means of* [300] these, the twain—Cosmos and Man [301]—but *by* [302] the One.

---

[297] Cf. Philo, *De Som.*, § 20; M. i. 639; P. 584 (Ri. iii. 241): "not for those who *are called* men, but for those who *are truly so.*"
[298] Or animal.
[299] ἐκστάσεως, lit. extension, or consciousness.
[300] διά.
[301] Cf. P. S. A., x. 3.
[302] ὑπό.

COMMENTARY

THE CONSUMMATION OF THE "GENERAL SERMONS"

What "yesterday's sermon," which Hermes addressed to Asclepius, may have been, we have no means of deciding. The similarity of the phrase with the opening words of *C. H.*, ix. (x.) is noticeable, and points, perhaps, to a collection of Sermons to Asclepius and Tat strung together in some chronological order, as delivered day by day. If this be the fact, however, we must assume that such introductions were prefixed by the editor of that collection.

"The Key of Thrice-greatest Hermes" must have been considered one of the most remarkable documents of the school, for, as we have already mentioned in the case of "The Cup" treatise, the apocryphal "Books of Moses" plagiarize the title. [303]

That it was an important treatise may also be seen from the fact that Stobæus reproduces no less than five extracts from it under the title, "From the [Sermons] of Hermes to Tat," or simply "Of Hermes." Strangely enough in *two* cases (xxxix. 8 and xl. 3) Stobæus makes the persons of the dialogue Asclepius and Tat; this, however, must be a mistake, for it contradicts his own headings, it contradicts the nature of the sermon, it contradicts the supposed introduction of the editor of the collection from whom the redactor of our Corpus has taken his text, and it contradicts Chalcidius, who quotes from our treatise as a treatise of Hermes. [304]

Nevertheless, in spite of the importance of the treatise, it purports to be an epitome, [305] an abridgment of the "General Sermons" (οἱ γενικοὶ λόγοι)[306] addressed to Tat.

The sermon itself, however, has by no means the appearance of being an abridgment; on the contrary, it is one of the most complete and fundamental expositions that we have.

I would, therefore, suggest that the general reference in the words, "as we have shown in treating of the rest" (§ 1), and the precise reference to "The General Sermons," in § 7, have originated this wording of the introduction

---

[303] R. 182, 3; 190, 2.
[304] Chalcid., *Comment. in Timæum* (ed. Fabric.), p. 350.
[305] Compare also the introduction to *C. H.*, xvi. (see R. 191, 1); and also Ex. i. 16 and Comment.
[306] *Cf.* § 7, below; *C. H.*, xiii. (xiv.) 1; and Exs. ix. 1 and xviii. 1. The title must be so translated, I think, in spite of the fact that in the introductory words of the above treatise the term is immediately followed by the antithesis "rebirth" (παλιγγενεσία), as though the Sermons were on birth or genesis (γένεσις),—which, as we know from the Naassene Document, was the subject of the Lesser Mysteries, whereas Rebirth was that of the Greater. Everard gives "in the general speeches"; Parthey, "*in communibus*"; Ménard, "*dans les discours généraux*"; Chambers, "in the Generalities."

with the editor of the collection of Asclepius and Tat Sermons which I have previously supposed. It is a gloss of the editor and no part of the original text.

If this argument holds good, "The Key," instead of being an epitome, is a further teaching that presupposes a prior instruction already given in "The General Sermons," and so stands out as a more intimate exposition of the inward doctrine of the higher grades of the school.

Reitzenstein (p. 461) would have it that the doctrine of Sermons, ix. (x.) and x. (xi.), is a mediate one between the dualism of vi. (vii.) and the pronounced pantheistic mysticism of v. (vi.) and xi. (xii.); but I should fancy that these labels, even if they are correctly attached, would not represent such overwhelming contradictions to the Trismegistic doctors as they appear to do to their modern critics. There were different points of view; there were different grades of instruction; every doctrine had more truth in it at the proper time and in the right place. In any case this sermon is one of the most beautiful tractates preserved to us.

THE WILL OF GOD

1. Our treatise begins with the statement that the universe and all therein is due to the Energy or Effective Working of God—that is to say, His Will. This Will is immutable and constant—the Law of the universe.

How subtly these philosophers in their most intimate circles used these terms may be seen from the Gnostic Doctor, Basilides, who writes:

"Naught was,—neither matter, nor substance, nor voidness of substance, nor simplicity, nor impossibility of composition, nor inconceptibility, nor imperceptibility, neither man, nor angel [Hermeticè, daimon], nor God; in fine, neither anything at all for which man has ever found a name, nor any operation which falls within the range either of his perception or conception.

"Such, or rather far more removed from the power of man's comprehension, was the state of Non-Being, when the Deity beyond Being, without thinking, or feeling, or determining, or choosing, or being compelled, or desiring, willed to create universality."

"When I use the term will," writes Basilides, "I do so merely to suggest the idea of an operation transcending all volition, thought, or sensible action."

2. God's Energy, or Self-realization, is, then, His Will ($\theta\acute{\epsilon}\lambda\eta\sigma\iota\varsigma$); His Essence ($o\mathring{\upsilon}\sigma\acute{\iota}\alpha$) or Substance is "to will the being of all things"; in brief, He is the Very Subsistence ($\mathring{\upsilon}\pi\alpha\rho\xi\iota\varsigma$) of all—a term which subsequently came into great prominence in the later Platonic philosophy.

3. In § 3 we have a clear distinction drawn between the transcendent idea of God as Creator or Willer, and the ordinary conception of God as Maker or Fabricator or Demiurge—a distinction that meets us in almost every

Gnostic system. In our treatise, however, there is no setting of the one idea over against the other in any sense of antagonism. It is only stated that the self-operation of Deity transcends all such limited conceptions as that of a Maker or Fabricator.

OF GNOSIS AND ECSTASIS

4. The distinctive feature of God as the Good, or the Desirable, the Supreme Consummation, is "that He should be known" (τὸ γνωρίζεσθαι); in other words, the science of all sciences is the Gnosis of God.

5. The Vision Glorious, the One Sight, is next spoken of under the simile of the shining of a Ray of the Light[307] and Life of the Spiritual Sun into the mind. This consummation of Ecstasis, [308] we are told, was a transcending of the limitations of body, and was a faculty possessed by the forebears (πρόγονοι) of the "race" into which Hermes and now Tat are being born; these ancestors are mentioned under symbolic Greek names, evidently a substitute for Egyptian ones, for the reference is clearly to the priesthood of some past civilization of the Nile Land. At the same time, it can be referred to certain grades of super-men, regarded as gods, who had reached to certain stages of celestial dignity.[309]

To this idea of ancient Masters of the Gnosis in Egypt, Lactantius refers as follows:

"And so it appears that he [Cronus] was not born from Heaven (which is impossible), but from that man who was called Uranus; and that this is so, Trismegistus bears witness, when, in stating that there have been very few in whom the perfect science has been found, he mentioned in their number Uranus, Cronus, and Hermes his kinsfolk."[310]

Lactantius seems to be somewhat under the fascination of the theory of Euhemerus, and has no credence in the Heaven-born, in spite of the Christ Birth. We, however, learn from him that he knew of a statement by Hermes in this connection in which, besides Uranus and Cronus, an ancient Hermes was mentioned. Now in our treatise this is not the case, and Tat and not Hermes is the speaker; whereas in *P. S. A.*, xxxvii., where Hermes speaks of his progenitor Hermes, no mention is made of Uranus and Cronus. Therefore Lactantius refers to a lost treatise of Hermes.

---

[307] Hipp., *Philos.*, vii. 21 (ed. D. and S., p. 358); *F. F. F.*, pp. 257, 258.

[308] *Cf.* § 25, where ecstasis is explained as an extension of consciousness,—a certain "greatness" (μέγεθος).

[309] See the "Chart of Orphic Cosmogony," facing p. 87 of my Orpheus (London, 1896), where Uranus and Cronus are referred to the two lower of the three Noëtic "planes" transcending the Sensible Universe.

[310] *Div. Institt.*, i. 11 (ed. Fritz., i. 29, 30).

OF APOTHEOSIS

6. The nature of Ecstasy is then further explained; it is the fruit of meditation or contemplation, the consummation of the Theoretic Life.

"The Gnosis of the Good is holy silence and a giving holiday (καταργία) to every sense."

The Holy Silence reminds us of the Sigē of the Christian Gnostics; here, however, instead of the Mother-Æon of Cosmos, it is used in the sense of the pure mother-nature of the little cosmos of man, the divine womb that brings to birth the true man.

With this may be compared *C. H.*, xiii. (xiv.) 2:

"Wisdom conceived by mind in silence, such is the matter and the womb from out which *man* is born, and the true Good the seed."

It is hardly necessary to add that this is the Yoga of the Upaniṣhads. Indeed, the first part of § 6 might be taken word for word from those sublime treatises of Vaidik theosophy, and shows how identical is the thought of those who have first-hand experience of the higher consciousness.

"For it is possible, my son, that a man's soul should be made like to God (ἀποθεωθῆναι), e'en while it still is in a body, if it doth contemplate the Beauty of the Good."

This is the "deification" (ἀποθέωσις), or "apotheōsis" of a man; he becomes like unto God, in that he becomes a god. The Beauty of the Good is the Cosmic Order; and the mode of this meditation was to bring the soul into sympathy with the Cosmic Soul.

THE METAMORPHOSES OF THE SOUL

7. The secret of this divine operation (or theurgy) is based upon the fact that the soul can be transformed into every likeness. The Great Likeness of God is the Cosmic Order, the making oneself into this Likeness is the supreme transformation or transfiguration of the soul.

The separated or individual soul is in perpetual pilgrimage, revolving on the wheel of transformation. This doctrine was shared in by many other faiths, and it was also Egyptian.

In this connection we may refer instructively to Hippolytus' quotations from the Naassene Document (§ 3 S.):

"And they [311] say that the soul is very difficult to discover, and hard to understand; for it never remains of the same appearance, or form, or in the

---

[311] The quotation is from the text of the Hellenistic Commentator, who is referring to the Chaldæans.

same state, so that we can describe it by a general type, or comprehend it by an essential quality."

On this Hippolytus comments:

"These variegated metamorphoses they [312]have laid down in the Gospel superscribed 'According to the Egyptians.'"

The *Gospel according to the Egyptians* is lost, with the exception of a few fragments. We, however, here learn that it described the metamorphoses of the soul. It was a Gospel having its origin in Egypt and suited to Egyptian modes of thought. It follows, therefore, that the doctrine of the soul's transformation was Egyptian. [313]

THE LADDER OF BEING

The Hermetic doctrine of the evolution of the soul, by means of multitudinous transformations, is characterised by certain main moments, for in the course of it it passes through definite stages of existence designated as animal, human, daimonic, and god-like; there being, further, two grades of being within the choir of gods—the errant and inerrant. The final stage is the most perfect glory (δόξα) or power of the soul.

With all of this there is a strikingly exact parallel of ideas in the Pauline Letters.

"But some one will say: How do the dead rise, and with what body do they come [? back]?

"Thou foolish one! That which thou sowest is not made quick unless it die.

"And that which thou sowest—'tis not the body that shall be thou sowest, but a naked grain of wheat or of one of the other seeds. [314]

"'Tis God that gives to it [315]a body as he will,—yea to every one of the seeds its proper body.

"Not every flesh is the same flesh; but there is one of men, another flesh of beasts, another flesh of birds, and another of fishes.

"There are also bodies celestial, as well as bodies terrestrial. But the glory of the celestial [bodies] is one, and the glory of the terrestrial is another.

---

[312] The Gnostics Hippolytus calls the Naassenes.
[313] Reitzenstein (p. 22, 2) says that it was in error that the Greeks stated the Egyptians believed in metempsychosis; in this I believe that Reitzenstein is himself in error. The Egyptians at any rate demonstrably believed in soul metamorphosis; and when we find people who lived in Egypt teaching this metamorphosis in connection with metempsychosis, it is but natural to conclude that the Greeks, who were in touch with the living tradition of Egypt, knew more about the matter than modern scepticism.
[314] The "grain of mustard seed"—"wheat" if a good body comes therefrom, "tares" if an imperfect growth results.
[315] *Sc.* the soul as grain.

"[And of the former] the glory of the sun is one, and the glory of the moon is another, and [yet] another is the glory of the stars; for star differeth from star in glory.

"So also is the resurrection of the dead." [316]

And by "resurrection of the dead," I believe that Paul meant what all the instructed of the time meant—namely, the "reaching the first step of deathlessness," as Hermes has it in our treatise. The death or vice of the soul is ignorance, the virtue or life of the soul is Gnosis.

"For he who knows, he good and pious is, and still while on the earth, divine."

CONCERNING TRANSMIGRATION

8. With § 8, however, we are confronted with what appears to be a great difficulty. Hermes here seems to teach distinctly that a vicious (that is, an ignorant) soul, one who has not attained to Gnosis, goes back to attachment to animal bodies, while in §§ 19 ff., he at great length denies that a human soul can possibly do so. Is there any solution of this apparently complete self-contradiction in one and the same treatise?

Far as I am from desiring to play the apologist for any scripture, I am prevented from appending an impatient "No" to this query, for the following considerations:

In the first place, Hermes in § 8 is speaking of the vicious or ignorant soul, while in § 19 he is speaking not only of the "human" soul, but of the human soul that hath the Good Mind (§ 23); whereas the ignorant soul "doth not have Mind, and, therefore, such an one should not be called a *man*" (§ 24). Here, then, we have a fundamental distinction in souls incarnated into the "body of a man" (§ 8); they are of two classes.

The doctrine of § 8 applies to one class, the doctrine of § 19 to another.

Metempsychosis, in the sense of continued revolution on the wheel of life and death, is only for him who "persisteth in his vice"—that is to say, is still ignorant. Gnosis thus means the freedom from *saṁsāra*, to use a common Brāhmanical and Buddhistic term.

The ignorant soul does not see the Light, being "blinded by the body's passions, and tossed about"; this is the "turmoil" of which Plato speaks in the *Timæus*.

And here I must refer the reader to "Plato Concerning Metempsychosis," in the "Prolegomena," a chapter which I have written mainly in elucidation of the problems raised by our treatise.

---

[316] I Cor. xv. 35-42.

GNOSIS THE VIRTUE OF THE SOUL

9. So much, then, for the soul which persisteth in its vice or ignorance; but the virtue of the soul is Gnosis.

"For he who knows, he good and pious is, and still while on the earth, divine."

This is precisely the same idea as that of the Jīvanmukta in Indian theosophy—namely, the man who has reached Mukti or Liberation while still living in the body.

Hermes thus proceeds to distinguish Gnosis, the end of human science, from sense or opinion. Gnosis is the apotheosis of the mind, its immediate perception of the things-that-are—namely, the Intelligible Cosmos.

11. The Sensible or Hylic Cosmos is then explained, and also the nature of man, and his relationship to the Cosmos and God.

THE VEHICLES OF THE SOUL

13. The vehicles of man's "Soul" are then categorized (ψυχὴ δὲ ἀνθρώπου ὀχεῖται τὸν τρόπον τοῦτον), the Soul being here used in the sense of the Self, and as distinguished from the "soul" in the category. They are as follows, one within the other, in the sense of being respectively more intimate to the true nature of man:

Mind (νοῦς); reason (λόγος); soul (ψυχή); spirit (πνεῦμα); body (σῶμα).

The remarkable similarity of this category with the psychology of the Upaniṣhads cannot fail to strike the student of those mother-treatises of Vaidik theosophy. Thus we read in the *Kaṭhopaniṣhad*, I. iii. 10, 11:

"Beyond the senses are the rudiments[317]; beyond the rudiments impulsive mind; beyond the mind, the reason; beyond the reason, the Great Self.

"Beyond the Great, the Increate[318]; beyond the Increate, the Man [319]; beyond the Man, not any thing; That is the goal; That is the final end."

The analogy is striking. Body = gross elements; spirit = subtle elements; soul = impulsive mind (*manas*); reason = reason (*buddhi* [320]); Mind = the Great (*Mahat*); Source (ἀρχή) = the Increate; the One and Only (τὸ ἕν καὶ μόνον) = the Man.

---

[317] The subtler elements.
[318] *Avyakta*, undifferentiated cosmic substance.
[319] *Purusha*, the True Man.
[320] The *manas* and *buddhi* of the Upaniṣhads are not to be confounded with these terms as at present employed in modern Theosophical literature.

These so-called "vehicles," "envelopes," or "sheaths" (*koshas*), are elsewhere given in the Upaniṣhads as: *anna-maya-kosha*—that is, the *kosha* composed of, or resulting from, food (body); *prāṇa-maya-k.*, of life (spirit); *mano-maya-k.*, of impulse (soul); *vijñāna-maya-k.*, of discrimination (reason); *ānanda-maya-k.*, of bliss (Mind).

"Spirit" is thus seen to correspond to life (*prāna*); it is that which "bestows upon the living creature motion, and, as it were, doth bear it" (*i.e.* support it) "in a way" (§ 13). It is not Life, but individualized life, and in the Aupaniṣhad literature is differentiated into five modes, which may be almost translated as etheric currents or modes of motion in the body. [321]

The quotation from Proclus in "Plato Concerning Metempsychosis," will have sufficiently shown that this "life" is of the same nature as the animal life. It is that principle of soul which man shares with the animals.

THE DUAL SOUL

And here we may refer to Jamblichus (*De Myst.*, viii. 6), when referring to the "Hermaic writings" he says:

"Man has two souls, as these writings say. The one is from the first Mind, and partakes also of the power of the Creator, while the other, the soul under constraint, comes from the revolution of the celestial [spheres]; into the latter the former, the soul that is the seer of God, [322] insinuates itself at a later period.

"This being so, the soul that descends into us from the worlds [or spheres] keeps time with the circuit of these worlds, while the soul from the Mind existing in us in an intelligible fashion is free from the whirl of genesis; by this the bonds of Destiny are burst asunder; by this the Path up to the Gods whom mind alone can see is brought to birth; by such a life as this is that Great Art Divine, which leads us up to That beyond the spheres of genesis, brought to its consummation."

Hermes in our treatise is, however, more precise as to the so-called "vehicles" or "souls," for he writes (§ 17):

"Mind taketh, then, the soul for, as it were, an envelope. And soul itself being, too, a thing divine, [323] doth use the spirit as *its* envelope, while spirit doth pervade the living creature." [324]

---

[321] *Cf.* K. K., 44, 45, Comment.
[322] *Cf.* C. H., ix. (x.) 3: "The daimon who's illumined by God's Light."
[323] That is, being *logos*, as from the Creator or Second Mind.
[324] *Cf.* Exx. iv. 2; xv. 2; xix. 3; and Frag. xviii.

"HE WHO STANDS"

The Supreme Principle of all, the One and Only One, who "standeth perpetually" (§ 14), is the Intelligible Logos (ἡ νοητὴ στάσις, cf. § 11), the ὁ ἑστὼς of the Christianized Gnosis, as seen especially in the Simonian *Great Announcement*. He is the Cause of the perpetual motion of the Hylic Cosmos. Compare this with the following passage of Numenius:

"Now there are two modes of life, the first of the First and the second of the Second God. For it is evident that the First God should be standing (ἑστώς), and the Second, on the contrary, moved. The First, then, is occupied about things intelligible, and the Second about things intelligible and sensible.

"Marvel not that I say this; for thou shalt hear what is still more marvellous. For I say that it is not the motion that appertains to the Second, but the rest that pertains to the First, which is the innate 'motion' from which both their cosmic order and their eternal community and their preservation [or salvation] is poured forth on things universal."[325]

THE OLYMPIAN PATH

15. In § 15 the Gnosis is again declared to be the only Path of Salvation or Safety.[326] It is the Way Up to the Mount,[327] the Olympian Path.

The term Eleusis was also interpreted as Anabasis, or the Way Up.[328] Compare the Jewish commentator in the Naassene Document (§ 27):

"First is the Mystery called 'Eleusis' and 'Anaktoreion'—Eleusis because we come from Above,[329] streaming down from Adamas,[330] . . . and Anaktoreion from 'Returning Above.'"

"WHEN MIND BECOMES A DAIMON"

---

[325] Quoted by Eusebius, *Præp. Evang.*, XI. xviii. 20, 21 (539 B), ed. Dindorf (Leipzig, 1867), ii. 41. We do not know Numenius' date, but it was probably about the first half of the first century A.D. Though Numenius is almost invariably designated as a Pythagorean, he was rather a universalist, for his object was not only to trace the doctrines of Plato up to Pythagoras, but to show that they were not at variance with the doctrines and mysteries of the Brāhmans, Jews, Magi and Egyptians.

[326] *Cf.* the passage from Jamblichus quoted above.

[327] *Cf. C. H.*, xiii. (xiv.) 1: "The Passing o'er the Mount."

[328] *Cf. C. H.*, i. 24.

[329] Eleusis meaning Coming, Advent.

[330] The Man or Mind.

16. The next main doctrine touched on is one of immense importance, for it gives us the inner teaching which illuminates the "dark saying" in the "Pœmandres" (§ 24), when treating of the Way Up (ἄνοδος):

"And thou surrenderest thy way of life unto the daimon."

For in our treatise Hermes tells us that at death:

"The mind stript of its wrappings, and naturally divine, taking unto itself a fiery body, doth traverse every space, after abandoning the soul unto its judgment and whatever chastisement it hath deserved."

The key to this is the sentence (§ 21):

"When mind becomes a daimon, the law requires that it should take a fiery body to execute the services of God."

At death, the mind, of its own nature, perforce becomes a "servant of God," a Therapeut [331]; the man is his own judge and his own chastizer.

The "fire of hell" is then but the reflection of the light of the mind; it is the burning remorse of a mind that now sees the inevitable results of every selfish action—thought, word, and deed; that each of these comes inevitably back on the sender forth of it.

The soul, thus, lives out (and that too in the most realistic fashion, it *realizes* the actuality of the law in all its most minute details) the inevitable consequences of its past vicious deeds in body.

Here we have the hint of a psychology and of an inner teaching that persuades us there was a profound wisdom at the back of the intermediate instruction of these schools.

Compare this most reasonable theory of after-death "illumination" with the crudities of the eternal torment idea of popular religion with which we are so familiar, and reflect on what a "falling off" there has been from the Gnosis of the early days.

And what is the "fiery body" of the mind but the ray-like or starry vehicle of the man, the αὐγοειδὲς ἢ ἀστροειδὲς of Philoponus? [332]

This is the true "Astral Body" of a man, and not the "watery vesture" which is referred to under the term in modern nomenclature.

This is the true Body of Purification, that burns up all impurities, and in the light of the conflagration burns into man the memory of the Gnosis.

The soul is thus "chastised by its own self"; and if Hermes had taught us nothing else, he would have amply deserved the gratitude of humanity, and the title of Thrice-greatest. Yet is "Hermes" no single man, but a mind illuminated by the Mind.

---

[331] *Cf.* 23: "The mind in service."
[332] See my *Orpheus*, pp. 292 ff.

THE "SCOURGE" OF THE CHRIST

21. So then "the impious soul, scourged with its own sins, is plunged in murders, outrage, blasphemy, in violence of all kinds, and all the other things whereby mankind is wronged."

This is the "scourge" by which the Christ drives the unworthy out of His Temple. It does not mean that the soul is driven into *doing* these things, but that it is made to realize or *suffer* them—the consequences of its prior misdeeds. Whatever wrong it has done to its fellows, such it suffers, in the realization of its true nature, whereby the Light of Gnosis brings into amazing contrast the darkness or ignorance of its past actions.[333]

THE DISPENSATION OF THE UNIVERSE

22. And so Hermes explains the nature of "the dispensation of the universe"—the interlinking of the grades of being from God downwards the intercourse or communion of souls.

God, Cosmos and Man are grades of being. Each is a sun, as it were, in their operations, or powers or rays. God's rays are His energies or self-realizing operations; those of Cosmos are the natures of things, those of Man are the arts and sciences.

This communion or intercourse of higher with lower natures is to be realized on the side of man by the consummation of the sacred marriage, whereby man becomes a god, and finally God.

He only is blessed who is filled with God—that is to say, the true Gnostic who has received the consecration of the Fullness or Plērōma.[334]

Whereas the soul that is empty of God is deprived of that Fullness, cut off from it, and so empty of the Mind. This is the state of Emptiness (κένωμα) or Insufficiency (ὑστέρημα).

24. Such souls, says Hermes, should not be called *men*. For a true *man* is not only equal to a god, but even higher than the gods. Such a man we should, in Christian nomenclature, call a Christ—one animated or illuminated by the Mind or Spirit of God.

---

[333] With this compare the function of the Mind on the soul in incarnation, as described in *C. H.*, xii. (xiii.) 4.
[334] *Cf.* John i. 16: "Of His Fullness have we all received."

CORPUS HERMETICUM XI. (XII.)

MIND UNTO HERMES

(Text: P. 85-99; Pat. 20b-23.)

1. *Mind.* Master this sermon (*logos*), [335] then, Thrice-greatest Hermes, and bear in mind the spoken words; and as it hath come unto Me to speak, I will no more delay.

Hermes. As many men say many things, and these diverse, about the All and Good, I have not learned the truth. Make it, then, clear to me, O Master mine! For I can trust the explanation of these things, which comes from Thee alone.

2. *Mind.* Hear [then], My son, how standeth God and All.

God; Æon[336]; Cosmos; Time; Becoming. [337]

God maketh Æon; Æon, Cosmos; Cosmos, Time; and Time, Becoming.

The Good,—the Beautiful, Wisdom, Blessedness,—is essence, as it were, [338] of God; of Æon, Sameness [339]; of Cosmos, Order; of Time, Change; and of Becoming, Life and Death.

The energies of God are Mind and Soul; of Æon, lastingness [340] and deathlessness; of Cosmos, restoration and the opposite thereof [341]; of Time, increase and decrease; and of Becoming, quality.

Æon is, then, in God; Cosmos, in Æon; in Cosmos, Time; in Time, Becoming.

Æon stands firm round God; Cosmos is moved in Æon; Time hath its limits [342] in the Cosmos; Becoming doth become in Time.

3. The source, [343] therefore, of all is God; their essence, Æon; their matter, Cosmos.

God's power is Æon; Æon's work is Cosmos—which never *hath* become, yet ever *doth* become by Æon.

---

[335] Or thy reason.
[336] Eternity; the ideal world, beyond time. Cf. P. S. A., xxx., xxxi.
[337] Genesis.
[338] That is to say, the term "*ess*-ence" cannot really be applied to God, for He is beyond "*be*-ing."
[339] Or identity.
[340] Or duration.
[341] ἀνταποκατάστασις.
[342] Or is accomplished.
[343] πηγή.

Therefore will Cosmos never be destroyed, for Æon's indestructible; nor doth a whit of things in Cosmos perish, for Cosmos is enwrapped by Æon round on every side.

Her. But God's Wisdom—what is that?

Mind. The Good and Beautiful, and Blessedness, and Virtue's all, and Æon. Æon, then, ordereth [344] [Cosmos], imparting deathlessness and lastingness to matter.

4. For its [345] becoming doth depend on Æon, as Æon doth on God.

Now Genesis [346] and Time, in Heaven and on the Earth, are of two natures.

In Heaven they are unchangeable and indestructible, but on the Earth they're subject unto change and to destruction.

Further, the Æon's soul is God; the Cosmos' soul is Æon; the Earth's soul, Heaven.

And God's in Mind; and Mind, in Soul; and Soul, in Matter; and all of them through Æon.

But all this Body, [347] in which are all the bodies, is full of Soul; and Soul is full of Mind, and [Mind] of God.

It [348] fills it [349] from within, and from without encircles it, making the All to live.

Without, this vast and perfect Life [350] [encircles] Cosmos; within, it fills [it with] all lives [351]; above, in Heaven, continuing in sameness; below, on Earth, changing becoming.

5. And Æon doth preserve this [Cosmos], or by Necessity, or by Foreknowledge, or by Nature, or by whatever else a man supposes or shall suppose. And all is this,—God energizing.

The Energy of God is Power that naught can e'er surpass, a Power with which no one can make comparison of any human thing at all, or any thing divine.

Wherefore, O Hermes, never think that aught of things above or things below is like to God, for thou wilt fall from truth. For naught is like to That which hath no like, and is Alone and One.

And do not ever think that any other can possibly possess His power; for what apart from Him is there of life, and deathlessness and change of quality? For what else should He make [352]?

---

[344] Or adorneth.
[345] *Sc.* Matter's Becoming or Genesis.
[346] Or Becoming.
[347] *Sc.* Cosmos.
[348] *Sc.* Soul.
[349] *Sc.* Body, of Universe or Cosmos.
[350] Or Animal; that is, Soul.
[351] Or animals.
[352] *Sc.* than those which are Himself.

God's not inactive,[353] since all things [then] would lack activity; for all are full of God.

But neither in the Cosmos anywhere, nor in aught else, is there inaction. For that "inaction" is a name that cannot be applied to either what doth make or what is made. [354]

6. But all things must be made; both ever made, and also in accordance with the influence of every space. [355]

For He who makes, is in them all; not stablished in some one of them, nor making one thing only, but making all.

For being Power, He energiseth in the things He makes and is not independent of them,—although the things He makes are subject to Him.

Now gaze through Me [356] upon the Cosmos that's now subject to thy sight; regard its Beauty carefully—Body in pure perfection, though one than which there's no more ancient one, ever in prime of life, and ever-young, nay, rather, in even fuller and yet fuller prime!

7. Behold, again, the seven subject Worlds [357]; ordered [358] by Æon's order, [359] and with their varied course full-filling Æon!

[See how] all things [are] full of light, and nowhere [is there] fire; for 'tis the love and blending of the contraries and the dissimilar that doth give birth to light down shining by the energy of God, [360] the Father of all good, the Leader of all order, and Ruler of the seven world-orderings!

[Behold] the Moon, forerunner of them all, the instrument of nature, and the transmuter of its lower matter!

[Look at] the Earth set in the midst of All, foundation of the Cosmos Beautiful, feeder and nurse of things on Earth!

And contemplate the multitude of deathless lives, how great it is, and that of lives subject to death; and midway, between both, immortal [lives] and mortal, [see thou] the circling Moon.

8. And all are full of Soul, and all are moved by it, each in its proper way; some round the Heaven, others around the Earth; [see] how the right

---

[353] ἀργός. There is a word-play in the terms ἔργον (work), ἐνεργῶν (working in, energizing), ἐνεργής (active, energetic), ἐνέργεια (in-working, activity), and ἀργός (not-working, inactive, idle), ἀργία (inactivity, idleness), which it is impossible to bring out fully in English.
[354] Or what becomes.
[355] This seems to mean, that all things in the world of genesis (making, creating, or becoming) have their root-activity, first from the sameness of becoming of the one sphere or space, and then their differentiated activity from the seven spheres, spaces, or planes, which are the instruments of God in the differentiation of the Cosmos.
[356] Mind—*i.e.* with the mind's eye, or spiritual sight, or by the help of the Master's illuminating power. Cf. C. H., i. 7 and xiii. (xiv.) 11.
[357] κόσμους, cosmoi or world-orders.
[358] Or adorned, or made beautiful.
[359] The order of the Æon (Eternity, the Spiritual Space), æonian or everlasting order.
[360] The text from "Now gaze . . ." to here is given in R. 36, n. 1.

[move] not unto left, nor yet the left unto the right; nor the above below, nor the below above.

And that all these are subject unto Genesis,[361] My dearest Hermes, thou hast no longer need to learn of Me. For that they bodies are, have souls, and they are moved.

But 'tis impossible for them to come together into one without some one to bring them [all] together. It must, then, be that such a one as this must be some one who's wholly One.

9. For as the many motions of them [all] are different, and as their bodies are not like, yet has one speed been ordered for them all, it is impossible that there should be two or more makers for them.

For that one single order is not kept among "the many"; but rivalry will follow of the weaker with the stronger, and they will strive.

And if the maker of the lives that suffer change and death, should be another,[362] he would desire to make the deathless ones as well; just as the maker of the deathless ones, [to make the lives] that suffer death.

But come! if there be two,[363]—if Matter's one, and Soul is one, in whose hands would there be the distribution [364]for the making? Again, if both of them have some of it, in whose hands may there be the greater part?

10. But thus conceive it, then; that every living body doth consist of soul and matter, whether [that body be] of an immortal, or a mortal, or an irrational [life].

For that all living bodies are ensouled; whereas, upon the other hand, those that live not, are matter by itself. And, in like fashion, Soul when in its self is, after its own maker, cause of life; but *the* cause of all life is He who makes the things that cannot die.

Her. How, then, is it that, first, lives subject unto death are other than the deathless ones? And, next, how is it that that Life which knows no death, and maketh deathlessness, doth not make animals immortal?

11. Mind. First, that there is some one who does these things, is clear; and, next, that He is also One, is very manifest. For, also, Soul is one, and Life is one, and Matter one.

Her. But who is He?

Mind. Who may it other be than the One God? Whom else should it beseem to put Soul into lives but God alone? One, then, is God.

It would indeed be most ridiculous, if when thou dost confess the Cosmos to be one, Sun one, Moon one, and Godhead [365]one, thou shouldst wish God Himself to be some one or other of a number!

---

[361] Or becoming.
[362] From the maker of the immortals.
[363] *Sc.* makers.
[364] *Sc.* of matter and life.
[365] Or Divinity.

12. All things, therefore, He makes, in many [ways]. And what great thing is it for God to make life, soul, and deathlessness, and change, when thou [thyself] dost do [366]so many things?

For thou dost see, and speak, and hear, and smell, and taste, and touch, and walk, and think, and breathe. And it is not one man who smells, a second one who speaks, a third who touches, another one who smells, another one who walks, another one who thinks, and [yet] another one who breathes. But *one* is he who doth all these.

And yet no one of these could be apart from God. For just as, shouldst thou cease from[367] these, thou wouldst no longer be a living thing, so also, should God cease from them (a thing not law to say), no longer is He God.

13. For if it hath been shown that no thing can inactive [368]be, how much less God? For if there's aught He doth not make (if it be law to say), He is imperfect. But if He is not only not inactive, but perfect [God], then He doth make all things.

Give thou thyself to Me, My Hermes, for a little while, [369] and thou shalt understand more easily how that God's work is one, in order that all things may be—that are being made, or once have been, or that are going to be made. And *this* [370] is, My belovèd, Life; this is the Beautiful; this is the Good; this, God.

14. And if thou wouldst in practice [371] understand [this work], behold what taketh place with thee desiring to beget. Yet this is not like unto that, for He doth not enjoy.

For that indeed He hath no other one to share in what He works, for working by Himself, He ever is at work, Himself being what He doth. [372] For did He separate Himself from it, [373] all things would [then] collapse, and all must die, Life ceasing.

But if all things are lives, and also Life is one; then, one is God. And, furthermore, if all are lives, both those in Heaven and those on Earth, and One Life in them all is made to be by God, and God is it [374]—then, all are made by God.

---

[366] Or make; a play on the double meaning of the Greek verb.
[367] Lit. become inactive of (**καταργηθῇς**).
[368] A word has here dropped out in the text, which I have supplied by ἀργὸν (inactive), and not by the usual conjecture "apart from God."
[369] Cf. P. S. A., iii. 1: "Now lend to me the whole of thee."

[370] Sc. work, doing, making, or creating.
[371] ἔργῳ, in deed, in work.
[372] Or makes.
[373] Sc. His work, or creation.
[374] Viz., this Life.

Life is the making-one of Mind and Soul; accordingly Death is not the destruction of those that are at-oned, [375] but the dissolving of their union.

15. Æon, moreover, is God's image; Cosmos [is] Æon's; the Sun, of Cosmos; and Man, [the image] of the Sun.

The people call change death, because the body is dissolved, and life, when it's dissolved, withdraws to the unmanifest. But in this sermon (*logos*), Hermes, my beloved, as thou dost hear, I say the Cosmos also suffers change,—for that a part of it each day is made to be in the unmanifest,—yet it is ne'er dissolved.

These are the passions of the Cosmos—revolvings and concealments; revolving is conversion and concealment renovation.

16. The Cosmos is all-formed,—not having forms external to itself, but changing them itself within itself. Since, then, Cosmos is made to be all-formed, what may its maker be? For that, on the one hand, He should not be void of all form; and, on the other hand, if He's all-formed, He will be like the Cosmos. Whereas, again, has He a single form, He will thereby be less than Cosmos.

What, then, say we He is?—that we may not bring round our sermon (*logos*) into doubt; for naught that mind conceives of God is doubtful.

He, then, hath one *idea*, [376] which is His own alone, which doth not fall beneath the sight, being bodiless, and [yet] by means of bodies manifesteth all [ideas]. [377] And marvel not that there's a bodiless idea.

17. For it is like the form of reason (*logos*) [378] and mountain-tops in pictures. [379] For they appear to stand out strongly from the rest, but really are quite smooth and flat.

And now consider what is said more boldly, but more truly!

Just as man cannot live apart from Life, so neither can God live without [His] doing good. [380] For this is as it were the life and motion as it were of God—to move all things and make them live.

18. Now some of the things said [381] should bear a sense peculiar to themselves. So understand, for instance, what I'm going to say.

All are in God, [but] not as lying in a place. For place is both a body and immovable, and things that lie do not have motion.

Now things lie one way in the bodiless, another way in being made manifest.

---

[375] That is, Mind and Soul, *sc.* the Logos and World-Soul, or ego and animal soul.
[376] The root of form; used also loosely in Greek to denote form.
[377] Or forms.
[378] Or idea of the sermon.
[379] καὶ ἐν ταῖς γραφαῖς ἀκρώρειαι. All the translators talk of "margins" in MSS., and make entire nonsense of the passage. I can find absolutely no authority for translating ἀκρώρειαι margins.
[380] Or making the Good; that is, Æon.
[381] Or points of the sermon.

Think, [then,] of Him who doth contain them all; and think, that than the bodiless naught is more comprehensive, or swifter, or more potent, but *it* is the most comprehensive, the swiftest, and most potent of them all.

19. And, thus, think from thyself, and bid thy soul go unto any land; and there more quickly than thy bidding will it be. And bid it journey oceanwards; and there, again, immediately 'twill be, not as if passing on from place to place, but as if being there.

And bid it also mount to heaven; and it will need no wings, nor will aught hinder it, nor fire of sun, nor æther, nor vortex-swirl, [382] nor bodies of the other stars; but, cutting through them all, it will soar up to the last Body [of them all]. [383] And shouldst thou will to break through this as well, and contemplate what is beyond—if there be aught beyond the Cosmos [384]; it is permitted thee.

20. Behold what power, what swiftness, thou dost have! And canst thou do all of these things, and God not [do them]?

Then, in this way know [385] God; as having all things in Himself as thoughts, the whole Cosmos itself.

If, then, thou dost not make thyself like unto God, thou canst not know Him. For like is knowable to like [alone].

Make, [then,] thyself to grow to the same stature as the Greatness which transcends all measure; leap forth from every body; transcend all Time; become Eternity[386]; and [thus] shalt thou know God.

Conceiving nothing is impossible unto thyself, think thyself deathless and able to know all,—all arts, all sciences, the way of every life. [387]

Become more lofty than all height, and lower than all depth. Collect into thyself all senses of [all] creatures,—of fire, [and] water, dry and moist. Think that thou art at the same time in every place,—in earth, in sea, in sky; not yet begotten, in the womb, young, old, [and] dead, in after-death conditions.[388]

And if thou knowest all these things at once, [389]—times, places, doings, qualities, and quantities; thou canst know God.[390]

21. But if thou lockest up thy soul within thy body, and dost debase it, saying: I nothing know; I nothing can; I fear the sea; I cannot scale the sky; I know not who I was, who I shall be;—what is there [then] between [thy] God and thee?

---

[382] ἡ δίνη, presumably the vortex or "whorl" of the solar system (*cf.* "Vision of Er").
[383] *Sc.* the body or limit of the whole cosmos.
[384] *Cf. C. H.*, iv. (v.) 5: "And things above the heaven—if there be aught."
[385] Or think.
[386] Lit. Æon.
[387] παντὸς ζῴου ἦθος,—or nature of every animal.
[388] *Cf. C. H.*, xiii. (xiv.) 11.
[389] Or art simultaneously conscious of.
[390] A critical text from "Make, then, thy self" to here is given by R., p. 238.

For thou canst know naught of things beautiful and good so long as thou dost love thy body and art bad.

The greatest bad there is, is not to know God's Good [391]; but to be able to know [Good], and will, and hope, is a Straight Way, the Good's own [Path], both leading there and easy. [392]

If thou but sett'st thy foot thereon, 'twill meet thee everywhere, 'twill everywhere be seen, both where and when thou dost expect it not,—waking, sleeping, sailing, journeying, by night, by day, speaking, [and] saying naught. For there is naught that is not image of the Good.

22. *Her.* Is God unseen?

Mind. Hush! Who is more manifest than He? For this one reason hath He made all things, that through them all thou mayest see Him.

This is the Good of God, this [is] His Virtue,—that He may be made manifest through all. [393]

For naught's *unseen*, even of things that are without a body. Mind sees itself [394] in thinking, God in making. [395]

So far these things have been made manifest to thee, Thrice-greatest one! Reflect on all the rest in the same way within thyself, and thou shalt not be led astray.

---

[391] τὸ θεῖον—lit. the Godly, or Divine.
[392] *Cf.* Ex. i. 4.
[393] The preceding question and answer is quoted with very slight verbal variants by Cyril, *Contra Julianum*, ii. 52.
[394] Or is seen.
[395] Or doing.

COMMENTARY
TITLE AND FORM

The title in the MSS. is simply "Mind to Hermes." When, therefore, Cyril, in quoting the first three paragraphs of § 22 of our treatise, says that Hermes wrote these words "to his own mind," [396] he is evidently either a very careless reader, [397] or had not seen at first hand the treatise from which he quotes.

From its contents, moreover, it is very evident that our treatise, as far as its form is concerned, looks back to the "Pœmandres" as the type of instruction to Hermes (or to *a* Hermes).

This highly authoritative form of enunciating doctrine was evidently chosen because it was desired to impart a more intimate instruction than that of the "General Sermons" and the like,—to wit, the inculcation of the Æon-doctrine, in connection with the marvellous doctrine of At-one-ment with all things which constitutes the Path of the Good. The doctrine is no longer "Become (or make thyself like) Cosmos," but "Become Æon" (§ 20).

Now it is remarkable that the instruction given in our treatise by the Mind to Hermes is, almost point for point, the "esoteric" teaching of which the Sermon of Hermes to Tat, entitled the "Cup or Monad"—*C. H.*, iv. (v.)—is the "exoteric" form.

That the instruction in these Trismegistic schools of initiation was divided into grades is manifest on all sides; and, therefore, nothing is more natural than to find these two sermons standing in such intimate relations to one another as to doctrine, the one containing the more intimate and advanced explanation of the more general instruction of the other.

And that this inner instruction on the "Cup" doctrine must have been thought to be of very great value, is evident when we reflect that "The Cup" sermon was one of the most famous of all the treatises of Hermes, for, as we have seen, its title was worth being plagiarized, and the Baptism of the Cup, of which it treated, constituted the goal of the endeavour of the disciples of the School, as Zosimus tells us.

Mystically, then, the main interest of our treatise centres in the doctrine of the At-one-ment (as the inner consummation of the Baptism in the Cup or Monad), to which the Æon-idea is but a formal introduction; historically, however, the introduction of the Æon-idea presents itself as a critical problem, for the term is not found in the "Pœmandres," and, therefore, presumably was not used in the earliest documents of the School.

---

[396] *C. Jul.*, ii. 52; ed. Migne, col. 580 B.
[397] *Cf.* R. 128, i.; 196, 3.

THE ÆON-LORE

When, then, did this Æon-idea impose itself upon the older form of tradition of the Trismegistic schools? This is a most important question; for if we can in any way answer it, we shall be in a position to assign a *terminus ad quem* for the earlier forms of Hermetic doctrine.

The answer to the question seems to me to be involved in the supposition that the Æon-doctrine must have influenced "Hermeticism" at more or less the same date as that at which it influenced "Gnosticism."

Now "Gnosticism," in its Christianized forms, is practically never found without the Æon-lore.

The earliest forms of Christian Gnosis referred to by the later Patristic hæresiologists are bound up with Æonology. Not only so, but the very earliest reference to Gnosticism by any Christian writer presupposes the Æon-doctrine, and uses it in illustration of the spiritual state of the writer. [398]

The widespread influence of the Æon-doctrine can thus be traced back to at least the origins of Christianity.

Now as the Gnosis existed before any Christian form of it was developed, the question of the date when the Æon-doctrine was introduced into it must be referred to pre-Christian times.

And, indeed, the very simple character of the Æon-lore in our treatise, [399] as compared with the mind-bewildering complexity and transcendency of first and second century Christian Gnosticism, is all in favour of an early date for its introduction into "Hermeticism," which is only another name for "Gnosticism" of a preponderatingly Hellenic form.

If this line of reasoning holds good, we have in it a very strong presumption that the older forms of the Trismegistic treatises were pre-Christian.

And that this is so may be seen by the absolute identity of the teaching of our treatise (§ 2) with that of Philo, when he writes:

"But God is the Artificer of Time as well. For He is Father of its Father; and Time's Father is the Cosmos, which manifests its motion in the genesis of Time. . . .

"This [Cosmos] then, the Younger Son, the Sensible, being set a-moving, has caused Time's nature to appear and disappear; so that there nothing is which future is with God, who has the very Bounds of Time subject to Him. For 'tis not Time, but Time's Archetype and Paradigm, Eternity (or

---

[398] Namely, Paul in his Letters, which are the earliest of all Christian documents. See my article, "Some Notes on the Gnostics," in *The Nineteenth Century and After* (Nov. 1902), pp. 822-835; and *D. J. L.*, pp. 353 ff.

[399] Perhaps the clearest exposition is to be found in *P. S. A.*, xxx. and xxxi.

Æon), which is His Life. [400] But in Eternity naught is past, and naught is future, but all is present only."[401]

This passage of Philo is of the utmost importance for estimating the date of our treatises; for not only does it prove that the oldest forms of the Trismegistic literature were pre-Christian, but it further persuades us that our treatise, which belongs to a later type of this literature, may be dated as contemporary with Philo.

Chapter xi. in the Prolegomena, "Concerning the Æon-Doctrine," should be taken in close connection with this treatise, for it is not only introductory to it, but frequently refers directly to it.

For the rest, it is not necessary to attempt any detailed comments, since the instruction of the writer is clear enough for any careful reader to follow with ease after making himself acquainted with the general ideas in the preceding treatises. One or two notes on special points, however, may be attempted.

THE ROOT OF FORM

Thus in § 16, the sentence: "The Cosmos is all-formed (παντόμορφος),—not having forms external to itself, but changing them itself within itself,"—reminds us of *P. S. A.*, xix. 3: "The 'Thirty-six' who have the name of Horoscopes are in the self-same space as the fixed stars; of these the essence-chief, or prince, is he whom they call Pantomorph, or Omniform (παντόμορφος, *vel omniformis*),who fashioneth the various forms for various species"; and also of *P. S. A.*, xxxv.: "But they are changed as many times as there are moments in the hour of that revolving circle in which abides that God whom we have called All-form."

Compare also *C. H.*, xiii. (xiv.) 12, where, speaking of the "Circle of the types of life," Hermes says it is "composed of elements, twelve in number, but of one nature, an omniform idea."

With this compare Hermes-Prayer iv., addressed to Thoth as the Logos:

"Thee I invoke alone, thou who alone in all the Cosmos dost impose order on gods and men, who dost transform thyself in holy forms, making to be from things that are not, and from the things that are, making the not to be."

But the main interest of our treatise is not that the Intelligible Cosmos or Logos can create and destroy and transmute all forms at will, but that man as the microcosm has potential in him this great magic power.

---

[400] *Cf. C. H.*, i. 6; the Union of the Logos and Mind—or First-Born Son and Father—is Life; they are united in Æon.
[401] *Quod Deus Im.*, § 6; M. i. 277; P. 298 (Ri. ii. 72, 73).

"BECOME ALL THINGS"

The daring instruction given to Hermes in §§ 19 and 20 is distinctly a discipline of the Egyptian Wisdom; for though it is here set forth plainly and without circumlocution, as a straightforward intimate instruction, stripped of all mysterious hints or hesitating subterfuges, [402] it is clearly in the same circle of ideas of which popular Egyptian theurgy had some inkling. But whereas the philosopher-mystic was bidden to do this for himself of his own volition and achievement, the theurgist had to beg some god to do it for him.

Thus in the same Prayer, to which we have already referred, we read (§§ 2, 3):

"O holy Thoth, the true sight of whose face none of the gods endures! Make me to be in every creature's name [or 'true form'],—wolf, dog, or lion, fire, tree, or vulture, wall, or water, or what thou will'st, for thou art able so to do."

So also in *P. S. A.*, vii., we have the same idea, for certainly the phrasing of the sentences suggests something beyond the ordinary powers of the mind or imagination.

"He mingles with the elements by reason of the swiftness of his mind. He plunges into the sea's depths by means of its profundity. He puts his values on all things.

"Heaven does not seem too high for him; for it is measured by the wisdom of his mind as though it were quite near.

"No darkness of the air obstructs the penetration of his mind. No density of earth impedes his work. No depth of water blunts his sight.

"Though still the same, yet is he all, and everywhere is he the same."

It is indeed a marvellous "yoga" system that is sketched for us in our treatise. There is no question here of abstraction or negation, but a courageous identification or At-one-ment of oneself with all that lives and breathes. This is the Path of the Gnosis, the Way to Know God.

In other words, man is to copy his prototype, the Mind, and just as the Mind or Man, in the "Pœmandres" treatise, "had a mind to break right through the Boundary of the spheres" (§ 13), so is our philosopher bidden to "soar up to the Last Body of them all" (§ 19), that Last Body being the One Element of Cosmos itself.

"And shouldst thou will to break through this as well, and contemplate what is beyond—if there be aught beyond the Cosmos; it is permitted thee."

That the hard and fast distinctions which modern commentators would draw between words, in considering these mystical treatises, would have

---

[402] Or, as the writer of the *Pistis Sophia* would say, ἐν παρρησία, "face to face without a parable."

been laughed at by the writers of them, is amply manifested when the writer with enthusiastic fervour bursts forth:

"Then in this way know God, as having in Himself as thoughts the whole Cosmos itself.

"If, then, thou dost not make thyself like unto God, [403] thou canst not know Him. [404] For like is knowable to like [alone]. Make, then, thyself to grow to the same stature as the Greatness which transcends all measure; leap forth from every body; transcend all time; become Eternity; and thus shalt thou know God."

Every body or space must be transcended, even the Body of Cosmos itself; for the man must grow into the "stature of the Greatness that transcends all measure," that is, the intelligible superspatial Plērōma, the Æon as the Logos and Paradigm of Cosmos. And every time and all Time must also be transcended; for the man must become Eternity—that is, the Æon as the Paradigm of Time.

THE GOOD'S OWN PATH

In no scripture that I know is this Path more admirably set forth—the Good's own Path. All things, all spaces, and all times have to be realized as being within oneself *simultaneously*; if this is realized or known, not only imagined, then a man becomes a true Knower of God, a Gnostic.

Nor has ever a truer sentence been written than the wonderful words concerning this Path to the Supreme:

"If thou but sett'st thy foot thereon, 'twill meet thee everywhere, 'twill everywhere be seen, both where and when thou dost expect it not—waking, sleeping, sailing, journeying, by night, by day, speaking, and saying naught. For there is naught that is not image of the Good."

CONCERNING INDIA

In conclusion, I would only point out that if for the hopeless reading in the first sentence of § 19 we were to take Patrizzi's emendation, which has been adopted by Parthey, we should have the interesting sentence:

"And, thus, think from thyself, and bid thy soul go unto India."

If this should be the original reading, it is remarkable that India should have been selected of all places. We know, however, from a study of what is known of the life of Apollonius of Tyana, that this "Gnostic" philosopher made an enormous propaganda of Indian ideas among the philosophic and mystic communities and schools of the first century.

---

[403] *Sc.* as Cosmos.
[404] *Sc.* as Father of this Only Son.

Apollonius must have known something, perhaps a great deal, concerning the *siddhis* acquired by *yoga*-practices. At any rate, we find his biographer Philostratus making him write the following letter to his Eastern hosts on his return from India:

"I came to you by land and ye have given me the sea; nay, rather, by sharing with me your wisdom ye have given me power to travel through heaven. These things will I bring back to the mind of the Greeks, and I will hold converse with you as though ye were present, if it be that I have not drunk of the Cup of Tantalus in vain." [405]

That an intensely great interest was taken in Indian ideas at Alexandria is shown by the fact that we find Plotinus himself in 242 starting off with the expedition of Gordian to the East in the hope of coming in contact with the Indian Wisdom.

But all these considerations, though interesting in themselves, do not immediately concern us, unless we are subjectively persuaded that the emendation of Patrizzi is firmly established. Should, however, this reading in any way be confirmed by objective evidence, we should have to reconsider the question of date by the light of it, though, I fear, with little chance of any definite result. For though the propaganda of Indian ideas by Apollonius could not have begun prior to the middle of the first century, we have in this fact no very sure criterion, for "India" must have been in the air, and strongly in the air, even prior to Apollonius' visit to India, or why should he have been induced to make so long and dangerous a journey? Indeed, "India" had been in the air ever since the expedition of Alexander—that is, from the beginning of the Alexandrian period—the second quarter of the fourth century B.C. onwards.

---

[405] Philos., *Vit. Ap.*, iii. 51. Cf. my *Apollonius of Tyana, the Philosopher Reformer of the First Century A.D.* (London, 1901), p. 88.

CORPUS HERMETICUM XII. (XIII.)

ABOUT THE COMMON MIND

OF HERMES TO TAT

(Text: P. 99-113; Pat. 23b-25b.)

1. *Hermes.* The Mind, O Tat, is of God's very essence—(if such a thing as *essence* of God [406] there be)—and what *that* is, it and it only knows precisely.

The Mind, then, is not separated off from God's essentiality, but is united unto it, as light to sun.

This Mind in men is God, and for this cause some of mankind are gods, and their humanity is nigh unto divinity.

For the Good Daimon said: "Gods are immortal men, and men are mortal gods."

2. But in irrational lives Mind is their *nature*. For where is Soul, there too is Mind; just as where Life, there is there also Soul.

But in irrational lives their soul is life devoid of mind [407]; for Mind is the in-worker of the souls of men for good;—He works on them for their own good.

In lives irrational He doth co-operate with each one's nature; but in the souls of men He counteracteth them.

For every soul, when it becomes embodied, is instantly depraved by pleasure and by pain.

For in a compound body, just like juices, pain and pleasure seethe, and into them the soul, on entering in, is plunged. [408]

3. O'er whatsoever souls the Mind doth, then, preside, to these it showeth its own light, by acting counter to their prepossessions, just as a good physician doth upon the body prepossessed by sickness, pain inflict, burning or lancing it for sake of health.

In just the selfsame way the Mind inflicteth pain upon the soul, to rescue it from pleasure, whence comes its every ill.

The great ill of the soul is godlessness [409]; then followeth fancy [410] for all evil things and nothing good.

---

[406] That is, if we can use such a term with respect to God.
[407] That is, of the mind manifested in man as distinguished from the general Mind.
[408] βαπτίζεται.

So, then, Mind counteracting it doth work good on the soul, as the physician health upon the body.

4. But whatsoever human souls have not the Mind as pilot, they share in the same fate as souls of lives irrational.

For [Mind] becomes co-worker with them, giving full play to the desires towards which [such souls] are borne,—[desires] that from the rush of lust strain after the irrational; [so that such human souls,] just like irrational animals, cease not irrationally to rage and lust, nor ever are they satiate of ills.

For passions and irrational desires are ills exceeding great; and over these God hath set up the Mind to play the part of judge and executioner.

5. *Tat.* In that case, father mine, the teaching (*logos*) as to Fate, [411] which previously thou didst explain to me, risks to be over-set.

For that if it be absolutely fated for a man to fornicate, or commit sacrilege, or do some other evil deed, why is he punished,—when he hath done the deed from Fate's necessity?

Her. All works, my son, are Fate's; and without Fate naught of things corporal—or good, or ill—can come to pass.

But it is fated too, that he who doeth ill, shall suffer. And for this cause he doth it—that he may suffer what he suffereth, because he did it.

6. But for the moment, [Tat,] let be the teaching (*logos*) as to vice and Fate, for we have spoken of these things in other [of our sermons]; but now our teaching (*logos*) is about the Mind:—what Mind can do, and how it is [so] different,—in men being such and such, and in irrational lives [so] changed; and [then] again that in irrational lives it is not of a beneficial nature, while that in men it quencheth out the wrathful and the lustful elements.

Of men, again, we must class some as led by reason, and others as unreasoning.

7. But all men are subject to Fate, and genesis and change, for these [412] are the beginning and the end of Fate.

And though all men do suffer fated things, those led by reason (those whom we said the Mind doth guide) do not endure like suffering with the rest; but, since they've freed themselves from viciousness, not being bad, they do not suffer bad.

Tat. How meanest thou again, my father? Is not the fornicator bad; the murderer bad; and [so with] all the rest?

Her. [I meant not that;] but that the Mind-led man, my son, though not a fornicator, will suffer just as though he had committed fornication, and though he be no murderer, as though he had committed murder.

---

[409] ἀθεότης. *Cf. C. H.*, x. (xi.) 8, 9: "And the soul's vice is ignorance"; and § 20: "What greater chastisement of any human soul, can there be, son, than lack of piety?" The only way of salvation from the bonds of Fate is thus "piety" or "godliness." See R. 102, 1, for references.

[410] δόξα.

[411] Heimarmenē.

[412] *Sc.* genesis and change.

The quality of change he can no more escape than that of genesis.

But it *is* possible for one who hath the Mind, to free himself from vice.

8. Wherefore I've ever heard, my son, Good Daimon also say—(and had He set it down in written words, He would have greatly helped the race of men; for He alone, my son, doth truly, as the First-born God, gazing upon all things, give voice to words (*logoi*) divine)—yea, once I heard Him say:

"All things are one, and most of all the bodies which the mind alone perceives. Our life is owing to [God's] Energy and Power and Æon. His Mind is Good, so is His Soul as well. And this being so, intelligible things know naught of separation. So, then, Mind, being Ruler of all things, and being Soul of God, can do whate'er it wills."

9. So do thou understand, and carry back this word (*logos*) unto the question thou didst ask before,—I mean about Mind's Fate.

For if thou dost with accuracy, son, eliminate [all] captious arguments (*logoi*), thou wilt discover that of very truth the Mind, the Soul of God, doth rule o'er all—o'er Fate, and Law, and all things else; and nothing is impossible to it,—neither o'er Fate to set a human soul,[413] nor under Fate to set [a soul] neglectful of what comes to pass. Let this so far suffice from the Good Daimon's most good [words].[414]

Tat. Yea, [words] divinely spoken, father mine, truly and helpfully. But further still explain me this.

10. Thou said'st that Mind in lives irrational worked in them as [their] nature, co-working with their impulses.

But impulses of lives irrational, as I do think, are passions.

Now if the Mind co-worketh with [these] impulses, and if the impulses of [lives] irrational be passions, then is Mind also passion, taking its colour from the passions.

Her. Well put, my son! Thou questionest right nobly, and it is just that I as well should answer [nobly].

11. All things incorporal when in a body are subject unto passion, and in the proper sense they are [themselves] all passions.

For every thing that moves [another] is incorporal; while every thing that's moved is body.

Incorporals are further moved by Mind, and movement's passion.

Both, then, are subject unto passion—both mover and the moved, the former being ruler and the latter ruled.

But when a man hath freed himself from body, then is he also freed from passion.

But, more precisely, son, naught is impossible, but all are possible.

---

[413] *Cf.* Lact., *D. I.*, ii. 15.
[414] The critical text of this paragraph is given R. 78.

Yet passion differeth from possibility; for that the one is active, while the other's passive.

Incorporals [415]moreover act upon themselves, for either they are motionless [416] or they are moved; but whichsoe'er it be, it's passion.

But bodies are invariably acted on, and therefore are they passible.

Do not, then, let terms trouble thee; action and passion are both the selfsame thing. To use the fairer sounding term, however, does no harm.

12. *Tat.* Most clearly hast thou, father mine, set forth the teaching (*logos*).

Her. Consider this as well, my son; that these two things God hath bestowed on man beyond all mortal lives—both mind and speech (*logos*) equal to immortality. He hath the mind for knowing God and uttered speech (*logos*) for eulogy of Him. [417]

And if one useth these for what he ought, he'll differ not a whit from the immortals. [418] Nay, rather, on departing from the body, he will be guided by the twain unto the Choir of Gods and Blessed Ones.

13. *Tat.* Why, father mine!—do not the other lives make use of speech (*logos*)?

Her. Nay, son; but use of voice; speech is far different from voice. For speech is general among all men, while voice doth differ in each class of living thing.

Tat. But with men also, father mine, according to each race, speech differs.

Her. Yea, son, but man is one; so also speech is one and is interpreted, and it is found the same in Egypt, and in Persia, and in Greece.

Thou seemest, son, to be in ignorance of Reason's (*Logos*) [419] worth and greatness. For that the Blessed God, Good Daimon, hath declared:

"Soul is in Body, Mind in Soul; but Reason (*Logos*) is in Mind, and Mind in God; and God is Father of [all] these."

14. The Reason, then, is the Mind's image, and Mind God's [image]; while Body is [the image] of the Form; and Form [the image] of the Soul.

The subtlest part of Matter is, then, Air; of Air, Soul; of Soul, Mind; and of Mind, God. [420]

And God surroundeth all and permeateth all [421]; while Mind surroundeth Soul, Soul Air, Air Matter.

---

[415] Reading ἀσώματα for σώματα.
[416] The words I have translated by "act," "active" and "action," may be more literally rendered by "energize," "energic" and "energy." The "motionless" has "energy" because it is the cause of motion to that which it moves.
[417] Following the emendation of R.
[418] The critical text of the above paragraphs is given R. 156, n. 6.
[419] It is impossible to bring out the word-play of the original in English; and so the double meaning is lost.
[420] This sentence is tagged on to the end of *C. H.,* v. (vi.) by some scribe.

Necessity [422]and Providence and Nature are instruments of Cosmos and of Matter's ordering; while of intelligible things each is Essence, and Sameness is their Essence.

But of the Bodies [423] of the Cosmos each is many; for through possessing Sameness, [*these*] composed Bodies, though they do change from one into another of themselves, do natheless ever keep the incorruption of their Sameness.

15. Whereas in all the rest of composed bodies, of each there is a certain number; for without number structure cannot be, or composition, or decomposition.

Now it is units that give birth to number and increase it, and, being decomposed, are taken back again into themselves.

Matter is one; and this whole Cosmos—the mighty God and image of the mightier One, both with Him unified, and the conserver of the Will and Order of the Father—is filled full of Life. [424]

Naught is there in it throughout the whole of Æon, the Father's [everlasting] Re-establishment, [425]—nor of the whole, nor of its parts,—which doth not live.

For not a single thing that's dead, hath been, or is, or shall be in [this] Cosmos.

For that the Father willed it should have Life as long as it should be. Wherefore it needs must be a God.

16. How, then, O son, could there be in the God, the image of the Father, [426] in the plenitude [427]of Life—dead things [428]?

For that death is corruption, and corruption is destruction.

How then could any part of that which knoweth no corruption be corrupted, or any whit of him the God destroyed?

Tat. Do they not, then, my father, die—the lives in it, that are its parts?

Her. Hush, son!—led into error by the term in use for what takes place.

They do not die, my son, but are dissolved as compound bodies.

Now dissolution is not death, but dissolution of a compound; it is dissolved not so that it may be destroyed, but that it may become renewed.

---

[421] *Cf.* § 20 below.
[422] Reading ἀνάγκη for ἀνάγκῃ; see § 21 below.
[423] *Sc.* the elements.
[424] Lit. a Plērōma of Life.
[425] ἀποκατάστασις.
[426] Reading πατρός for παντός.
[427] Plērōma.
[428] A critical text of the last five paragraphs is given R. 25, n. 1.

For what is the activity of life? Is it not motion? What then in Cosmos is there that hath no motion? Naught is there, son!

17. *Tat.* Doth not Earth even, father, seem to thee to have no motion?

Her. Nay, son; but rather that she is the only thing which, though in very rapid motion, is also stable.

For how would it not be a thing to laugh at, that the Nurse of all should have no motion, when she engenders and brings forth all things?

For 'tis impossible that without motion one who doth engender, should do so.

That thou shouldst ask if the fourth part [429] is not inert, is most ridiculous; for that the body which doth have no motion, gives sign of nothing but inertia.

18. Know, therefore, generally, my son, that all that is in Cosmos is being moved for decrease or for increase.

Now that which is kept moving, also lives; but there is no necessity that that which lives, should be all same. For being simultaneous, the Cosmos, as a whole, is not subject to change, my son, but all its parts are subject unto it; yet naught [of it] is subject to corruption, or destroyed.

It is the terms employed that confuse men. For 'tis not genesis that constituteth life, but 'tis sensation; it is not change that constituteth death, but 'tis forgetfulness.

Since, then, these things are so, they are immortal all,—Matter, [and] Life, [and] Spirit, Mind [and] Soul, of which whatever liveth, is composed.

19. Whatever then doth live, oweth its immortality unto the Mind, and most of all doth man, he who is both recipient of God, and co-essential with Him.

For with this life alone doth God consort; by visions in the night, by tokens in the day, and by all things doth He foretell the future unto him,—by birds, by inward parts, by wind, by tree.

Wherefore doth man lay claim to know things past, things present and to come.

20. Observe this, too, my son; that each one of the other lives inhabiteth one portion of the Cosmos,—aquatic creatures water, terrene earth, and aery creatures air; while man doth use all these,—earth, water, air, [and] fire; he seeth heaven, too, and doth contact it with [his] sense.

But God surroundeth all, and permeateth all, [430] for He is energy and power; and it is nothing difficult, my son, to *conceive* God.

21. But if thou wouldst Him also *contemplate*, behold the ordering of the Cosmos, and [see] the orderly behaviour of its ordering; behold thou the Necessity of things made manifest, and [see] the Providence of things become

---

[429] *Sc.* element.
[430] *Cf.* § 14 above.

and things becoming; behold how Matter is all-full of Life; [behold] this so great God in movement, with all the good and noble [ones]—gods, daimones and men!

Tat. But these are purely energies, O father mine!

Her. If, then, they're purely energies, my son,—by whom, then, are they energized except by God?

Or art thou ignorant, that just as Heaven, Earth, Water, Air, are parts of Cosmos, in just the selfsame way God's parts are Life and Immortality, [and] Energy, and Spirit, and Necessity, and Providence, and Nature, Soul, and Mind, and the Duration [431] of all these that is called Good?

And there is naught of things that have become, or are becoming, in which God is not.

22. *Tat.* Is He in Matter, father, then?

Her. Matter, my son, is separate from God, in order that thou may'st attribute unto it the quality of space. But what thing else than mass [432] think'st thou it is, if it's not energized? Whereas if it be energized, by whom is it made so? For energies, we said, are parts of God.

By whom are, then, all lives enlivened? By whom are things immortal made immortal? By whom changed things made changeable?

And whether thou dost speak of Matter, or of Body, or of Essence, know that these too are energies of God; and that materiality is Matter's energy, that corporality is Bodies' energy, and that essentiality doth constitute the energy of Essence; and this is God—the All.

23. And in the All is naught that is not God. Wherefore nor size, nor space, nor quality, nor form, nor time, surroundeth God; for He is All, and All surroundeth all, and permeateth all.

Unto this Reason (*Logos*), son, thy adoration and thy worship pay. There is one way alone to worship God; [it is] not to be bad. [433]

---

[431] *Sc.* Æon.
[432] Probably in the sense of "quantity."
[433] Lactantius, *D. I.*, vi. 25, translates the last two sentences into Latin, with the strange remark that Hermes so spake in treating "About Justice." See the following Commentary on § 6, and Ex. xi.

COMMENTARY

THE SAYINGS OF THE GOOD DAIMON

This Sermon has as its subject the Common or General Mind—Great Mind, Good Mind, Good Daimon. For Mind, as we are told (§ 2), is the Benefactor of men (εὐεργέτης ἀνθρώπων); He is the Good Shepherd, the Good Husbandman, the Good Physician, as He is called in different tractates.

From a critical standpoint, the point of greatest interest is that our Hermes in no less than three places (§§ 1, 8, 13) quotes certain Sayings of the Good Daimon.

Now the first of these quotations (§ 1)—"Gods are immortal men, and men are mortal Gods"—is one of the most cited Sayings of Heracleitus.[434] Hermes, however, does not mean to say that Heracleitus was Agothodaimon, but that Heracleitus was the mouthpiece of the Good Mind when he uttered this "word" (*logos*).

Nor was this the opinion of Hermes only; it was the belief apparently of Heracleitus himself when he declared:

"Not because you hear me say so, but because you hear the Reason (*Logos*) so declare, is it wise to confess that All are One."[435]

At any rate the term Logos, as used by Heracleitus, in connection with such a declaration, is taken by Hippolytus[436] to mean the All-pervading Reason, and not the normal reason of man.

What, then, is our surprise to find the second of Hermes' quotations of a Saying of the Good Daimon qualified by the words (§ 8): "And had He set it down in written words" or "in writing," when that quotation begins with the words: "All are One"[437]—the root-formula of Heracleitus.

Such Sayings of Heracleitus must have been the common property of all the philosophers of the time and of their pupils. But the quotation of Hermes does not end with the formula of Heracleitus; it continues, how far exactly it is difficult to determine. Reitzenstein (p. 127) would apparently make it end with the word "Æon," but I am inclined to think it goes to the end of § 8. In either case it includes the term "Æon."

If, now, we turn to the third quotation from the Sayings of the Good Daimon (§ 13), we are at once struck with its remarkable resemblance to the form of teaching in *C. H.*, xi. (xii.) 4. Though there is no precise verbal agreement, there is a striking identity of style of formula.

---

[434] Diels, 62; Bywater, 67; Fairbanks, 67 (p. 40), which see for references to ancient authors who quote it.
[435] Diels, 50; Bywater, I; Fairbanks, I (p. 24).
[436] *Philos.*, ix. 9.
[437] *Cf. C. H.*, x. (xi.) 25, and xvi. ("Definitions of Asclepius") 3; for references to the Magical and Alchemical literature, see R. 39, 1; 106, 5; 127, 3.

In our treatise, however, the Saying is used in authoritative illustration of the meaning of the Reason (*Logos*), whereas in the "Mind to Hermes,"—that is, in the Sermon of the Good Daimon Himself to Hermes—Reason is omitted, Mind and Reason being there transcended by Æon and Mind.

Moreover, the whole style of what follows this quotation in our treatise is exactly the same as the style of instruction in *C. H.*, xi. (xii.)—short categorical formulæ; and, further, the previous quotation (§ 8) contains the key-word Æon, which characterizes the teaching of the "Mind to Hermes."

I therefore conclude that our Hermes is using a more intimate instruction, known only to the Hermes-grade, and not published for the Tat-degree; and that this is the meaning of his saying that it has not been written down. He means simply that it has not yet been allowed to be published for those in the Tat-stage.

There were, then, other treatises now lost of the same type as that of the "Mind to Hermes"; in them there were quotations from the Sayings of Heracleitus; the "Obscure Philosopher" being regarded as one who had come into direct contact with the Logos or Mind, and as one, therefore, who spoke with the authority of direct revelation.

HERMES AND BASILIDES

The next point of critical interest is the sentence in § 7:

"I meant not that, but that the Mind-led man, my son, though not a fornicator, will suffer just as though he had committed fornication, and though he be no murderer, as though he had committed murder."

If we now turn to the quotation which Clement of Alexandria [438] gives us from Book XXIII. of the *Exegetica*, of Basilides, we read:

"For just as the babe, who, although it hath done no wrong previously, or actively committed any sin, yet hath the capacity of sin in it,—whenever it is subjected to suffering, is advantaged and reaps many benefits, which otherwise are difficult to gain; in just the selfsame way is it, that although a perfect man may not have sinned in act, and yet doth suffer pains, he suffereth them in just the selfsame fashion as a babe; having within himself the tendency to sin, but refusing to embrace the opportunity to sin, he doth not sin. So that even for such a man as this we ought not to suppose the incapacity for sin.

"For just as it is the will to commit fornication that constitutes the fornicator, even though he does not find the opportunity of actually committing fornication, and the will to commit murder that constitutes the murderer, although he may not be actually able to effect his purpose; so also in

---

[438] *Strom.*, IV. xii., § 82 (P. 600; S. 217): Dindorf., ii. 363.

the case of the 'sinless' man I mean, if I see him suffering, even if he has actually *done* no sin, I shall say he is evil by his *will* to sin. For I will say anything rather than that Providence is evil." [439]

Providence, as in our treatise, is here the instrument of the Good (§ 14), of the Will of God; it is the will of man that is the source of evil, as we learn from *C. H.*, iv. (v.) 8: "For 'tis not God, 'tis we who are the cause of evil things, preferring them to good."

In our treatise, then, the very same problem is treated as in the *Exegetica* of Basilides. Hermes speaks of the "Mind-led man," the "man who has the Logos in him"; Basilides speaks of the "perfect man." So also in *C. H.*, iv. (v.) 4, the "perfect man" is he who has "received the Mind."

The ideas of Hermes and of Basilides are practically identical; the words of both are strikingly similar when they cite fornication and murder as typical sins, and these and no others.

Compare again with this idea of the babe in Basilides the words of Hermes in *C. H.*, x. (xi.) 15:

"Behold an infant's soul, my son, that is not yet cut off, because its body is still small and not as yet come unto its full bulk. . . . A thing of beauty altogether is such a soul to see, not yet befouled with body's passions, still all but hanging from the Cosmic Soul."

And with this compare what Hippolytus [440] tells us of Valentinus:

"Valentinus says that he once saw a babe that had only just been born, and that he proceeded to question it to find out who it was. And the babe replied and said it was the Logos."

And also the Psalm of Valentinus quoted by the same heresiologist [441]:

All things depending from Spirit I see;

All things supported by Spirit I view;

Flesh from Soul depending;

Soul by Air supported;

Air from Æther hanging;

Fruits borne of the Deep;

Babe borne of the Womb.

Here, then, as in other instances, we have intimate points of contact between the Hermetic and Christian Gnosis. Is there, however, any question of direct plagiarism? I think not; but that the Christian doctors and the Hermetic philosophers were both in contact with the same body of inner teaching.

---

[439] See *F. F. F.*, 274, 275.
[440] *Philos.*, vi. 42 (D. and S., 302); *F. F. F.*, p. 306.
[441] *Philos.*, vi. 37 (D. and S., 290); see emended text in Hilgenfeld (A.), *Die Ketzergeschichte des Urchristenthums* (Leipzig, 1884), p. 304; *F. F. F.*, p. 307.

4. With the action of the Mind on the soul in incarnation (§ 4) compare *C. H.*, x. (xi.), 18, 19, where the office of the Mind in respect to the soul out of incarnation is graphically described.

THE SERMONS ON FATE

6. In § 6 Hermes tells us that he has already spoken about Fate in others of his Sermons; while in §§ 14 and 21 he three times refers to Necessity and Providence.

In this connection it is to be noticed that Lactantius (*D. I.*, vi. 25), in quoting the last two sentences of our treatise, says that he takes them from a Sermon by Hermes "On Justice."

Now, Stobæus has preserved for us an Extract (xi.) from a Sermon dealing with Justice, Providence, Necessity and Fate; also an Extract (x.) from a Sermon of Hermes to Tat dealing with Fate, and ending with the words: "Such is the Sermon on the rule of Providence, Necessity and Fate." We have also an Extract (xiii.) "Of Hermes from the Books to Ammon," entitled "Of the General Economy," which deals with Providence, Necessity and Fate.

There were, then, according to Hermes, already existing not one but several Sermons on Fate, and, as we learn from Stobæus, not only in the Tat-literature but also in the Ammon-literature. It seems, then, probable that in the collection used by Lactantius the Tat-Sermons on Fate immediately preceded our treatise, and that one of these sermons (the one immediately preceding our treatise, presumably) was entitled "On Justice," thus confirming the title I have prefixed to the Stobæus Extract xi.

MATERIALITY AND CORPORALITY ARE ENERGIES OF GOD

22. Finally, in § 22 it has to be noticed that with the express teaching that Matter and Body are so far from being evil that they are Energies of God—His materiality and corporality—the charge of dualism against our philosophers must for ever be abandoned. Their doctrine was that of pan-monism; and, therefore, wherever we find signs of dualism, or even distinct statements of an indubitably dualistic nature, we must understand that this was a formal convenience for the better insistence upon the need of strenuous exertion to solve the mystery of the opposites, rather than an essential doctrine of the Gnosis.

CORPUS HERMETICUM XIII. (XIV.)

THE SECRET SERMON ON THE MOUNTAIN

CONCERNING REBIRTH AND THE PROMISE OF SILENCE OF THRICE-GREATEST HERMES UNTO TAT HIS SON

(Text: R. 339-348; P. 114-128; Pat. 15b-17b.)

1. *Tat.* [Now] in the General Sermons, [442] father, thou didst speak in riddles most unclear, conversing on Divinity; and when thou saidst no man could e'er be saved before Rebirth, [443] thy meaning thou didst hide.

Further, when I became thy Suppliant, in Wending up the Mount, [444] after thou hadst conversed with me, and when I longed to learn the Sermon (*Logos*) on Rebirth (for this beyond all other things is just the thing I know not), thou saidst, that thou wouldst give it me—"when thou shalt have become a stranger to the world." [445]

Wherefore I got me ready and made the thought in me a stranger [446] to the world-illusion.

And now do thou fill up the things that fall short [447] in me with what thou saidst would give me the tradition [448] of Rebirth, setting it forth in speech or in the secret way.

I know not, O Thrice-greatest one, from out what matter and what womb Man comes to birth, or of what seed. [449]

2. *Hermes.* Wisdom that understands [450] in silence [451] [such is the matter and the womb from out which Man is born], and the True Good the seed.

---

[442] ἐν τοῖς γενικοῖς. *Cf. C. H.,* x. (xi.) 1 and 7.
[443] παλιγγενεσία.
[444] Reading ἐπὶ τῆς τοῦ ὄρους μεταβάσεως with P., and not κατα-βάσεως with R. *Cf. C. H.,* x. (xi.) 15; Jamb., *D. M.,* viii. 6.
[445] κόσμου.
[446] Reading ἀπηλλοτρίωσα with the majority of the editors, and not the ἀπήδρισα of R.
[447] τὰ ὑστερήματα ἀναπλήρωσον.
[448] παραδοῦναι, the word used for the giving of this lesson or inner instruction is the technical term for the "handing on" of a doctrine or being initiated into it.
[449] R.'s reading would make this refer to Hermes: "I know not from what womb thou com'st to birth." But the whole instruction seems to favour the usually accepted reading.
[450] σοφία νοερά.
[451] *Cf. C. H.,* x. (xi.) 5.

Tat. Who is the sower, father? For I am altogether at a loss.

Her. It is the Will of God, my son.

Tat. And of what kind is he that is begotten, father? For I have no share of that essence in me, which doth transcend the senses. [452] The one that is begot will be another one from God, God's Son?

Her. All in all, out of all powers composed.

Tat. Thou tellest me a riddle, father, and dost not speak as father unto son.

Her. This Race, [453] my son, is never taught; but when He willeth it, its memory is restored by God.

3. *Tat.* Thou sayest things impossible, O father, things that are forced. Hence answers would I have direct unto these things. Am I a son strange to my father's race?

Keep it not, father, back from me. I am a true-born son; explain to me the manner of Rebirth.

Her. What may I say, my son? I can but tell thee *this*. Whene'er I see within myself the Simple Vision [454] brought to birth out of God's mercy, [455] I have passed through myself into a Body that can never die. And now I am not what I was before; but I am born in Mind.

The way to do this is not taught, and it cannot be seen by the compounded [456] element by means of which thou seest.

Yea, I have had my former composed form dismembered for me. I am no longer touched, yet have I touch; I have dimension too; and [yet] am I a stranger to them now.

Thou seest me with eyes, my son; but what I am thou dost not understand [even] with fullest strain of body and of sight.

4. *Tat.* Into fierce frenzy and mind-fury hast thou plunged me, father, for now no longer do I see myself.

Her. I would, my son, that thou hadst e'en passed right through thyself, as they who dream in sleep yet sleepless.

Tat. Tell me this too! Who is the author [457] of Rebirth?

Her. The Son of God, the One Man, by God's Will.

5. *Tat.* Now hast thou brought me, father, unto pure stupefaction. Arrested from the senses which I had before, ... [458]; for [now] I see thy Greatness identical with thy distinctive form.

---

[452] τῆς ἐν ἐμοὶ οὐσίας τῆς νοητῆς.
[453] *Cf.* Ex. i. 3.
[454] ἄπλαστον, that is to say, not made up, non-fictitious, not compounded; that is, simple—the opposite of compounded.
[455] *Cf.* below, § 7: the man "who hath been taken pity on by God"; and also §10.
[456] πλαστόν.
[457] γενεσιουργός.
[458] A lacuna unfortunately follows.

Her. Even in this thou art untrue [459]; the mortal form doth change with every day. 'Tis turned by time to growth and waning, as being an untrue thing. [460]

6. *Tat.* What then is true, Thrice-greatest One?

Her. That which is never troubled, son, which cannot be defined; that which no colour hath, nor any figure, which is not turned, which hath no garment, which giveth light; that which is comprehensible unto itself [alone], which doth not suffer change; that which no body can contain. [461]

Tat. In very truth I lose my reason, father. Just when I thought to be made wise by thee, I find the senses of this mind of mine blocked up.

Her. Thus is it, son: That which is upward borne like fire, yet is borne down like earth, that which is moist like water, yet blows like air, [462] how shalt thou *this* perceive with sense—the that which is not solid nor yet moist, which naught can bind or loose, of which in power and energy alone can man have any notion,—and even then it wants a man who can [463]perceive the Way of Birth in God [464]?

7. *Tat.* I am incapable of this, O father, then?

Her. Nay, God forbid, my son! Withdraw into thyself, and it will come; *will*, and it comes to pass; throw out of work the body's senses, and thy Divinity shall come to birth; purge from thyself the brutish torments—things of matter.

Tat. I have tormentors then in me, O father?

Her. Ay, no few, my son; nay, fearful ones and manifold.

Tat. I do not know them, father.

Her. Torment the first is this Not-knowing, [465] son; the second one is Grief; the third, Intemperance; the fourth, Concupiscence; the fifth, Unrighteousness; the sixth is Avarice; the seventh, Error [466]; the eighth is Envy; the ninth, Guile [467]; the tenth is Anger; eleventh, Rashness; the twelfth is Malice.

These are in number twelve; but under them are many more, my son; and creeping through the prison of the body [468] they force the man that's placed within [469] to suffer in his senses. But they depart (although not all at

---

[459] ψεύδη.
[460] ὡς ψεῦδος.
[461] *Cf. P. S. A.*, xxxi..3.
[462] *Cf. C. H.*, iv. (v.) 1.
[463] Retaining the reading δεόμενου δὲ τοῦ δυναμένου.
[464] τὴν ἐν θεῷ γένεσιν—*cf.* § 10.
[465] ἄγνοια.
[466] ἀπάτη.
[467] δόλος.
[468] *Cf. C. H.*, xvi. 15.
[469] ἐνδιάθετον.

once) from him who hath been taken pity on by God [470]; and this it is which constitutes the manner of Rebirth. And . . . . [471] the Reason (*Logos*).

8. And now, my son, be still and solemn silence keep! Thus shall the mercy that flows on us from God not cease.

Henceforth rejoice, O son, for by the Powers of God thou art being purified for the articulation of the Reason (*Logos*). Gnosis of God hath come to us, and when this comes, my son, Not-knowing is cast out.

Gnosis of Joy hath come to us, and on its coming, son, Sorrow will flee away to them who give it room. The Power that follows Joy do I invoke, thy Self-control. O Power most sweet! Let us most gladly bid it welcome, son! How with its coming doth it chase Intemperance away!

9. Now fourth, on Continence I call, the Power against Desire.

. . . . [472] This step, my son, is Righteousness' firm seat. For without judgment [473] see how she hath chased Unrighteousness away. We are made righteous, son, by the departure of Unrighteousness.

Power sixth I call to us,—that against Avarice, Sharing-with-all. [474]

And now that Avarice is gone, I call on Truth. And Error flees, and Truth is with us.

See how [the measure of] the Good is full, my son, upon Truth's coming. For Envy hath gone from us; and unto Truth is joined the Good as well, with Life and Light.

And now no more doth any torment of the Darkness venture nigh, but vanquished [all] have fled with whirring wings.

10. Thou knowest [now], my son, the manner of Rebirth. And when the Ten is come, my son, that driveth out the Twelve, the Birth in understanding [475] is complete, and by this Birth we are made into Gods.

Who then doth by His mercy gain this Birth in God, abandoning the body's senses, knows himself [to be of Light and Life [476]] and that he doth consist of these, and [thus] is filled with Bliss.

---

[470] *Cf.* above, § 3: "brought to birth out of God's mercy"; and also § 10.
[471] A lacuna in the text.
[472] Something has here evidently fallen out in the text.
[473] χωρὶς κρίσεως. If, however, we must read κτίσεως with the majority of the editors, I cannot understand the various translations. Everard gives "without labour"; Parthey, "*nulla contentione*"; Ménard, "*sans combat*"; Chambers, "without contention." I would, therefore, render it: "See how she hath chased out Unrighteousness without a home"; for it seems to me that in χωρὶς κτίσεως we have the exact antithesis of ἕδρασμα. Righteousness has here her firm seat or abode, and Unrighteousness is thus naturally without a home.
[474] κοινωνίαν.
[475] νοερὰ γένεσις, lit., intellectual birth.
[476] Completed from *C. H.*, i. 22.

11. *Tat.* By God made steadfast, father, no longer with the sight my eyes afford I look on things, but with the energy the Mind doth give me through the Powers. [477]

In heaven am I, in earth, in water, air; I am in animals, in plants; I'm in the womb, before the womb, after the womb; I'm everywhere!

But further tell me this: How are the torments of the Darkness, when they are twelve in number, driven out by the ten Powers? What is the way of it, Thrice-greatest one?

12. *Her.* This dwelling-place [478]through which we have just passed, my son, is constituted from the circle of the types-of-life, this being composed of elements, twelve in number, but of one nature, an omniform [479]idea. For man's delusion there are disunions [480] in them, son, while in their action they are one. Not only can we never part Rashness from Wrath; they cannot even be distinguished.

According to right reason (*logos*), then, they [481] naturally withdraw once and for all, in as much as they are chased out by no less than ten powers, that is, the Ten.

For, son, the Ten is that which giveth birth to souls. And Life and Light are unified there, where the One hath being from the Spirit. According then to reason (*logos*) the One contains the Ten, the Ten the One.

13. *Tat.* Father, I see the All, I see myself in Mind.

Her. This is, my son, Rebirth—no more to look on things from body's view-point (a thing three ways in space extended), [482] . . . [483] though this Sermon (*Logos*) on Rebirth, on which I did not comment [484];—in order that we may not be calumniators [485]of the All unto the multitude, to whom indeed the God Himself doth will we should not.

14. *Tat.* Tell me, O father: This Body which is made up of the Powers, is it at any time dissolved?

Her. Hush, [son]! Speak not of things impossible, else wilt thou sin and thy Mind's eye be quenched.

The natural body which our sense perceives is far removed from this *essential* birth.

The first must be dissolved, the last can never be; the first must die, the last death cannot touch.

---

[477] τῇ διὰ δινάμεων νοητικῇ ἐνεργείᾳ.

[478] σκῆνος,—tent or tabernacle of the human soul. *Cf.* below, § 15.

[479] *Cf.* commentary on *C. H.,* xi. (xii.) 16.

[480] διαζυγαὶ—the opposite of συζυγίαι.

[481] That is, the Twelve.

[482] As opposed to some other dimension, presumably.

[483] Some words are evidently missing.

[484] See § 1.

[485] διάβολοι, compare § 22. The lacuna probably contained some reference to keeping silence.

Dost thou not know thou hast been born a God, Son of the One, even as I myself?

15. *Tat.* I would, O father, hear the Praise-giving with hymn which thou didst say thou heardest then when thou wert at the Eight [the Ogdoad] of Powers.

Her. Just as the Shepherd did foretell [I should], my son, [when I came to] the Eight. [486]

Well dost thou haste to "strike thy tent," [487] for thou hast been made pure.

The Shepherd, Mind of all masterhood, [488] hath not passed on to me more than hath been writ down, for full well did He know that I should of myself be able to learn all, and hear what I should wish, and see all things.

He left to me the making of fair things [489]; wherefore the Powers within me, e'en as they are in all, [490] break into song.

16. *Tat.* Father, I wish to hear; I long to know these things.

Her. Be still, my son; hear the Praise-giving now that keeps [the soul] in tune, Hymn of Re-birth—a hymn I would not have thought fit so readily to tell, had'st thou not reached the end of all.

Wherefore this is not taught, but is kept hid in silence.

Thus then, my son, stand in a place uncovered to the sky, facing the southern wind, [491] about the sinking of the setting sun, and make thy worship; so in like manner too when he doth rise, with face to the east wind.

Now, son, be still!

THE SECRET HYMNODY

17. Let every nature of the World receive the utterance of my hymn!

Open thou Earth! Let every bolt of the Abyss be drawn for me. Stir not, ye Trees!

I am about to hymn creation's Lord, both All and One.

Ye Heavens open, and ye Winds stay still; [and] let God's deathless Sphere receive my word (*logos*)!

For I will sing the praise of Him who founded all; who fixed the Earth, and hung up Heaven, and gave command that Ocean should afford

---

[486] *Cf. C. H.*, i. 26.
[487] λῦσαι τὸ σκῆνος. *Cf.* above, § 12. The meaning is generally to free oneself from the trammels of the body. Compare the Pythian Oracle concerning Plotinus: "But now since thou hast struck thy tent and left the tomb of thy daimonic soul" (νῦν δ' ὅτε δὴ σκῆνος μέν ἐλύσαο, σῆμα δ' ἔλειψας ψυχῆς δαιμονίς). Porphyry, *Plotini Vita*, xxii.; *cf.* Ex. vii. 3; Ex. iii. 1.
[488] *Cf. C. H.*, i. 2.
[489] *Sc.* psalms and praise-giving.
[490] *Sc.* prophets.
[491] Also used of the south-west quarter. The "south wind" is thought to have extended from SSE. to W.

sweet water [to the Earth], to both those parts that are inhabited and those that are not, for the support and use of every man; who made the Fire to shine for gods and men for every act.

Let us together all give praise to Him, sublime above the Heavens, of every nature Lord!

'Tis He who is the Eye of Mind; may He accept the praise of these my Powers!

18. Ye Powers that are within me, hymn the One and All; sing with my Will, Powers all that are within me!

O blessed Gnosis, by thee illumined, hymning through thee the Light that mind alone can see, [492] I joy in Joy of Mind.

Sing with me praises all ye Powers!

Sing praise, my Self-control; sing thou through me, my Righteousness, the praises of the Righteous; sing thou, my Sharing-all, the praises of the All; through me sing, Truth, Truth's praises!

Sing thou, O Good, the Good! O Life and Light, from us to you our praises flow!

Father, I give Thee thanks, to Thee Thou Energy of all my Powers; I give Thee thanks, O God, Thou Power of all my Energies!

19. Thy Reason (*Logos*) sings through me Thy praises. Take back through me the All into [Thy] Reason—[my] reasonable oblation [493]!

Thus cry the Powers in me. They sing Thy praise, Thou All; they do Thy Will.

From Thee Thy Will [494]; *to* Thee the All. Receive from all their reasonable oblation. The All that is in us, O Life, preserve; O Light illumine it; O God in-spirit it. [495]

It is Thy Mind that plays the Shepherd [496] to Thy Word, [497] O Thou Creator, Bestower of the Spirit [upon all]. [498]

20. [For] Thou art God; Thy Man [499] thus cries to Thee through Fire, through Air, through Earth, through Water, [and] through Spirit, through Thy creatures.

'Tis from Thy Æon I have found Praise-giving; and in Thy Will, [500] the object of my search, have I found rest.

---

[492] τὸ νοητὸν φῶς.
[493] *Cf.* below, 21.
[494] *Cf. P. S. A.*, Comment, and R. 39, n. 1.
[495] The Spirit being Light and Life.
[496] ποιμαίνει, acts as a shepherd or feeds; Pœmandres is thus the Shepherd of men or the feeder of men, He who gives them the heavenly food.
[497] The Word or Reason or true Man in man.
[498] πνευματοφόρε δημιουργέ.
[499] *Cf. C. H.*, i. 32.
[500] βουλή.

Tat. By thy good pleasure [501]have I seen this Praise-giving being *sung*, [502] O father; I have set it in *my* Cosmos too.

Her. Say in the Cosmos that thy mind alone can see, my son.

Tat. Yea, father, in the Cosmos that the mind alone can see; for I have been made able by thy Hymn, and by thy Praise-giving my mind hath been illumined. But further I myself as well would from my natural mind send praise-giving to God.

21. *Her.* But not unheedfully, my son.

Tat. Ay. What I behold in mind, that do I say.

To thee, thou Parent of my Bringing into Birth, as unto God I, Tat, send reasonable offerings. [503] O God and Father, thou art the Lord, thou art the Mind. Receive from me oblations reasonable as thou would'st wish; for by thy Will all things have been perfected.

Her. Send thou oblation, son, acceptable to God, the Sire of all; but add, my son, too, "through the Word" (*Logos*).

Tat. I give thee, father, thanks for showing me to sing such hymns.

22. *Her.* Happy am I, my son, that thou hast brought the good fruits forth of Truth, products that cannot die.

And now that thou hast learnt this lesson from me, make promise to keep silence [504] on thy virtue, and to no soul, my son, make known the handing on to thee the manner of Rebirth, that we may not be thought to be calumniators. [505]

And now we both of us have given heed sufficiently, both I the speaker and the hearer thou.

In Mind [506]hast thou become a Knower of thyself and of our [common] Sire.

---

[501] θέλημα.
[502] Cf., for instance, *The Ascension of Isaiah*, i. 6: "In the twentieth year of the reign of Hezekiah, Isaiah had *seen* the words of this prophecy."—Charles' Trans. (London, 1900), p. 5.
[503] *Cf.* above, § 18.
[504] *Cf. P. S. A.*, xxxii. 4.
[505] διάβολοι, slanderers, calumniators; compare § 13; also Ex. i. 16.
[506] νοερῶς.

COMMENTARY

CONCERNING THE TITLE

"The Secret Sermon on the Mountain" is the main title given in all the MSS., with the exception of A; the subsidiary contents-title is evidently derived from the same edition to which we owe the other contents-titles preserved in our Corpus. Reitzenstein (p. 193), however, thinks that the main title has arisen by mistake. What the mistake is he does not tell us; perhaps he means that in our Sermon there is no mention of "*On* a Mountain," but rather, as in § I, if we accept his reading, of "*Down* a Mountain." But in this we cannot follow him; for the whole teaching is precisely "On the Mount"—to the top of which Tat has now come. For the "Mountain" was symbolic of stages of inner development, and in § 9 we are told precisely: "This *step* (the fifth) is Righteousness' firm seat,"—showing that the Mountain was conceived as an ascent or stair of steps as is so often seen in Egyptian frescoes.

THE TERM APOCRYPHON

Again, with regard to the title, the term "Secret" (ἀπόκρυφος—apocryphal) is used in its original sense of hidden away, meaning esoteric or not put into circulation, as applied to a *logos* or sermon, or a collection of *logoi* or sayings.

A *logos* in this sense had very much the same meaning for our Ancients as the Sanskrit *mahā-vākyam* ("great saying") has to-day for an Indian theosophist who applies the term to the great mystical utterances of the Upaniṣhads; such as: "That art thou" (*Tat tvam asi*), etc.

In classical antiquity these *logoi* or *logia* were regarded as words of wisdom, and were the most sacred legacies of the sages to humanity. These oracular utterances were frequently collected together, and even prior to the days of syncretism formed the most sacred "deposits" (διαθῆκαι) of various nations; the same term being subsequently given to the Christian Bible.

Thus Herodotus calls Onomacritus, the first collector of the archaic Orphic Hymns, a "depository of oracles" (διαθέτην χρησμῶν),—the word carrying the meaning of "one who arranges," corresponding exactly to the term Vyāsa in Sanskrit, the supposed "author" of the *Mahābhārata*.

Such collections of *logoi* or *logia* were then generally called "deposits," the word also sometimes bearing the meaning of "testaments" as containing the expression of the Divine will or dispensation. The same term is used by Strabo (x. 482) of the Laws of Lycurgus; it was also applied by the

Orphics and Pythagoreans to such sacred laws [507]; while Ecclesiastical writers subsequently used it in reference to the Canonical Books. [508]

The Orphics and Pythagoreans also called these collections "sacred utterances" (ἱεροὶ λόγοι); and even Clement of Alexandria refers to such a saying of Orpheus as "that truly sacred utterance" (τὸν ὄντως ἱερὸν λόγον).

That such collections were kept secret is not surprising; indeed, such must have been the case from time immemorial. But even on the ground of purely Greek and Roman history, we are not without information of collections of oracles carefully guarded as the secret scriptures or bibles of nations.

Cicero [509] speaks of such a bible of the Veii. The Athenians, in the time of the Kings, possessed a similar bible of *logia* [510]; and Dinarchus [511] tells us that the safety of the State depended on this secret scripture (ἀπορρήτους διαθήκας) These occult sayings (ἀπόθεντα ἔπη) are further called by Suidas (*s.v.*) "withdrawn volumes" (βιβλία ἀνακεχωρηκότα)—that is to say, books withdrawn from public perusal, or, in other words, apocryphal, hidden or secret (ἀπόκρυφα).

And not only was this the case with the ancient writings themselves, but also with the commentaries upon them, and by degrees with everything referring to them, until finally we find Themistius the rhetorician, in the fourth century, speaking of that "mass of Archaic wisdom not open to the public or in general circulation, but scarce and occult." [512]

We have, therefore, translated the term by "secret" as conveying the proper meaning of the epithet in the title, and not by "apocryphal," a word that nowadays connotes the judgment of a theological canon.

THE THREE STAGES OF PROBATION

I. In the first paragraph Tat definitely refers to *three* Stages of Probation, before he is deemed fit to hear the Sermon on Rebirth.

(i) First there is the General or Preliminary Instruction contained in a collection of discourses called the General Sermons (Γενικοὶ Λόγοι).

(ii) Next is the Stage where Tat becomes the Suppliant of Hermes, a stage characterized by Conversation or Dialogue (διαλεχθῆναι); that is to say, Tat was allowed to ask questions. This is further symbolically described by a

---

[507] Grotius, *ap.* Jablonski, ii. 397; Lobeck, *Aglaoph.*, p. 714.
[508] Euseb., *Chron.*, 99 A.
[509] *De Div.*, i. 44.
[510] Herod., v. 90.
[511] *Or. c. Demos.*, 91, 20.
[512] *Or.*, IV. 60: "στῖφος ἀρχαιας σοφίας, οὐ κοινῆς οὐδε ἐν μέσῳ κυλινδουμένης ἀλλὰ σπανίου καὶ ἀποθέτου."

phrase, ἐπὶ τῆς τοῦ ὄρους μεταβάσεως, which is difficult to translate, but which seems to mean either Passing up, or Wending up, the Mountain, or Wending over the Mountain. That is to say, that Hermes was gradually leading Tat to the top of the Mountain, in plain words, as far as his normal intellect could carry him; the Top of the Mountain representing the highest point of unaided mental faculty.

This stage was, I believe, represented by the collection of Sermons to Tat, or Dialogues with Tat, known as the Διεξοδικοὶ Λόγοι—a term somewhat difficult to translate precisely.

The fundamental meaning of διέξοδος is a "way through and out," a "pathway" or "passage," or "means of escape." It thus comes to mean the course of a narrative, or a detailed narrative, exposition, discussion. Hence also a "passage" of Scripture. As set over against γενικὸς (General), therefore, διεξοδικὸς would mean Detailed or Expository; but at the same time it would to the Greek ear suggest the meaning of the Means of Escape or the Way out of Ignorance.

(iii) The third Stage is that of Moral and Mental Purification. "Wherefore I got me ready and made the thought (τὸ φρόνημα) in me a stranger to the world-illusion" (τῆς τοῦ κόσμου ἀπάτης)—the Error that in § 7 sums up the first six vices, and is in § 9 driven out by Truth.

Stage ii. may have been technically known as that of the Suppliant, though, of course, of this we cannot be sure. In any case the term must be considered in close connection with Philo's treatise *On the Contemplative Life*, which, as Conybeare tells us, most probably formed Book IV. of Philo's voluminous work, or rather apology, *De Legatione*. The alternative title of this work was *The Suppliants*. By "Suppliant" Philo tells us he means "one who has fled to God and taken refuge with Him." [513]

Here, however, the term is used in a narrower sense, as adapted to the personal relationship of disciple to master, who, during the time of probation, stands to him as the representative of God. The master is his spiritual father, the image of God the Father. [514]

THE HOLY MOUNT OF INITIATION

As to the symbolic use of the term Mountain, I need hardly remind my readers that it was perhaps the most common figure employed in the apocalypses of the time. Instances come immediately crowding into the mind, such as the "Mount of Galilee" in the Askew and Bruce Gnostic Codices, on which all the great initiations and rites are performed by the Risen Lord; or the

---

[513] *De Sac. Ab. et C.*, i. 186, 33.
[514] See the praise-giving of Tat, § 21.

Mount Tabor [515] of *The Gospel according to the Hebrews*, "My Mother the Holy Spirit took me by one of the hairs of the head and carried me unto Mount Tabor"; or in the *Acts of John*, where the Vision of the Spiritual Crucifixion is shown to John on the Mount; or in *The Gospel of Eve*, where the Vision of the Great and Little Man is seen on the Mount; or in *The Shepherd of Hermas*, where the Angel of Repentance bears off Hermas to the Mount of Arcadia, etc. In every case the Mountain is no physical mountain, but the height of contemplation, an interior state of spiritual consciousness.

Stage iii., again, is of interest because of the terms in which it is described; they may be compared with the same teaching in the Behnesa *logos*:

Jesus saith: "Except ye fast to the world, ye shall in nowise find the Kingdom of God."

Again, in Tat's prayer for the consummation of his probation: "And now do thou fill up the things that fall short in me" (τὰ ὑστερήματα ἀναπλήρωσον), it should be noticed that we have the well-known technical terms of the Christianized Gnosis, the Plērōma and Hysterēma, or Fullness and Insufficiency.

THE BIRTH FROM ABOVE

The time has come for Tat to receive, through his master, the touch of the true Mind-consciousness, the Christ is to be born in his heart, the light of the Plērōma is to shine into his inmost being. It is to be a New Birth, a Regeneration (παλιγγένεσις), or Re-birth (ἀναγέννησις), in the sense of being born from Above (ἄνωθεν).

Compare John iii. 3: "Amen, Amen, I say unto thee; Except a man be born from Above, he cannot see the Kingdom of God." And also 7: "Marvel not that I said unto thee, Ye (*pl.*) must be born from Above,"—where the comment on a prior saying, "*Ye* must be born from Above," formally unsuited to the scheme of a dialogue between Jeschu and Rabbi Nakdimon, reveals the work of the Haggadist.

So also in I Pet. i. 22, 23: "Having made your souls holy by hearkening to the Truth [516] . . . being Re-born (ἀναγεγεννημένοι) not from the seed of destruction, but from the Seed that cannot be destroyed, through the Word [517] (*Logos*) of God, who lives and endures." [518]

These passages from the New Testament Scriptures are not, of course, cited to show any dependence of our Hermetic authors on the New Testament writers; but simply to show how they mutually explain one another. For indeed the doctrine of the New Birth and of the Sacred Marriage was

---

[515] "The Mountain of Light," the traditional scene of the Transfiguration.
[516] Precisely as did Tat.
[517] *Cf.* precisely the same formula in our treatise, § 21.
[518] That is, of God as Æon and God as Life, which is the union of God as Mind and Logos.

beyond all else the crowning mystery of the Spiritual Way for all the mystic schools of the time. [519]

THE VIRGIN BIRTH

2. The secret that Tat would learn is the Mystery of the Birth from the Virgin Womb—the Birth of Man, the Great Mystery of Regeneration. Many illustrations of the meaning of this pivot-doctrine of the Christian teaching might be quoted from Gnostic writings, but it will be sufficient to remind the reader of what the Jewish Commentator in the Naassene Document (§ 28) has written in contrasting the Great Mysteries (or the heavenly ones) with the Little Mysteries (those of fleshly generation). Speaking of the Mysteries of Regeneration, he writes:

"For this is the Gate of Heaven, and this is the House of God, where the Good God dwells alone; into which no impure [man] shall come, but it is kept under guard for the spiritual alone,—where when they come, they must cast away their garments, and all become bridegrooms, obtaining their true manhood, through the Virginal Spirit. For this is the Virgin big with child, conceiving and bearing a Son."

And to this the Christian Commentator adds:—"not psychic, not fleshly, but a blessed Æon of Æons."

The Jewish Commentator uses the language of Philo, who, as we have shown, centred his ideas round the conception of the Sacred Marriage and the Virginal Spirit.

So, too, does our treatise. The Womb is Silence, the silence of contemplation, the image of the Great Silence the Mother of the Æons in many a Christianized Gnostic System; the Matter is Wisdom; the Æon's coming to consciousness in man is the Birth of Man the Son of God; and the Seed is the Good or Logos sown by the Will of the Father. This is the Birth of the Christ in man, the Great Mystery that awaits us when we have made ourselves strangers to the world-illusion.

Is this Son then, asks Tat, other than God? No, answers Hermes; it is the Mystery of Sameness, not of Difference; it is the Plērōma, not the Insufficiency,—"All in all, out of all powers composed," the Common Fruit of the Plērōma, as the Valentinians would have expressed it.

---

[519] The antiquity of the ideas connected with this spiritual mystery may be seen from what Reitzenstein (pp. 227 ff.) has to say concerning mystic συνουσία or congress; of it, as perhaps of nothing so much in the world, may it be said *corruptio optimi pessima*.

THE RACE OF THE LOGOS

It is a Race, not an individual; it is We and no longer I. [520] This is the Race of the Logos; the Self-taught Race of Philo; or, as Hermes says: "This Race, my son, is never taught, but when He willeth it, its memory is restored by God."

This is the ἀνάμνησις of Pythagoras and Plato,—the regaining of the consciousness of the Divine State; it must be self-perceived. And so Philo tells us:

"But as for the Race of Devotees who are taught ever more and more to see, let them strive for the intuition of That-which-is; let them transcend the sun which men perceive [and gaze upon the Light beyond, the True Sun or Logos], nor ever leave this rank which leads to Perfect Blessedness. Now they who betake themselves to the [Divine] Service, [do so] not because of any custom, or *some one's advice or appeal*, but are carried away by Heavenly Love." [521]

They are of the Race of Elxai, the Hidden Power or Holy Spirit, the Spouse of Iexai, the Hidden Lord or Logos. [522]

THE SELF-TAUGHT

3. Hermes cannot teach to Tat this Birth in words, even as Isis is not permitted to declare it openly to Horus (*K. K.*, 36):

"I may not tell the story of this Birth; for it is not permitted to describe the origin of thy descent, O Horus, son of mighty power, lest afterward the Way-of-Birth of the immortal Gods should be known unto men"—that is, the Mystery of the Birth of Horus.

Hermes can only guide Tat towards the realisation of the Blessed Sight, by putting himself into that sublime state of consciousness, so that Tat, so to speak, bathes, or is baptized in, his master's spiritual presence, the Cup of the Mind. This, as we have seen already from several treatises, was the way of transmission of the Power of the powers, the true Laying-on of Hands.

Hermes describes the change that takes place in himself when he passes into the higher spiritual consciousness. He seems to "pass through himself"—to "involve" himself, as it is said somewhere in the *Mahābhārata* of the Ṛiṣhis—"into a Body that can never die," that is, into a, or rather *the*, Essential or Cosmic Body, [523] that embraces the cosmos within it. The way to do this is not taught, for it cannot be understood from any sensible experience,

---

[520] Compare the Song of the Powers in *Pistis Sophia* (pp. 16, 17), where the "We" alternates with the "I."
[521] *D. V. C.*, M. 473, 10; P. 891.
[522] See *D. J. L.*, pp. 374, 375.
[523] *Cf.* R. 52. But compare especially § 6, and *C. H.*, iv. (v.) 1.

the outer physical form of the adept remaining as it was before. It is an inner change. The Birth of a Christ is the striking of a new keynote; everything remains apparently as it was before, but all things receive a new interpretation.

No physical sight, even of the greatest intensity, can penetrate the Veil of this Mystery.

"Thou seest me with eyes, my son; but what I am thou dost not understand."

With this compare the marvellous Ritual of Initiation in *The Acts of John*:

"Who I am thou shalt know when I depart.[524] What I am seen to be, that am I not; but what I am, thou shalt see when thou comest."[525]

None but those who have reached the Christ-state can know it; no teaching will avail to explain its manner and its mysteries. It must be realized.

THE NEW CREATION

4. But Tat, who has "made himself ready," is becoming quickened by the power of his master. His spiritual senses are being born; already he is losing touch with the physical; he no longer sees himself. But this is not enough; he must not only be able to lose consciousness of his physical body, and see and hear as though with the mind alone, but he must "invert" himself, pass right through himself, and no longer see things as without him, but all things as within him.

All this is a New Creation to be accomplished in the man himself. The Author or Genesiurge of Re-birth, as contrasted with the Maker or Demiurge of Birth, is the One Man, the Logos, the Energic Reason and Will of God; the one is the Creator of the Immortal Body, the other is the Maker of the mortal frame.

THE WAY OF BIRTH IN GOD

5. The reading of the next sentence is faulty, and it is impossible to extract the correct meaning. The "Greatness" (τὸ μέγεθος) and "distinctive form" (χαρακτήρ) are terms familiar enough to us in Christian Gnostic writings.[526] Greatness connotes the same idea as Æon; "character" or

---

[524] That is, when the Presence is withdrawn,—by contrast.
[525] *Texts and Studies*, V. i. 14.
[526] The term "Greatness," however, is probably of Egyptian derivation. In the *Papyrus Insinger*, written somewhere during the last half of the first century B.C. and first half of the first century A.D., according to Spiegelberg, God's Wisdom and Providence are praised (coll. xxxv., xxxvi.). The superscription of this section runs: "The Four-and-Twentieth Teaching: The Instruction: Learn the Greatness of God, that thou mayest let it come into thine heart" (xxxv. 17); and later on: "He knoweth the Blasphemer who thinketh wickedness, He knoweth the Pious with the Greatness of God in his heart. The tongue, before even it is questioned—its words God knoweth" (xxxvi. 3-5).

"distinctive form" or "rank" is generally the impression from a typical original, and here stands for the form by which a man is recognised.

6. Hermes then proceeds to describe the nature of this Greatness or Æon, or Sameness, manifested in difference. It is, alchemically speaking, the One Element, which can only be comprehended by one Born in God—that is, by a God.

7. The way of this Birth is then described as a de-energizing, or throwing out of work of the body's senses, with a corresponding energizing of the One Sense, the Æonic Consciousness; or as a purging out of the tendencies of the lower nature, and replacing them by the energies of the Divine Powers.

This is the Mystery of Repentance (μετανοῖα), not a change of mind only, but a change throughout the whole nature; all things in the man turn towards God.

The forces or energies of the soul have no direction in themselves; it is the will of man that can turn them "downwards" or "upwards," so that they become vices or virtues.

OF THE TEN AND THE TWELVE

8., But not only does Hermes set forth a formal exposition of this Repentance in terms of the conquest and driving out of the Horde of Vices by the Company of Virtues, but at the same time he performs an efficacious theurgic rite of invocation whereby he enables Tat to realize the instruction in immediate experience.

The Virtues that Hermes invokes are not abstractions, but definite substantial powers; they are, in fact, the "filling up" of Tat's "insufficiency"; in other words, they are what the Christian Gnostics would have called the Æons of the Plērōma.

Behind all there is a definite scheme of numbering. There is a Twelve and a Ten and a Seven and a Three and a One.

The Torments of the Darkness are the Twelve; they are not torments in themselves, but only for him who is in Error. They are Twelve yet are they one, for though they are "pantomorph" or "omniform," yet are they of one nature; the Twelve are thus conditioned by the main irrational "types of life," or animal natures,—the so-called zodiac.

These divisions are not, however, fundamental, they are solely for man's delusion or error; in action they are one—that is, they keep man in Error or Ignorance. Thus they can be regarded as one, or two, or three, or four, or six; and so combined and recombined.

This is further explained by the sentence: "Thoth is heart and tongue of the Pious; lo! his house is God!" (xxxv. 19). R. 237.

Twelve, then, is the nature of the "animal soul" in man—the number of his going-forth into externality. This out-going is arrested when man repents, and turns himself to return, to go within; the cosmogonical is transformed by the soteriological; the "enformation according to substance" gives place to the "enformation according to gnosis." As Ignorance characterized the Twelve, so does Gnosis characterize the Ten, the Perfect Number or Number of Perfection.

The Going-forth was that of the multiplication of species—Twelve (3 × 4 or 2 × 6); the Return is Ten, that is the Seven and the Three; and Seven is addition (3 + 4) and not multiplication.

Multiplication seems here to mean the generation, by two parents, of things of the same kind and power; while addition signifies the intensification of the same nature to a higher power.

The Ten is "that which giveth birth to souls"—that is, human souls; and not only human souls, but, in its consummation, to divine souls.

It may, perhaps, be of interest here to set down simple lists of the vices and virtues as given in our treatise, and to append to them the list of vices in *C. H.*, i. 24 and 26.

1. Not-knowing.	1. Gnosis.
2. Grief.	2. Joy.
3. Intemperance.	3. Self-control.
4. Concupiscence.	4. Continence.
5. Unrighteousness.	5. Righteousness.
6. Avarice.	6. Sharing-with-all
7. Error.	7. Truth.
8. Envy.	
9. Guile.	8. The Good.
10. Anger.	9. Life.
11. Rashness.	10. Light.
12. Malice.	

1. Growth and Waning.	First Zone.
2. Device of Evils.	Second Zone.
3. Guile of the Desires.	Third Zone.
4. Arrogance.	Fourth Zone.
5. Daring and Rashness.	Fifth Zone.
6. Getting Wealth.	Sixth Zone.
7. Falsehood.	Seventh Zone.

8. Those-that-are.	Eighth.
9. The Powers in a band.	Ninth.
10. The Father.	Tenth.

It is at once seen that the first seven virtues are arranged so as to be the direct antitheses of the first seven vices. The root of the Twelve is Ignorance; indeed, all the Twelve are permutations of Ignorance. They seem to be twelve, whereas they are but one in nature; again, not only are they twelve, but manifold (§ 12).

Thus, for instance, Rashness and Wrath or Anger are but one, and so of the rest; the permutations are infinite. This may be seen from the septenary classification in "The Shepherd" treatise, where we have: Guile of the Desires (3), a combination of Guile (9) and Desire or Concupiscence (4); Device of Evils (2), a combination of Guile (9) and Malice (12); Unholy Daring and Rashness (5), a combination of Unrighteousness (5) and Rashness (11); Getting Wealth by evil means (6), a combination of Guile (9) and Avarice (6). So also just as Anger (10) and Rashness (11) are one, so are Envy (8) and Avarice (6) but aspects of the same thing; and so again Intemperance (3) and Concupiscence or Desire (4), Grief (2) and Ignorance (1), etc.

All are summed up in Ignorance, or Error, just as the seven virtues are summed up in Gnosis or Truth. [527] And just as Ignorance is the source of vice, so is Knowledge or Gnosis the beginning of Truth. Gnosis is not the end but the beginning of the Path, the end of it is God or the Good.

The difference between the "Pœmandres" arrangement and the categories of our treatise is conditioned by the fact that in the former the process of transformation in the case of a good man *after death* is described, whereas in the latter the Way of Rebirth in a living man is set forth.

That the Virtues (and Vices, therefore) were categorized according to the fundamental numbers of the Gnosis may be seen in most systems of Christian Gnostic æonology; indeed, it was a common plan of the general Gnostic theosophy of the time. In our treatise we have set forth the manner of the immediate practical ethical realization of what might be taken by a superficial student of Gnostic æonology as an empty schematology of purely metaphysical abstractions. [528] These things, however, meant *everything* to the Gnostic; they were fullnesses—no abstractions, but transcendent realities.

So also in the *Shepherd of Hermas* (Vis. iii. 8, 7), just as in our treatise, we are presented with the Vision of a Band of seven Women, each the mother of the next, seven Virtues, called: Faith, Continence, Simplicity, Freedom-from-malice, Seriousness, Gnosis (ἐπιστήμη), Love.

And not only do we have the Seven, but also the Twelve, twelve Maidens (Sim. xv. 1-3): Faith, Continence, Power, Long-suffering, Simplicity,

---

[527] Cf. *P. S. A.*, xxix. 2.
[528] The usual way, indeed, in which it is taken.

Freedom-from-malice, Chastity, Joyfulness, Truth, Understanding, Concord, Love.

To these are opposed twelve Women in dark robes: Infidelity, Incontinence, Disobedience, Error, Grief, Depravity, Wantonness, Quickness-to-wrath, Falsehood, Folly, Slander, Hate.

Zosimus also speaks of the Twelve Fates (Μοῖραι) of Death, and associates them with the Passions.[529]

But, indeed, the subject is infinite, for it is the consummation of all right endeavour and all true progress in humanity. We must, then, leave it for the present, to avoid running to too great length in these comments. Sufficient for the moment to point to the fact that the Ten is not only the Wedding Garment of Purity, but also the Robe of Power or Glory. In its consummation also it is the Garment of the Christ, the One Robe without seam throughout, for the Ten contains the One, and the One contains the Ten.

THE DAWN OF COSMIC CONSCIOUSNESS

13. The result of this Potent Invocation of the Powers,—that is to say, the realization of the full meaning of the sacred rite which consummates itself in the consciousness of Hermes, and so communicates itself in some measure to Tat,[530]—is that Tat begins to "see"; "I see the All, I see myself in Mind."

"In heaven am I, in earth, in water, air; I am in animals, in plants; I'm in the womb, before the womb, after the womb,—I'm everywhere" (§ 11).

Compare this with *C. H.*, xi. (xii.) 22, where Hermes is himself being taught by Mind:

"Collect into thyself all senses of all creatures,—of fire, and water, dry and moist. Think that thou art at the same time in every place, in earth, in sea, in sky; not yet begotten, in the womb, young, old and dead, in after-death conditions."

This is, as we have seen, a pure Egyptian formula, and connotes the opening of the "cosmic consciousness."

This consciousness, whatever else it may be, is a transcending of our three-dimensional limitation of consciousness,—that of the "body's view-point,—a thing three ways in space extended."

THE VOW OF SILENCE

The mystery of this New Birth in consciousness is to be kept secret; therefore Hermes has not commented on it, presumably in the Expository

---

[529] Berthelot, 244; R. 214.
[530] *Cf. C. H.*, i. 7; xi. (ixi.) 6.

Sermons; moreover, it must even now be kept secret (§ 22), and therefore is the treatise a Secret Sermon. The reason for this is given both here and in § 22: "That we may not be thought to be calumniators" (διάβολοι), by the Many or Unknowing. What may be the precise meaning of this phrase I do not know, and can only speculate.

Those who had reached the full grade of Hermes are to keep silence on their "virtue" or power (§ 22); they were never to boast of their Gnosis. If they did, it would only bring the Gnosis into contempt; for they would still appear as ordinary men, would probably often say and do things, when they were not in the higher state of consciousness, which fell below the standard of their high ideals, and so they would be slanderers or calumniators of the Gnosis before the world.

14. The New Birth is further characterized as the Essential Birth (ἡ οὐσιώδης γένεσις); it was the birth of the Essential Man, the God, Son of the One, to which other treatises refer. [531]

OF THE OGDOAD

15. Tat now desires to hear the Praise-giving of the Powers, which only those can sing who have reached the stage called Eighth, or the Ogdoad; this is the state above the Harmony or the Hebdomad of Fate (*C. H.*, i. 26). The man is now free and no longer a slave. It is the power of prophetic hymnody, for the man now hears the True Harmony of things and is above the Concatenation of Difference; it is the state "that keeps the soul in tune." He who has reached this height can ever sing in tune; it is the state of the Hearer of the Eternal Praise-giving, and those who reach it can express it infinitely, each in his own fashion.

The idea of the Ogdoad is represented in many a Christian Gnostic system, especially in the Valentinian tradition, which has many Egyptian elements in it.

So we read in the *Excerpts from Theodotus* appended to the writings of Clement of Alexandria:

"Him whom the Mother [532] brings to birth, she leadeth unto Death and to the world; but him whom Christ brings to rebirth, He changeth into Life, unto the Ogdoad." [533]

Many were the names given to the Ogdoad by the Christian Gnostics,—such as the Jerusalem Above, Wisdom, the Land flowing with milk and honey, the Holy Spirit, the Land of the Lord, the Mesotes.

---

[531] *Cf. P. S. A.*, vii. 2.
[532] *Sc.* the Lower Mother, Nature.
[533] *Exx. ex Theodot.*, § 80 (ed. Dindorf, iii. 453).

These terms were, however, with the exception of the last, Jewish synonyms; the term Ogdoad itself was in all probability Egyptian. Thus in one of the Magic Papyri we read:

"Having known the power of the book, thou shalt hide it, my son. For in it there is stored the Authentic Name, which is the Name Ogdoad,—He who doth order and doth regulate all things." [534]

A HYMN FOR MORNING AND FOR EVENING PRAYER

16. The Hymn that follows is to be kept secret—that is to say, it is to be taken by Tat as an example of the form of prayer he is now to use in his private devotions, and is therefore probably intended to replace some other form of prayer which he had hitherto been using, as was the custom in such communities.

The instruction to use it at sunset and sunrise, in the open air, reminds us of the appended passages to "The Shepherd" treatise, where we read (§ 29):

"And when even was come and all sun's beams began to set, I bade them all give thanks to God." [535]

Compare also what Philo tells us of the Therapeuts:

"Twice a day, at dawn and even, they are accustomed to offer up prayers; as the sun rises praying for the sunshine, the real Sunshine, that their minds may be filled with Heavenly Light, and as it sets praying that their soul, completely lightened of the lust of the senses and sensations, may withdraw to its own Congregation and Council-chamber, there to track out Truth." [536]

So also Apollonius of Tyana is said to have prayed and meditated three times a day: at daybreak (Phil., *V. A.*, vi. 10, 18; vii. 31), at mid-day (vii. 10), and at sundown (viii. 13); and with regard to "keeping silence on their virtue," we are told of the Later Pythagoreans, of whom he was so conspicuous an example:

"In particular they kept the rule of silence regarding the Divine Service [that is, the Gnosis]. For they heard within them many Divine and unspeakable things on which it would have been difficult for them to keep silence, had they not first learned that it was just this Silence which spoke to them" (i. 1). [537]

And so the Hymn has to be heard in silence; all earthly sounds must be stilled for the Heavenly Harmony to be heard.

---

[534] *Leyden Papyrus W. S.*, 139, 45 (Leemans); *cf.* also *ibid.*, 141, 5; R. 54. For further comments on the Ogdoad, see Commentary on *C. H.*, i. 26.
[535] *Cf.* also *P. S. A.*, xli. 1.
[536] *D. V. C.*, M. ii. 475; P. 893.
[537] See my *Apollonius of Tyana*, pp. 123 and 120.

17. It is to be noticed that in four out of the five MSS. the title "Secret Hymnody" is followed by the indication "Logos IV."

Reitzenstein (p. 345, n. 21) thinks that the three prior "Logoi" were:

I. "Holy art Thou, O God"—*C. H.*, i. 31, 32.

II. "The Glory of all things is God"—*C. H.*, iii. (iv.).

III. "Whither stumble ye, sots?"—*C. H.*, vii. (viii.).

The latter two, however, are not hymns; the only other hymn in our Corpus being:

"Who then may sing Thee praise of Thee?"—*C. H.*, v. (vi.) 10, 11.

Our Hymn is a Hymn to the Sun, it is true, but to the Spiritual Sun, not the physical orb of day. It is to the Eye of Mind that these orisons are addressed—to the All-seeing Light.

Nor is this Eulogy a formal *Te Deum*, but a potent theurgic Praise-giving. All nature is to thrill with the joy of this thankfulness.

Most beautiful is this Song of Praise, all of it, but we would specially call attention to the words:

"Thy Reason sings through me Thy praises. Take back through me the All into Thy Reason—my reasonable oblation [538]! *From* Thee Thy Will; *to* Thee the All!"

The Outbreathing of the Universe through the Reason or Logos[539] is the manifestation or realisation of the Will of God. The Logos is Son, Will is Mother and God Father.

The Inbreathing of the Universe is through Man ("Thy Man thus cries to Thee," § 20): "Take back through Me the All." This is accomplished in the first instance by the sacrifice of the reason, of man's small limited reason, to the Great Reason of things.

And yet the All, the Universe itself, is not something other than God; it is *all* God.

"*From Thee* Thy Will"; Thou art the Source of all. "*To Thee* the All"; Thou art the End of all, the Desirable One, The Good.

Compare with this the Hymn in the Jewish deposit of the Naassene Document:

"*From Thee* is Father, and *Through Thee* Mother,—the two Immortal Names, Parents of Æons, O Thou who hast the Heaven for thy City, O Man of Mighty Names!"

Also notice: "The All that is in us, O Life, preserve; O Light, illumine it; O God, in-spirit it!" And compare it with § 12, where we are told:

---

[538] *Cf.* I Pet. ii. 5: "Ye also as living stones are built up, a spiritual house for holy service, to offer up spiritual oblations acceptable to God through Jesus Christ," And also Rom. xii. 1: "I beseech you, therefore, brethren, to present your bodies as a living oblation, holy, well-pleasing unto God,—your reasonable service."

[539] Hesychius in his Lexicon defines Logos as the "Cause of Activity," or that which underlies action,—ἡ τοῦ δράματος ὑπόθεσις.

"While Life and Light are unified there, where the One hath being from the Spirit."

The Prayer is for the Baptism of Light—Illumination by the Gnosis [540]; this was the Dowsing in the Mind of "The Cup" treatise, even as true Baptism in primitive Christianity was called Illumination or φωτισμός.

"THROUGH THE WORD"

21. Tat now feels himself impelled to utter praises himself. He says what he feels. His master has given him the impulse, has made the conditions for him whereby he is conceived as a Child of God, a Prophet. But as yet he is not grown into the stature of a true Seer. His higher nature has received the germ, but this must have time to develop, and only gradually will its power descend into his lower mind.

At present his thankfulness is poured forth to his master, who has performed the theurgic rite of initiation ("All things have been perfected") for him.

But Hermes restrains him; it is not to the master that his thanks are due, but to God. And if he cannot as yet give thanks direct to God, then let him send those thanks—"acceptable oblations"—to God "Through the Word."

And that this was and is the practice of universal Christendom requires no pointing out;—the most striking parallel to the wording of our treatise being I Pet. ii. 5: "Spiritual oblations acceptable to God through Jesus Christ."

Tat has now passed from the rank of Hearer to that of Knower; he is now a true Gnostic: "Thou hast become a Knower of thyself, and of our Sire."

Compare *logos* 2 of the latest found Sayings at Oxyrhynchus: "(Strive therefore?) to know yourselves, and ye shall know ye are Sons of the (almighty?) Father; (and?) ye shall know that ye are in (the City of God? [541]), and ye are (the City? [542])."

---

[540] Compare γνῶσις ἁγία, φωτισθεὶς ἀπὸ σοῦ (§ 18); φῶτιζε φώς (§ 19); ἐπιφώτισταί μου ὁ νοῦς (§ 21).

[541] *Sc.* the Ogdoad.

[542] *Cf.* I. Pet. ii. 5: "Ye are built up as living stones, a spiritual house for service."

CORPUS HERMETICUM XIV. (XV.)

[A LETTER] OF THRICE-GREATEST HERMES TO ASCLEPIUS

UNTO ASCLEPIUS GOOD HEALTH OF SOUL! [543]

(Text: P. 128-134; Pat. 49, 50.)

1. SINCE in thy absence my son Tat desired to learn the nature of the things that are, and would not let me hold it over, as [natural to] a younger son fresh come to gnosis of the [teachings] on each single point,—I was compelled to tell [him] more, in order that the contemplation [544] [of them] might be the easier for him to follow.

I would, then, choosing out the chiefest heads of what was said, write them in brief to thee, explaining them more mystic-ly, [545] as unto one of greater age and one well versed in Nature.

2. If all things manifest have been and are being made, and made things are not made by their own selves but by another; [if] made things are the *many*,—nay more, are *all* things manifest and all things different and not alike; and things that are being made are being made by other [than themselves];—there is some one who makes these things; and He cannot be made, but is more ancient than the things that can.

For things that can be made, I say, are made by other [than themselves]; but of the things that owe their being to their being made, it is impossible that anything should be more ancient than them all, save only That which is not able to be made.

3. So He is both Supreme, and One, and Only, the truly wise in all, as having naught more ancient [than Himself].

For He doth rule o'er both the number, size and difference of things that are being made, and o'er the continuity of their making [too].

Again, things makeable are seeable; but He cannot be seen.

For for this cause He maketh,—that He may not be able to be seen.

He, therefore, ever maketh [546]; and therefore can He ne'er be seen.

---

[543] εὖ φρονεῖν. I do not know the exact meaning of this expression. Everard translates "to be truly wise"; Parthey, "*recte sapere*" following Patrizzi; Ménard, "*sagesse*"; Chambers, "to be rightly wise." I would suggest that εὖ φρονεῖν was the form used among these disciples of the Inner Way for the usual χαίρειν. Instead of wishing one another happiness, they wished each other wisdom, good thought, right thinking, good health of soul.
[544] θεωρία.
[545] That is to say, more fully and profoundly, as to one more advanced in the mystic science.
[546] Cf. *C. H.*, xvi. 18.

To comprehend Him thus is meet; and comprehending, [it is meet] to marvel; and marvelling, to count oneself as blessed, as having learnt to know one's Sire.

4. For what is sweeter than one's own true Sire? Who, then, is He; and how shall we learn how to know Him?

Is it not right to dedicate to Him alone the name of God, or that of Maker, or of Father, or rather [all] the three;—God for His Power, and Maker for His Energy, and Father for His Good?

Now Power doth differ from the things which are being made; while Energy consisteth in all things being made.

Wherefore we ought to put away verbosity and foolish talk, and understand these two—the made and Maker. For that of them there is no middle [term]; there is no third.

5. Wherefore in all that thou conceivest, in all thou nearest, these two recall to mind; and think all things are they, reckoning as doubtful naught, nor of the things above, nor of the things below, neither of things divine, nor things that suffer change or things that are in obscuration. [547]

For all things are [these] twain, Maker and made, and 'tis impossible that one should be without the other; for neither is it possible that "Maker" should exist without the "made," for each of them is one and the same thing.

Wherefore 'tis no more possible for one from other to be parted, than self from self.

6. Now if the Maker is naught else but That which makes, Alone, Simple, Uncompound, it needs must do this [making] to Itself,—to Which its Maker's making is "its being made." [548]

And as to all that's being made,—it cannot be [so made] by being made by its own self; but it must needs be made by being made by other. Without the "Maker" "made" is neither made nor is; for that the one without the other doth lose its proper nature by deprivation of that other.

---

[547] τῶν ἐν μυχῷ. I do not know what is the exact meaning of this expression. Everard translates "things that are in darkness or secret"; Parthey, "*quæ sunt in abdito*"; Ménard, "*dans les profondeurs*"; Chambers, "those in secrecy." I suggest that the technical term μυχός, signifying generally a shut-in or locked-up place (*conclave*, as Damascius translates it), is to be referred, along the line of Platonic and Pythagorean tradition, to Pherecydes. Porphyry (*De Antro Nymph.*, C. 31) tells us that the synonyms "μυχοί (chambers?), recesses (or pits), caverns, doors, gates" were used by Pherecydes as symbolical expressions to signify "the *geneses* and *apogeneses* of souls," whatever these terms may mean exactly. The "birth" and "decease" of a soul, in this connection, presumably mean its coming into the world of genesis out of the womb of the World-soul, and its reception back again into the bosom of the great Mother. If this be so, our text would seem to indicate that things are in two states,—in a state of change (that is, in the active condition), and again in a passive condition, in the state which Indian philosophers call *laya* or *pralaya*. See for the μυχοί of Pherecydes Sturz's *Pherecydis Fragmenta*, pp. 43 ff. (Leipzig, 1824).

[548] Or genesis.

If, [549] then, all things have been admitted to be two,—the "that which is being made" and "that which makes,"—[all then] are one in union of these,—the "that which leadeth" and the "that which followeth."

The making God is "that which leadeth"; the "that which is being made," whatever it be, the "that which followeth."

7. And do not thou be chary of things made because of their variety, from fear of attribution of a low estate and lack of glory unto God.

For that His Glory's one,—to make all things; and this is as it were God's Body, the making [of them]. [550]

But by the Maker's self naught is there thought or bad or base.

These things are passions which accompany the making process, as rust doth brass and filth doth body; but neither doth the brass-smith make the rust, nor the begetters of the body filth, nor God [make] evil.

It is continuance in the state of being made that makes them lose, as though it were, their bloom; and 'tis because of this God hath made change, as though it were the making clean of genesis.

8. Is it, then, possible for one and the same painter man to make both heaven, and gods, and earth, and sea, and men, and all the animals, and lifeless things, and trees, and yet impossible for God to make all things?

What monstraus lack of understanding; what want of knowledge as to God! [551]

For such the strangest lot of all do suffer; for though they say they worship piously and sing the praise of God, yet by their not ascribing unto Him the making of all things, they know not God; and, added unto this not-knowing, they're guilty even of the worst impiety to Him—passions to Him attributing, or arrogance, or impotency.

For if He doth not make all things, from arrogance He doth not make, or not being able,—which is impiety [to think].

9. One Passion hath God only—Good; and He who's Good, is neither arrogant nor impotent.

For this is God—the Good, which hath all power of making all.

And all that can be made is made by God,—that is, by [Him who is] the Good and who can make all things. [552]

But would'st thou learn how He doth make, and how things made are made, thou may'st do so.

10. Behold a very fair and most resemblant image—a husbandman casting the seed into the ground; here wheat, there barley, and there [again] some other of the seeds!

---

[549] From here to the end of the sermon, with the exception of the final sentences of § 7 and § 10, and the third sentence of § 9, and with a few very slight verbal variants, is quoted by Cyril, *Contra Julianum*, ii. 64 (Migne, col. 598 D).
[550] *Cf. C. H.*, xvi. 18.
[551] Or genesis.
[552] This sentence, which appears to be very tautological, is omitted by Cyril.

Behold one and the same man planting the vine, the apple, and [all] other trees!

In just the selfsame way doth God sow Immortality in Heaven, and Change on Earth, and Life and Motion in the universe.

These are not many, but few and easy to be numbered; for four in all are they,—and God Himself and Genesis, in whom are all that are.

COMMENTARY

ASCLEPIUS AND TAT

Fabricius, in his *Bibliotheca Græca*,[553] says that the title should be "On the Nature of the All," and that he has recovered it from Cyril, *C. Jul.*, ii., but I cannot verify this statement.

The form of this treatise is different from any of the preceding, being that of a letter. It evidently belongs to the Asclepius-Tat type of tradition, as in *C. H.*, x. (xi.): "My yesterday's discourse I did devote to thee, Asclepius, and so 'tis only right I should devote to-day's to Tat."

The distinction drawn between Tat and Asclepius is of interest; Tat is the younger,—who has only "just come to Gnosis of the teaching on each single point." Can this mean that he has only just been permitted to share in the "Expository Sermons" or "Detailed Discourses"? It is probable, for *C. H.*, x. (xi.) 1, continues: "And this the more because 'tis the abridgment (epitome) of the General Sermons which he has had addressed to him."

Asclepius is older, and already ἐπιστήμων τῆς φύσεως—well-versed in the study of Nature.

What may be the exact significance underlying these personifications it is very difficult to say; but the same facts, whatever they may have been, are clearly referred to in *K K.* (Stob., *Ecl.*, i. 49; p. 386, 24 W.); especially the later accession of "Asclepius" to the School, and the fact that "Tat," because of his too great "youth," could not have handed on to him the tradition of the complete or all-perfect contemplation (ὁλοτελὴς θεωρία)—that is, of the *mathēsis* or *gnōsis*, or, in other words, the "learning of the things that are, the contemplating of their nature and the knowing God" (*C. H.*, i. 3); or the "being taught the nature of the all and the Supreme Vision" (*ibid.*, 27).

This view of the tradition of the School seems to clash entirely with the other view set forth in *C. H.*, xiii. (xiv.), where Tat has handed on to him the "manner of Rebirth," but a probable explanation has already been attempted in the "Prolegomena," chap. xvi.: "The Disciples of Thrice-greatest Hermes."

COMPARE WITH "MIND UNTO HERMES"

The treatise itself requires little commentary; the similarity of its doctrine, however, with that of the "Mind unto Hermes" is remarkable. For instance, compare the last sentence of § 7 of our treatise with *C. H.*, xi. (xii.) 14: "For that indeed He hath no other one to share in what He works, for working by Himself, He ever is at work, Himself being what He doth."

---

[553] Ed. Harles (4th ed.), vol. i. lib. i. cap. vii.

Compare also the first sentence of § 8 with *C. H.*, xi. (xii.) 20: "Behold what power, what swiftness thou dost have! And canst thou do all of these things, and God not do them?"

THE GOOD HUSBANDMAN

With the Good Husbandman "image" (§ 10) compare:

"Come unto me, Good Husbandman, Good Daimon, Harpocrates, Chnouphis . . . who rollest down the stream of Nilus, [554] and minglest with the Sea . . . as man with woman." [555]

And in the Alchemical literature:

"[Come then], and coming contemplate, enquire of Acharantus (?), the Husbandman, and learn of Him, what is it that is sown, and what that which is reaped; and thou shalt learn that he who soweth corn shall reap corn also, and he who soweth barley shall in like manner reap barley." [556]

So also Zosimus in the "Book Concerning the Logos":

"And that I tell thee truth, I call to witness Hermes, when he says: Go unto Achaab (?), the Husbandman, and thou shalt learn that he who soweth corn gives birth to corn." [557]

---

[554] The Heavenly River of fructifying essence.
[555] *Abhandl. d. Berl. Akad.* (1865), p. 120, 26; R. 143.
[556] Berthelot, p. 30.
[557] Berthelot, p. 89.

CORPUS HERMETICUM (XVI.)

THE DEFINITIONS OF ASCLEPIUS UNTO KING AMMON
THE PERFECT SERMON OF ASCLEPIUS UNTO THE KING

(Text: R. 348-354; Pat. at end. [558])

1. GREAT is the sermon (*logos*) which I send to thee, O King—the summing up and digest, as it were, of all the rest.

For it is not composed to suit the many's prejudice, since it contains much that refuteth them.

Nay, it will seem to thee as well to contradict sometimes my sermons too.

Hermes, my master, in many a conversation, both when alone, and sometimes, too, when Tat was there, has said, that unto those who come across my books, their composition will seem most simple and [most] clear; but, on the contrary, as 'tis unclear, and has the [inner] meaning of its words concealed, it will be still unclearer, when, afterwards, the Greeks will want to turn our tongue into their own,—for this will be a very great distorting and obscuring of [even] what has been [already] written.

2. Turned into our own native tongue, [559] the sermon (*logos*) keepeth clear the meaning [560] of the words (*logoi*) [at any rate].

For that its very quality of sound, the [very] power of the Egyptian names, have in themselves the bringing into act of what is said.

As far as, then, thou canst, O King—(and thou canst [do] all things)—keep [this] our sermon from translation; in order that such mighty mysteries may not come to the Greeks, and the disdainful speech of Greece, with [all] its looseness, and its surface beauty, [561] so to speak, take all the strength out of [562] the solemn and the strong—the energetic [563] speech of Names.

The Greeks, O King, have novel words, energic of "argumentation" [only]; and thus is the philosophizing of the Greeks—the noise of words.

But we do not use words; but we use sounds full-filled with deeds.

3. Thus, then, will I begin the sermon by invocation unto God, the universals' Lord and Maker, [their] Sire, and [their] Encompasser; who though being All is One, [564] and though being One is All; for that the Fullness of all

---

[558] At the end after *P. S. A.*, but the pages are unnumbered.
[559] This presumably means from the hieroglyphic into the demotic—τῇ πατρῴᾳ διαλέκτῳ ἑρμηνευόμενος.
[560] Lit. the mind.
[561] Or, perhaps, smartness.
[562] Make jejune, so to say—ἐξίτηλον ποιήσῃ.
[563] That is, "words of power," words that *do* things.
[564] Cf. R. 127, 3; and *P. S. A.*, i. 1.

things is One, and [is] in One, this latter One not coming as a second [One], but both being One.

And this is the idea [565] that I would have thee keep, through the whole study of our sermon, Sire!

For should one try to separate what *seems* to be both All *and* One *and* Same from One,—he will be found to take [566] his epithet of "All" from [the idea of] multitude, and not from [that of] fullness [567]—which is impossible; for if he part All from the One, he will destroy the All. [568]

For all things *must* be One—if they indeed *are* One. Yea, they are One; and they shall never cease being One—in order that the Fullness may not be destroyed.

*   *   *   *   *

4. See then in Earth a host of founts of Water and of Fire forth-spirting in its midmost parts; in one and the same [space all] the three natures visible—of Fire, and Water, and of Earth, depending from one Root. [569]

Whence, too, it [570]is believed to be the Treasury [571]of every matter. It sendeth forth of its [572] abundance, and in the place [of what it sendeth forth] receiveth the subsistence from above. [573]

For thus the Demiurge [574]—I mean the Sun—eternally doth order Heaven and Earth, pouring down Essence, [575] and taking Matter up, drawing both round Himself and to Himself all things, and from Himself giving all things to all.

For He it is whose goodly energies extend not only through the Heaven and the Air, but also onto Earth, right down unto the lowest Depth and the Abyss.

6. And if there be an Essence which the mind alone can grasp, [576] this is his Substance, [577] the reservoir [578] of which would be His Light.

---

[565] Lit. mind.
[566] The construction is very elliptical; ἐκδεξάμενος simply.
[567] That is, completeness, perfection,—πληρώματος.
[568] *Cf.* Plato, *Soph.*, 259 D, E.
[569] *Cf. P. S. A.*, iv. 1.
[570] *Sc.* Earth.
[571] A magazine, a store-house,—ταμιεῖον. The term "treasure" (θησαυρός) is found in most lavish use in the Greek-Coptic Gnostic works, and also in Christian Gnostic literature and Jewish Apocalyptic.
[572] *Sc.* matter's.
[573] τὴν ἄνωθεν ὕπαρξιν,—*hyparxis*, substance or subsistence, a word of frequent use and highly technical meaning with the last of the Neo-Platonists, especially with Proclus. *Cf. C. H.*, x. (xi.) 2.
[574] *Cf. P. S. A.*, xxix. 4.
[575] Lit. bringing or drawing down; κατάγειν = *deducere, elicere*—used frequently of magic arts.
[576] νοητὴ οὐσία = *intelligibilis essentia*.

But whence this [Substance] doth arise, or floweth forth, He, [and He] only, knows.

※　　※　　※　　※　　※

Or rather, in space and nature, He is near unto Himself . . . though as He is not seen by us, . . . understand [Him] by conjecture. [579]

7. The spectacle of Him, however, is not left unto conjecture; nay [for] His very rays, [580] in greatest splendour, shine all round on all the Cosmos that doth lie above and lie below.

For He is stablished in the midst, wreathed with the Cosmos, [581] and just as a good charioteer, He safely drives the cosmic team, [582] and holds them in unto Himself, [583] lest they should run away in dire disorder.

The reins are Life, and Soul, and Spirit, Deathlessness, and Genesis. He lets it, then, drive [round] not far off from Himself—nay, if the truth be said, together with Himself.

8. And in this way He operates [584]all things. To the immortals He distributeth perpetual permanence; and with the upper hemisphere of His own Light—all that he sends above from out His other side, [585] [the side of him] which looks to Heaven—He nourisheth the deathless parts of Cosmos.

But with that side that sendeth down [its Light], and shineth round all of the hemisphere [586]of Water, and of Earth, and Air, He vivifieth, and by births and changes keepeth in movement to and fro the animals [587]in these [the lower] parts of Cosmos. . . .

9. He changes them in spiral fashion, and doth transform them into one another, genus to genus, species into species, their mutual changes into one

---

[577] ὄγκος = moles, mass, bulk, volume; in later philosophy it means "atom," and may mean so here, of course in the philosophical and mystic and not in the physical sense.

[578] ὑποδοχή = receptaculum.

[579] The text is very corrupt. Patrizzi translates: "*Vel quia ipso loco, et natura prope se ipsum existens, non a nobis conspicitur cogit nos per conjecturas intelligere*"—which certainly does not represent the Greek. Ménard conjectures brilliantly but in entire emancipation from the text: "*Pour comprendre par induction ce qui se dérobe à notre vue, il faudrait être près de lui et analogue à sa nature.*" Reitzenstein discovers two lacunas in the text, but does not attempt to fill them. As the text stands, then, all attempt at translation seems hopeless.

[580] Lit. his very sight,—αὐτὴ ἡ ὄψις, that is, his rays, ὄψις being used of the visual rays which were supposed by the science of the time to proceed from the eyes. Cf. Ex. vii. 4.

[581] Wearing the Cosmos as a wreath or crown; the visible sun being regarded as a "head." See "The Perfect Sermon."

[582] Lit. car or chariot—ἅρμα.

[583] Lit. binds it to himself—ἀναδήσας εἰς ἑαυτόν.

[584] δημιουργεῖ.

[585] Lit. part.

[586] κύτος = a, hollow, vase, or vessel.

[587] That is, those lives subject to death, as opposed to the immortals.

another being balanced—just as He does when He doth deal with the Great Bodies.

For in the case of every body, [its] permanence [consists in] transformation.

In case of an immortal one, there is no dissolution; but when it is a mortal one, it is accompanied with dissolution. [588]

And this is how the deathless body doth differ from the mortal, and how the mortal one doth differ from the deathless.

10. Moreover, as His Light's continuous, so is His Power of giving Life to lives continuous, and not to be brought to an end in space or in abundance.

For there are many choirs of daimons round Him, like unto hosts of very various kinds; who though they dwell with mortals, yet are not far from the immortals; but having as their lot from here unto the spaces of the Gods,[589] they watch o'er the affairs of men, and work out things appointed by the Gods—by means of storms, whirlwinds and hurricanes, by transmutations wrought by fire and shakings of the earth, [590] with famines also and with wars requiting [man's] impiety,—for this is in man's case the greatest ill against the Gods.

11. For that the duty of the Gods is to give benefits; the duty of mankind is to give worship [591]; the duty of the daimons is to give requital.

For as to all the other things men do, through error, or foolhardiness, or by necessity, which they call Fate, [592] or ignorance—these are not held requitable among the Gods; impiety alone is guilty at their bar.

12. The Sun is the preserver [593] and the nurse of every class. [594]

And just as the Intelligible World, [595] holding the Sensible in its embrace, fills it [all] full, distending it with forms of every kind and every shape—so, too, the Sun distendeth all in Cosmos, affording births to all, and strengtheneth them.

When they are weary or they fail, He takes them in His arms again.

13. And under Him is ranged the choir of daimons—or, rather, choirs; for these are multitudinous and very varied, ranked underneath the groups of Stars, [596] in equal number with each one of them.

---

[588] Compare "Sermon to Tat," I. (Ménard). *Cf.* Stob., *Ecl*, i. 61; 274, 24 W.
[589] Lit. "the land of these"—that is, of the immortals.
[590] *Cf.* Ex. ix. 5.
[591] Or, to be pious. *Cf. P. S. A.*, ix. 1.
[592] εἱμαρμένην.
[593] σωτήρ.
[594] Or genus.
[595] Or Cosmos.
[596] ὑπὸ τὰς τῶν ἀστέρων πλινθίδας. πλινθίς = πλινθίον, and is used of any rectangular figure, and also of groups of stars as in Eratosth. *apud* Strab., II. i. 35; v. 36 (*Lex.* Sophocles); compare αἱ τῶν πλινθίων ὑπογραφαί, the fields, or spaces, into which the Augurs divided the heavens, *templa*, or *regiones coeli* (*Lex.* Liddell and Scott).

So, marshalled in their ranks, they are the ministers of each one of the Stars, being in their natures good, and bad, that is, in their activities (for that a daimon's essence is activity); while some of them are [of] mixed [natures], good and bad.

14. To all of these has been allotted the authority o'er things upon the Earth; and it is they who bring about the multifold confusion of the turmoils on the Earth—for states and nations generally, and for each individual separately.

For they do shape our souls like to themselves, and set them moving with them,—obsessing nerves, and marrow, veins and arteries, the brain itself, down to the very heart.[597]

15. For on each one of us being born and made alive, the daimons take hold on us—those [daimones] who are in service at that moment [of the wheel] of Genesis, who are ranged under each one of the Stars.[598]

For that these change at every moment; they do not stay the same, but circle back again.

These, then, descending through the body [599] to the two parts [600] of the soul, set it [601] awhirling, each one towards its own activity.

But the soul's rational part is set above the lordship of the daimons—designed to be receptacle of God.

16. Who then doth have a Ray shining upon him through the Sun within his rational part—and these in all are few on them the daimons do not act; for no one of the daimons or of Gods has any power against one Ray of God.

As for the rest, they are all led and driven, soul and body, by the daimons—loving and hating the activities of these.

The reason (*logos*), [then,] is not the love that is deceived and that deceives.[602]

The daimons, therefore, exercise the whole of this terrene economy,[603] using our bodies as [their] instruments.

And this economy Hermes has called Heimarmenē.[604]

17. The World Intelligible,[605] then, depends from God; the Sensible from the Intelligible [World].

---

[597] Lit. viscera.
[598] *Cf. P. S. A.*, xxxv. 2.
[599] *Cf. C. H.*, xiii. (xiv.) 7.
[600] The two irrational parts, "passion" and "desire" (θυμὸς and ἐπιθυμία).
[601] The soul.
[602] This Erōs is the lower love (*cf. C. H.*, i. 18: "love, the cause of death"), not the Divine Love who inspires Hermes in "The Perfect Sermon" and who is mentioned *C. H.*, xviii. 14.
[603] διοίκησιν.
[604] Or, Fate; *cf. C. H.*, i. 9; and *P. S. A.*, xix.
[605] Or, Intelligible Cosmos.

The Sun, through the Intelligible and the Sensible Cosmos, pours forth abundantly the stream from God of Good,—that is, the demiurgic operation.

And round the Sun are the Eight Spheres, dependent from Him—the [Sphere] of the Non-wandering Ones, the Six [Spheres] of the Wanderers, and one Circumterrene.

And from the Spheres depend the daimones; and from these, men.

And thus all things and all [of them] depend from God. [606]

18. Wherefore God is the Sire of all; the Sun's [their] Demiurge; the Cosmos is the instrument of demiurgic operation.

Intelligible Essence regulateth Heaven; and Heaven, the Gods; the daimones, ranked underneath the Gods, regulate men.

This is the host [607] of Gods and daimones. [608]

Through these God makes all things for His own self.

And all [of them] are parts of God; and if they all [are] parts—then, God is all.

Thus, making all, He makes Himself; nor ever can He cease [His making], for He Himself is ceaseless. [609]

Just, then, as God doth have no end and no beginning, so doth His making have no end and no beginning. [610]

✻ ✻ ✻ ✻ ✻

---

[606] *Cf. P. S. A.*, iv. 1 n.; and xix.
[607] Or army, or hierarchy. Compare the "soldier" degree of the Mithriaca.
[608] *Cf. C. H.*, x. (xi.) 22; and *P. S. A.*, v. 1.
[609] *Cf. C. H.*, xiv. (xv.), 7 and 5.
[610] See Commentary to Frag. iv. (Lact., *D. I.*, ii. 15).

COMMENTARY

CONCERNING THE TITLE

Patrizzi has run (xvi.) and (xvii.) together, under the title "Definitions of Asclepius—Book I.," though he clearly saw that (xvii.) did not belong to (xvi.) by his remark, "*videntur sequentia ex alio libro sumpta.*" He also heads (xvii.) 1-10 "Definitions of Asclepius—Book II.," and 11-16 "D. of A.—Book III.," though the contents have evidently nothing to do with such a title.

In the MSS. a later hand has added to the general title a catalogue of contents as follows:

"Of God; Matter; Evil; Fate; the Sun; Intelligible Essence; Divine Essence; Man; the Economy of the Plērōma; the Seven Stars; the Man after the Likeness" [611]—for which largely irrelevant list Patrizzi substitutes the title: "Of the Sun and Daimons."

Reitzenstein (p. 192) is of opinion that this contents-list, and also the similar headings in (xviii.), are due to some Byzantine scribe, who also foolishly interpolated (xvii.).

But even to (xvi.) the title "Definitions of Asclepius" seems very inappropriate; while, on the other hand, we find Lactantius (*D. I.*, ii. 5), in referring to the "incursions of daimones," claiming that it was a doctrine also of Hermes, and adding:

"Asclepius, his hearer, has also explained the same idea at greater length in that 'Perfect Sermon' which he wrote to the King."

This is quite definite, and the authority of Lactantius should perhaps be preferred to that of the MSS., but as the title would clash with "The Perfect Sermon" of Hermes to Asclepius, and as Lactantius may just possibly mean "in that initiatory sermon,"—the term *perfectus* being used in a general and not in an appellative sense,—I have kept the traditional title and placed that of Lactantius second.

A TRADITION CONCERNING THE TRISMEGISTIC LITERATURE

1. Like "The Key"—*C. H.*, x. (xi.)—of Hermes, our treatise is an Epitome [612]; Asclepius has previously written a number of Sermons to the King.

The reference to the "Conversations" between Hermes and Asclepius and Tat, sometimes when both the latter were present and sometimes with

---

[611] R. 348 n.
[612] *Cf.* also Ex. i. 16, and Comment.

Asclepius alone, presupposes the existence of this class of Dialogue, and indicates that the Correspondence of Asclepius with the King is a later deposit of our literature. [613]

This literary activity of Asclepius is claimed in the introduction to be authorized by Hermes, and, moreover, purports to have been originally written in Demotic Egyptian. In other words, the writer would have us believe that the Greek is a translation from Egyptian. This it clearly is not; and we can only conclude that the "prophecy" as to direct translation is a literary fiction of our author.

2. On the other hand, it is highly probable that our author was in contact with a living tradition, to the effect that the Hermes-teaching was originally Egyptian, and that this was "interpreted" into Greek—that is, into Greek modes of thought, rather than "translated" in the ordinary sense into Greek.

In any case, the contempt shown by our author for the Greek language and "philosophizing," and his admiration for Hieroglyphic Egyptian as a "language of the Gods"—a magical tongue, that by its *māntric* power compelled the understanding of the hearer, by putting him in sympathy with the ideas pictured by the ideograms, or sounded forth by the "names of power" [614]—show that he was not only not a Greek, but also no lover of Greek Philosophy.

This is exceedingly puzzling, seeing not only that the majority of the writers of our tractates are plainly deep students and lovers of Plato, but also that the author of our tractate himself also writes very much in the same style as they do.

All of this seems to indicate that in his introduction he was using for his own purposes some tradition about the ancient Thoth-literature that was current in his time. A form of this tradition was also made use of by Philo of Byblus in the first century, when he makes the Phœnician priest Sanchuniathon discover the origin of the Phœnician cosmogony and mystery-teaching in the Books of Taautos, "whom the Egyptian called Thoyth, the Alexandrians Thoth, and the Greeks changed into Hermes."

Sanchuniathon, he says, "having come across the secret writings that had been discovered and brought from the shrines of the Temples of Ammon,—compositions which were not known to all,—practised by himself the science (τῆν μάθησιν) of all things." [615]

Philo also professes to quote from one of the earliest priests of Phœnicia, a certain Thabiōn, who is said apparently to have got his information from a writing of the Seven Kabiri, and of Asclepius, the pupil of

---

[613] This deduction, however, has to be modified by the view we hold as to the authorship of the introduction. See Comment., § 5.
[614] *Cf.* R. 269.
[615] *Ap.* Euseb., *Præp. Ev.*, I. ix. 29.

Taautos. This Thabiōn asserted that Taautos was made King of Egypt by Kronos—that is, Ammon. [616]

Here we are evidently in contact with certain traditions with regard to Thoth-Hermes, his ancestors and pupils, and secret writings. Presumably many such traditions were floating about, and were used according to the fancy and taste of Hellenistic writers for their own purposes.

But there was also another tradition concerning a certain King Ammon, used in one form by Jamblichus, when he writes:

"It was Hermes who first taught this Path [*sc.* the Way up to God]. And Bitys, [617] the Prophet, translated [his teachings concerning it] for King Ammon, discovering them in the inner temple in an inscription in the sacred characters at Saïs in Egypt." [618]

What our author and Jamblichus have in common is that there were certain secret teachings of Hermes in the Sacred Language of Ancient Egypt hidden away in the inner shrines of the temples, and that these were translated into the current Egyptian language of the time for a certain King Ammon.

It must, then, have been some tradition of this kind that our author or writer had in mind; he would have it believed that he was writing in the style or according to the model of a certain literature.

Who this King Ammon was can only be guessed at; but to my mind it is probable that the "translations" of Bitys were made in connection with the translation activity of Manetho for King Ptolemy, and this translation was into Greek. Our author, however, would refer it to some Egyptian King, and so seek to invoke the authority of a high antiquity for the treatise he was putting into circulation.

A SPECULATION AS TO DATE

5. What seems to differentiate our treatise from the rest of the tractates, is the prominence its author gives to the doctrine of the Sun as Demiurgic Orderer of all things. This so to speak pantheistic form of Sun-worship is peculiarly Egyptian. [619]

Now if we remember the disdainful way in which Greek "philosophizing" is spoken of in the introduction, we may be tempted to take the sentence, "And *if* there be any essence which the mind alone can grasp" (§ 6), as a somewhat patronizing reference to the Intelligible World of Greek Philosophy, as also the analogy in § 12; but when we turn to §§ 17 and 18 the exposition fully adopts the doctrine of the Intelligible and Sensible Worlds. This is so irreconcilable a contradiction that one is almost compelled to believe

---

[616] *Ibid.,* I. x. 38, 39.
[617] *Cf.* Zosimus (§ 8).
[618] *De Myst.,* viii. 5.
[619] *Cf.* R. 198, 1; and also Comment on § 17 below.

that the introduction is by another hand altogether, and that our sermon proper begins with § 3.

But even so, the sermon is addressed to some King or other—"The Perfect Sermon to the King" of Lactantius—without any further qualification. Who, however, this King may have been historically must remain a matter of pure conjecture.

7. When, then, Reitzenstein, pointing to § 7, says that the symbolism of the Sun as a chariot eer wearing a crown of rays corresponds with that of the pictures of the Aurelian Sun-god, and adds further it is the Roman Empire-god of the third century, we are quite prepared to acknowledge a similarity of symbolism. But if it is intended to suggest that, therefore, we are to date our document by this similarity, it must be admitted that the indications are far too vague; for the symbolism of the Sun as the ray-crowned charioteer is fundamental with the cult of Mithras, and is found in Greece long before the Aurelian period.

THE DELINEATION OF THE SUN

It is interesting, however, here to notice that the Sun is "wreathed with cosmos," and to compare this with the passage concerning the Macroprosopus in the *Untitled Apocalypse* of the Coptic Gnostic Codex Brucianus, and especially with the sentence:

"The Hair of His Head is the number of the Hidden Worlds, and the Outline of His Face is the Type of the Æons." [620]

In this *Untitled Apocalypse* there is a strong Egyptian undercolouring; that, however, the idea of a crown of powers was pre-eminently Egyptian may be seen from many a passage in the *Pistis Sophia*.

8. It is also of interest to notice that the delineation of the Sun in § 8 reminds us of the Orphic Phanes, especially the reference to the two hemispheres above and below,—the two parts of the Egg in Orphic symbolism.

9. The hint that the sun-life runs in some sort of spiral or serpentine fashion in animals, and that this also is the case with the Great Bodies or Celestial Animals, is of interest.

CONCERNING THE DAIMONES

10. Our author then proceeds to set forth his doctrine of the daimones or ministers of the Gods, who are assigned to the lower hemisphere of operation, from the Earth to the Sun, the Gods presumably occupying the higher hemisphere of activity. These daimones are what a Hindu or Buddhist

---

[620] *F. F. F.*, 549.

would call kārmic agents, for they are all connected with what is called the Fate-Sphere, the Instrument or the Wheel of Genesis, or Saṁsāra.

15. These daimones rule over the lower energies of the soul; the higher energy or rational part of the soul is set above them, and is designed to be the "receptacle of God,"—or rather of His Ray,—the Mind proper.

16. With § 16 compare the remarkable passage in one of the Letters of Valentinus:

"One [alone] is Good, whose free utterance is His manifestation through His Son; it is by Him alone that the heart can become pure, when every evil essence has been expelled from it.

"Now its purity is prevented by the many essences which take up their abode in it, for each of them accomplishes its own deeds, outraging it in divers fashions with unseemly lusts.

"As far as I can see, the heart seems to receive somewhat the same treatment as an inn [or caravanserai], which has holes and gaps made in its walls, and is frequently filled with dung, men living filthily in it and taking no care of the place as being someone else's property. Thus is it with the heart so long as it has no care taken of it, ever unclean and the abode of many daimons.

"But when the Alone Good Father hath regard unto it, it is sanctified and shineth with light; and he who possesseth such a heart is so blessed that 'he shall see God.'" [621]

The language of Valentinus is remarkably like that of our treatises; Valentinus himself was an Egyptian.

17. Entirely Egyptian also is the Scheme of Dependency given in § 17, as we have already pointed out on several occasions, quoting from a Hymn of Valentinus.

The sentence: "Wherefore God is the Sire of all; the Sun's [their] Demiurge"—distinctly contradicts Reitzenstein's (p. 198, 1) statement that the Sun in our treatise is worshipped as the All-god. The Sun is He "by whom all things are made,"—the Creative Logos of God. [622]

19. The treatise is evidently incomplete; if, however, we turn to the contents-title given at the beginning of these comments we can gain but little information as to what is missing, for the contents there given do not in any but the vaguest fashion correspond to the substance of our treatise, nor do the subjects treated of come in the same order as in the contents-heading. The Divine Essence, Man, the Economy of the Plērōma and the Man after the Likeness, which are clearly not treated of in our text, *may* then have been treated in the missing portion of our tractate; but this is all we can say.

---

[621] Quoted by Clemens Alexandrinus, *Strom.*, II. xx. 114; P. 489 (ed. Dindorf, ii. 219). See for further critical text, Hilgenfeld (A.), *Ketzergesch. d. Urchrist.*, p. 296; F. F. F., 300, 301.
[622] *Cf. P. S. A.*, xxix. 5.

CORPUS HERMETICUM (XVII.)

[OF ASCLEPIUS TO THE KING]

(Text: R. 354; Pat. at end of last piece.)

*   *   *   *   *
*   *   *   *   *
*   *   *   *   *
*   *   *   *   *
*   *   *   *   *
*   *   *   *   *

Asclepius. If thou dost think [of it], O King, even of bodies there are things bodiless. [623]

The King. What [are they]?—(asked the King.)

Asc. The bodies that appear in mirrors—do they not seem then to have no body?

The King. It is so, O Asclepius [624]; thou thinkest like a God [625]!—(the King replied.)

Asc. There are things bodiless as well as these; for instance, forms [626]—do not they seem to thee to have no body, but to appear in bodies not only of the things which are ensouled, but also of those which are not ensouled?

The King. Thou sayest well, Asclepius.

Asc. Thus, [then,] there are reflexions of things bodiless on bodies, and of bodies too upon things bodiless—that is to say, [reflexions] of the Sensible on the Intelligible World, and of the [World] Intelligible on the Sensible.

Wherefore, pay worship to the images, O King, since they too have their forms as from the World Intelligible.

(Thereon His Majesty arose and said:)

The King. It is the hour, [627] O Prophet, to see about the comfort of our guests. To-morrow, [then,] will we resume our sacred converse. [628]

---

[623] *Cf.* Plat., *Soph.*, 229 D, 240 A, 246 B.
[624] The corrector of B has changed the name Asclepius into Tat, as he has everywhere in *C. H.*, ii. (iii.); R. 193, 1.
[625] θείως.
[626] Or ideas.
[627] *Cf.* Plat., *Soph.*, 241 B.

COMMENTARY

ON THE ADORATION OF IMAGES

The loss of the end of the previous sermon, and also the loss of almost the whole of (xvii.), is to be accounted for by the falling out of one or more quires from the original MS. of our Corpus, [629] a phenomenon similar to that already remarked in the case of C. H., ii. (iii).

And that this is the fact is brought out interestingly by the note of Reitzenstein (p. 193, 1)—namely, that one of the correctors of one of the copies (Paris MS.) of this faulty original has precisely in these two places changed the name Asclepius into Tat. He was puzzled, and thought that his "correction" would set matters right; as a matter of fact, however, it only adds to the confusion.

What the main subject of our treatise may have been we can hardly conjecture; part of it, however, must have been devoted to an explanation of the *rationale* of image-adoration,—"Wherefore pay worship to the images, O King,"—of which we hear so much in *P. S. A.*

These symbolic images of the Gods are said to have their "forms" (ἰδέας) in sympathetic relation with the Intelligible World. These are mutual "reflections," the one of the other.

Now as the *Ka* of the God was thought to have immediate relation with the image-symbol of the God, and the Gods were of the Intelligible World,—the statues of the Gods were thought to be images of the Image in some special way; they were regarded as providing a straight path or line of connection between Earth and Heaven, just as a man who made himself like to the Man after the Likeness became in himself a Way Up.

---

[628] θεολογήσομεν.
[629] R. 198.

CORPUS HERMETICUM (XVIII.)

[THE ENCOMIUM OF KINGS]

(ABOUT THE SOUL'S BEING HINDERED BY THE PASSION OF THE BODY)

(Text: R. 355-360; Pat. at end.)

1. [NOW] in the case of those professing the harmonious art of muse-like melody—if, when the piece is played, the discord of the instruments doth hinder their intent, its rendering becomes ridiculous.

For when his instruments are quite too weak for what's required of them, the music-artist needs must be laughed at by the audience.

For He, with all good will, gives of His art unweariedly; they blame the [artist's] weakness.

He then who is the Natural Musician-God, not only in His making of the harmony of His [celestial] songs, but also in His sending forth the rhythm of the melody of His own song[s] right down unto the separate instruments, [630] is, as God, never wearied.

For that with God there is no growing weary.

2. So, then, if ever a musician desires to enter into the highest contest of his art he can—when now the trumpeters have rendered the same phrase of the [composer's] skill, and afterwards the flautists played the sweet notes of the melody upon their instruments, [631] and they complete the music of the piece with pipe and plectrum—[if any thing goes wrong,] one [632] does not lay the blame upon the inspiration [633] of the music-maker.

Nay, [by no means,]—to him one renders the respect that is his due; one blames the falseness of the instrument, in that it has become a hindrance to those who are most excellent—embarrassing the maker of the music in [the execution of] his melody, and robbing those who listen of the sweetness of the song.

---

[630] ἄχρι τῶν κατὰ μέρος ὀργάνων,—that is, to "parts" as opposed to "wholes"; "wholes" signifying generally noumenal or celestial essences, "parts" meaning the separate existences of the phenomenal or sensible world.

[631] ἄρτι δὲ καὶ αὐλητῶν τοῖς μελικοῖς τὸ τῆς μελῳδίας λιγυρὸν ἐργασαμένων.—I do not know what this means exactly. Ménard translates: *quand les joueurs de flûte ont exprimé les finesses de la mélodie*; Patrizzi gives: *melicis organis melodiæ dulcedinem*.

[632] Or perhaps "he," meaning the judge of the contest.

[633] τῷ πνεύματι.

3. In like way also, in our case, let no one of our audience for the weakness that inheres in body, blame impiously our Race. [634]

Nay, let him know God is Unwearied Spirit [635]—for ever in the self-same way possessed of His own science, unceasing in His joyous gifts, the self-same benefits bestowing everywhere.

4. And if the Pheidias—the Demiurge—is not responded to, by lack of matter to perfect His skilfulness, although for His own part the Artist has done all he can, let us not lay the blame on Him.

But let us, [rather,] blame the weakness of the string, [636] in that, because it is too slack or is too tight, it mars the rhythm of the harmony.

5. So when it is that the mischance occurs by reason of the instrument, no one doth blame the Artist.

Nay, [more;] the worse the instrument doth chance to be, the more the Artist gains in reputation by the frequency with which his hand doth strike the proper note, [637] and more the love the listeners pour upon that Music-maker, without [638]the slightest thought of blaming him.

So will we too, most noble [Sirs], set our own lyre in tune again, within, with the Musician!

6. Nay, I have seen one of the artist-folk [639]—although he had no power of playing on the lyre—when once he had been trained for the right noble theme, make frequent use of his own self as instrument, and tune the service of his string by means of mysteries, so that the listeners were amazed at how he turned necessitude into magnificence. [640]

Of course you know the story of the harper who won the favour of the God who is the president of music-work.

[One day,] when he was playing for a prize, and when the breaking of a string became a hindrance to him in the contest, the favour of the Better One supplied him with another string, and placed within his grasp the boon of fame.

A grasshopper was made to settle on his lyre, through the foreknowledge of the Better One, and [so] fill in the melody in substitution of the [broken] string. [641]

---

[634] The Race of the Prophets, or Gnostics—the Race of the Logos.
[635] Referring to the "inspiration" or "breath" above,—ὡς ἀκάματον μέν ἐστι πνεῦμα ὁ θεός. Compare John iv. 24: πνεῦμα ὁ θεός—God is Spirit.
[636] The metaphor has become somewhat mixed by the introduction of Pheidias, who was a "musician" in marble and ivory and gold, and not on strings and pipes.
[637] τῆς κρούσεως πολλάκις πρὸς τὸν τόνον ἐμπεσούσης.
[638] Reading ἔχοντες for ἔσχον.
[639] Meaning presumably prophets.
[640] It is difficult to follow the exact meaning of some of the writer's rhetorical sentences, even if our text is sound; here, however, the text, even after passing through Reitzenstein's hands, is still very halting, and so I venture on this translation with all hesitation.
[641] The song of the cicala was so pleasant to the ear of the Ancients, that we frequently find it used in poetry as a simile for sweet sounds. Plato calls the grasshoppers the "prophets of the Muses."

And so by mending of his string the harper's grief was stayed, and fame of victory was won.

7. And this I feel is my own case, most noble [Sirs]!

For but just now I seemed to make confession of my want of strength, and play the weakling for a little while; but now, by virtue of the strength of [that] Superior One, as though my song about the King had been perfected [by Him, I seem] to wake my muse.

For, you must know, the end of [this] our duty will be the glorious fame of Kings, and the good-will of our discourse (*logos*) [will occupy itself] about the triumphs which they win.

Come then, let us make haste! For that the singer willeth it, and hath attuned his lyre [642]for this; nay more, more sweetly will he play, more fitly will he sing, as he has for his song the greater subjects of his theme.

8. Since, then, he [643] has the [stringing] of his lyre tuned specially to Kings, and has the key of laudatory songs, and as his goal the Royal praises, let him first raise himself unto the highest King—the God of wholes.

Beginning, [then,] his song from the above, he, [thus,] in second place, descends to those after His likeness who hold the sceptre's power [644]; since Kings themselves, indeed, prefer the [topics] of the song should step by step descend from the above, and where they have their [gifts of] victory presided o'er for them, thence should their hopes be led in orderly succession.

9. Let, then, the singer start with God, the greatest King of wholes, who is for ever free from death, both everlasting and possessed of [all] the might of everlastingness, the Glorious Victor, the very first, from whom all victories descend to those who in succession do succeed to victory. [645]

10. Our sermon (*logos*) then, doth hasten to descend to [Kingly] praises and to the Presidents of common weal and peace, the Kings—whose lordship in most ancient times was placed upon the highest pinnacle by God Supreme; for whom the prizes have already been prepared even before their prowess in the war; of whom the trophies have been raised even before the shock of conflict.

For whom it is appointed not only to be Kings but also to be best.

At whom, before they even stir, the foreign land [646]doth quake.

✻ ✻ ✻ ✻ ✻

---

[642] For the idea of the prophet being the lyre of God, *cf.* Montanus (*ap.* Epiphan., *Hær.*, xlviii. 4). See also the references to Philo given by R. 204, n. 1.
[643] *Sc.* the singer.
[644] *Cf. K. K.*, 39 ff.
[645] But see Plasberg's reading. R. 370.
[646] τὸ βάρβαρον.

(ABOUT THE BLESSING OF THE BETTER [ONE] AND PRAISING OF THE KING)

11. But now our theme (*logos*) doth hasten on to blend its end with its beginnings—with blessing of the Better [One] [647]; and then to make a final end of its discourse (*logos*) on those divinest Kings who give us the [great] prize of peace.

For just as we began [by treating] of the Better [One] and of the Power Above, so let us make the end bend round again unto the same—the Better [One].

Just as the Sun, the nurse of all the things that grow, on his first rising, gathers unto himself the first-fruits of their yield with his most mighty hands, using his rays as though it were for plucking off their fruits—yea, [for] his rays are [truly] hands for him who plucketh first the most ambrosial [essences] of plants—so, too, should we, beginning from the Better [One], and [thus] recipient of His wisdom's stream, and turning it upon the garden of our souls above the heavens, [648]—we should [direct and] train these [streams] of blessing back again unto their source, [blessing] whose entire power of germination [in us] He hath Himself poured into us.

12. 'Tis fit ten thousand tongues and voices should be used to send His blessings back again unto the all-pure God, who is the Father of our souls; and though we cannot utter what is fit—for we are [far] unequal to the task—[yet will we say what best we can].

For Babes just born have not the strength to sing their Father's glory as it should be sung; but they give proper thanks for them, according to their strength, and meet with pardon for their feebleness. [649]

Nay, it is rather that God's glory doth consist in this [one] very thing—that He is greater than His children; and that the prelude and the source, the middle and the end, of blessings, is to confess the Father to be infinitely puissant and never knowing what a limit means.

13. So is it, too, in the King's case.

For that we men, as though we were the children of the King, feel it our natural duty to give praise to him. Still must we ask for pardon [for our insufficiency], e'en though 'tis granted by our Sire before we [even] ask.

And as it cannot be the Sire will turn from Babes new-born because they are so weak, but rather will rejoice when they begin to recognise [his

---

[647] τοῦ κρείττονος,—that is God, or the inner God, as in the last section.
[648] εἰς τὰ ἡμέτερα τῶν ψυχῶν ὑπερουράνια φυτά.
[649] Lit. "in this."

love] ⁶⁵⁰—so also will the Gnosis of the all [rejoice], which doth distribute life to all, and power of giving blessing back to God, which He hath given [us].

14. For God, being Good, and having in Himself eternally the limit of His own eternal fitness, and being deathless, and containing in Himself that lot of that inheritance that cannot come unto an end, and [thus] for ever everflowing from out that energy of His, He doth send tidings to this world down here [to urge us] to the rendering of praise that brings us home again. ⁶⁵¹

With Him, ⁶⁵² therefore, is there no difference with one another; there is no partiality ⁶⁵³with Him.

But they are one in Thought. One is the Prescience ⁶⁵⁴of all. They have one Mind—their Father.

One is the Sense that's active through them— their passion for each other.⁶⁵⁵ 'Tis Love ⁶⁵⁶ Himself who worketh the one harmony of all.

15. Thus, therefore, let us sing the praise of God.

Nay, rather, let us [first] descend to those who have received their sceptres from Him.

For that we ought to make beginning with our Kings, and so by practising ourselves on them, accustom us to songs of praise, and train ourselves in pious service to the Better [One].

[We ought] to make the very first beginnings of our exercise of praise begin from him, ⁶⁵⁷ and through him exercise the practice [of our praise], that so there may be in us both the exercising of our piety towards God, and of our praise to Kings.

16. For that we ought to make return to them, in that they have extended the prosperity of such great peace to us.

It is the virtue of the King, nay, 'tis his name alone, that doth establish peace.

He has his name of King because he levelleth the summits of dissension with his smooth tread, ⁶⁵⁸ and is the lord of reason (*logos*) that [makes] for peace.

And in as much, in sooth, as he hath made himself the natural protector of the kingdom which is not his native land, ⁶⁵⁹ his very name [is made] the sign of peace.

---

⁶⁵⁰ Lit. "at their recognition,"—ἐπὶ τῆς ἐπιγνώσεως—a play on *epignōsis* and *gnōsis*, and a parallel between the wisdom of God and the royal knowledge of the King.

⁶⁵¹ εἰς τόνδε τὸν κόσμον παρέχων τὴν ἀπαγγελίαν εἰς διασωστικὴν εὐφημίαν,—where it may be possible to connect ἀπαγγελία with the familiar εὐαγγέλιον.

⁶⁵² ἐκεῖσε.

⁶⁵³ τὸ ἀλλοπρόσαλλον.

⁶⁵⁴ πρόγνωσις.

⁶⁵⁵ τὸ εἰς ἀλλήλους φίλτρον.

⁶⁵⁶ ὁ ἔρως,—the Higher Love.

⁶⁵⁷ *Sc.* the King.

⁶⁵⁸ The word-play between βασιλεὺς and βάσει λεία is unreproducible in English.

For that, indeed, you know, the appellation of the King has frequently at once restrained the foe.

Nay, more, the very statues of the King are peaceful harbours for those most tempest-tossed.

The likeness of the King alone has to appear to win the victory, and to assure to all the citizens freedom from hurt and fear.

※   ※   ※   ※   ※

---

[659] τῆς βασιλείας τῆς βαρβαρικῆς.

COMMENTARY

THE APOLOGY OF A PŒMANDRIST

This, the last piece in our Corpus, differs so greatly both in style and form of contents from the rest of our sermons, that we are plainly dealing with a different order of endeavour.

The style is for the most part so very artificial and forced, that we are conscious of labour and effort, and sometimes of such obscurity as to make a clear rendering almost impossible. The contents are of the nature of an elaborate set Eulogy of Kings.

Whether or not this concluding piece ever bore a proper title it is impossible to say, for the existing headings are plainly added by a later redactor, [660]—as we have already seen in a number of other instances. I have therefore ventured to superscribe as the main title "The Encomium of Kings," [661] and have placed the contents-headings in parentheses.

Reitzenstein, in his analysis of the Corpus, concludes (p. 207) that this Eulogy was appended to the collection of treatises by the original redactor, or collector.

He was an Egyptian Rhetor, who was a follower of the Trismegistic tradition, and his object in making the collection was mainly to show the Rulers of the Empire that not only was there nothing in the Hermes religion that could excite their suspicion, but that, on the contrary, it was in its most fundamental teachings admirably calculated to inculcate Loyalty to the Rulers of the Empire's destinies.

It is, indeed, to this "Apology," so to speak, that we owe the good fortune of the preservation of our Corpus.

SPECULATIONS AS TO DATE

Who the "most noble [Sirs]" of §§ 5 and 7, to whom the Eulogy is immediately addressed, may be, is difficult to determine, for though the subject is the "Encomium of Kings" in general, some actual King was evidently in the mind of the writer when he penned § 16. Perhaps the "most noble" may have been the high officials of Egypt.

The lost conclusion of our Encomium, for our actual text is evidently incomplete, may have given clearer indications of the Emperor for whose ultimate perusal the Eulogy was intended. As it is, the indications are of the vaguest.

---

[660] In fact, are due to the first hand in B C D M. See R. 355, 1; 358, 12.

[661] See § 15—ἡ πρὸς τοὺς βασιλέας εὐφημία—and compare note to Clem. Alex., iii., in "Fragments from the Fathers."

Reitzenstein, however, is of opinion (pp. 207, 208) that the indications in § 16 best suit the reign of Diocletian (*imp.* 285-305 A.D.); but he is aware that, as far as these are concerned, an earlier date is not excluded (p. 208). It is only when he has treated, in his Addenda (pp. 371-374), the Encomium as an example of later Greek "art-prose," or rhythmic prose, the scheme of the accentuation of which has been of late years carefully studied, especially by Meyer and Wilamowitz, that he comes definitely to the conclusion that the external form of our Rhetor's effort fits precisely the time of Diocletian's Triumph, 302 A.D. I cannot, however, say that I am convinced by his arguments.

The strained and elaborate introduction (§§ 1-5) needs no further comment; no doubt it is very "fine writing," but it is difficult to pin some of it down to any precise meaning in translation.

THE STORY OF THE PYTHIC GRASSHOPPER

6. With § 6, however, our interest is awakened, for it reminds us of the famous Introduction to the *Protrepticus, or Exhortation to the Greeks*, of Clement of Alexandria, when he says:

"I could tell thee also of another—brother to these [662]—story and singer, of Eunomus the Locrian and the Pythic grasshopper.

"At Pytho there was gathered together a solemn assembly of Greeks to celebrate the Death of the Serpent, with Eunomus to sing the funeral song of the beast.

"Whether his song was a hymn or a dirge I cannot say; anyhow, there was a contest, and Eunomus had to harp it in the heat of the day, when the grasshoppers, warmed by the sun, were singing underneath the leaves along the hills.

"They were singing not to the Serpent, the dead thing, but to God the All-wise, a song of unrestrained mode far better than the modes of Eunomus.

"A cord breaks for the Locrian; the grasshopper flies on to the yoke; it chirped on the harp as on a branch; and the minstrel, modulating to the song of the grasshopper, filled up the missing string.

"It was not that the grasshopper was attracted by the song of Eunomus, as the story would have it, setting up a brazen statue at Pytho of Eunomus, harp and all, and his helper in the contest; it flew on naturally and sung naturally. The Greeks, however, thought it played the music." [663]

This passage shows that the story referred to by our author was well known, so well known indeed that Clement takes it as a text for a naturalistic explanation of Hellenic miracle. No literary dependence, however, of one or

---

[662] Amphion, Arion and Orpheus.
[663] Clem. Al., *Prot.*, i. 1; P. 2 (ed. Dindorf, i. 2).

the other can be entertained, for the similarity of the "τὴν νευρὰν ἀνεπλήρωσεν αὐτῷ" of our text and the "ὁ ᾠδὸς τὴν λείπουσαν ἀνεπλήρωσε χορδὴν" of Clement is far too slight a link to bear the weight of any argument of this nature. [664]

11. There is evidently a lacuna after § 10, and, judging by the opening words of § 11, it must be of some length, for the Praise of Kings so far is of a very brief description.

It is also of interest to notice how much easier the style of our author is when he treats of the Praises of God; his words seem to come far more easily, as though he had a subject to deal with with which he was more familiar, as, indeed, he ought to have been if he had studied the treatises he has collected together.

THE TRUE KING

13. The idea that all his subjects are the children of the King is Egyptian; or, rather, it is the tradition of all nations who believed in Divine Kings. The true King was he who, so to speak, contained all his subjects within himself; they were all "members," or, as we should say, cells, of his true Body. The nation was the King; the victory of the nation was ascribed to the virtue of the King. [665]

THE FELLOW-RULERS OF THE HEIGHT

14. The last three sentences of § 14 Reitzenstein (p. 208) would take as referring to the Kings under the suzerainty of the Emperor, who were bound to him by a common bond of love, in order that he may the more insist on the Diocletian date. [666] I would, however, refer the idea to the ideal of harmony and unity of the Beings of the Intelligible World, as described, for instance, by Plotinus, when he writes:

"They see themselves in others. For all things are transparent, and there is nothing dark or resisting, and everyone is manifest to everyone internally, and all things are made manifest; for light is manifest to light. For everyone has all things in himself, and again sees in another all things, so that all things are everywhere, and all in all, and each in all, and infinite the glory. For each of them is great, since the small also is great. And the sun there is all the stars, and, again, each and all are the sun. In each, one thing is pre-eminent above the rest, but it also shows forth all." [667]

---

[664] Cf. R. 205, 206.
[665] This belief, indeed, is the power of the Japanese in our own day.
[666] He thus, apparently, would take the ἐκεῖσε as referring to these subject kings and rulers.
[667] En., V. viii. 4.

Compare this also with the intuition of the seer in *The Untitled Apocalypse* of the Codex Brucianus:

"Their Crowns send forth Rays; the Brilliancy of their Bodies is as the life of the Space into which they are come; the Word (*Logos*) that comes out of their mouth is Eternal Life, and the Light that comes forth from their Eyes is Rest for them; the Movement of their Hands is their Flight to the Space out of which they are come, and their Gazing on their own Faces is Knowledge of themselves; their Giving to themselves is a repeated Return, and the Stretching out of their Hands establishes them; the Hearing of their Ears is the Perception in their Heart; and the Union of their Limbs is the Ingathering of Israel; their Holding to one another is their Fortification in the Logos." [668]

This is the Egyptian counterpart of the Plotinian Ecstasis; and Plotinus was by birth an Egyptian.

---

[668] *F. F. F.*, 557.

II
The Perfect Sermon

THE PERFECT SERMON
OR THE ASCLEPIUS

(Text: The Greek original is lost, and only a Latin version remains to us. I use the text of Hildebrand (G. F.), *L. Apuleii Opera Omnia ex Fide Optimorum Codicum* (Leipzig, 1842), Pars II., pp. 279-334; but have very occasionally preferred the text in Patrizzi's *Nova de Universis Philosophia* (Venice, 1593), or of the Bipontine edition of Appuleius, *Lucii Apuleji Madaurensis Platonici Philosophi Opera* (Biponti, 1788), pp. 285-325.)

I

1. [669] [I. M. [670]] [*Trismegistus.*] God, O Asclepius, hath brought thee unto us that thou mayest hear a Godly sermon, [671] a sermon such as well may seem of all the previous ones we've [either] uttered, or with which we've been inspired by the Divine, more Godly than the piety of [ordinary] faith.

If thou with eye of intellect [672]shalt *see* this Word [673]thou shalt in thy whole mind be filled quite full of all things good.

If that, indeed, the "many" be the "good," and not the "one," in which are "all." Indeed the difference between the two is found in their agreement,—"All" is of "One" [674] or "One" is "All." So closely bound is each to other, that neither can be parted from its mate.

But this with diligent attention shalt thou learn from out the sermon that shall follow [this].

But do thou, O Asclepius, go forth a moment and call in the one who is to hear. [675]

(And when he had come in, Asclepius proposed that Ammon too should be allowed to come. Thereon Thrice-greatest said:)

[*Tris.*] There is no cause why Ammon should be kept away from us. For we remember how we have ourselves set down in writing many things to

---

[669] I have added numbers to the paragraphs for greater convenience of reference.

[670] Ménard has divided the treatise into fifteen parts, which I have thus distinguished; the numbering of the chapters are those usually found.

[671] Or, a sermon about the Gods.

[672] *Intelligens.*

[673] Reason or sermon or *logos*; cf. iii. and below: "For that the Reason," etc.

[674] But ii. 1, referring again to this idea, has the reading: "'All' is 'One.'" Cf. *C. H.*, xvi. 3; and also xx. 2 below.

[675] This, as we shall see later on, is Tat. See xxxii. below.

his address,[676] as though unto a son most dear and most beloved, of physics many things, of ethics [too] as many as could be.

It is, however, with *thy* name I will inscribe this treatise.

But call, I prithee, no one else but Ammon, lest a most pious sermon on a so great theme be spoilt by the admission of the multitude.

For 'tis the mark of an unpious mind to publish to the knowledge of the crowd a tractate brimming o'er with the full Greatness of Divinity.

(When Ammon too had come within the holy place, and when the sacred group of four was now complete with piety and with God's goodly presence—to them, sunk in fit silence reverently, their souls and minds pendent on Hermes' lips, thus Love [677]Divine began to speak.)

II

1. [*Tris.*] The soul of every man, O [my] Asclepius, is deathless; yet not all in like fashion, but some in one way or [one] time, some in another.

Asc. Is not, then, O Thrice-greatest one, each soul of one [and the same] quality?

Tris. How quickly hast thou fallen, O Asclepius, from reason's true sobriety!

Did not I say that "All" is "One," and "One" is "All," [678] in as much as all things have been in the Creator before they were created. Nor is He called unfitly "All," in that His members are the "All."

Therefore, in all this argument, see that thou keep in mind Him who is "One"-"All," or who Himself is maker of the "All."

2. All things descend from Heaven to Earth, to Water and to Air.

'Tis Fire alone, in that it is borne upwards, giveth life; that which [is carried] downwards [is] subservient to Fire.

Further, whatever doth descend from the above, begetteth; what floweth upwards, nourisheth.

'Tis Earth alone, in that it resteth on itself, that is Receiver of all things, and [also] the Restorer of all genera that it receives.

This Whole, [679] therefore, as thou rememberest, [680] in that it is of all,—in other words, all things, embraced by nature under "Soul" and "World," [681] are in [perpetual] flux, so varied by the multiform equality of all their forms, that countless kinds of well-distinguished qualities may be

---

[676] Lit. to his name.
[677] *Cupido*; without doubt Erōs in the lost original; *cf.* xxi. 1 below; and Frag. xviii.
[678] This, as we have already noted, is a variant of the reading in i., where we find "*omnia unius esse*" ("all" is of "one") and not "*omnia unum esse*" ("all" is "one").
[679] *Sc.* the Cosmos.
[680] Presumably from some previous sermon.
[681] That is, Cosmos.

discerned, yet with this bond of union, that all should seem as One, and from "One" "All."⁶⁸²

III

1. That, then, from which the whole Cosmos is formed, consisteth of Four Elements—Fire, Water, Earth, and Air; Cosmos [itself is] one, [its] Soul [is] one, and God is one.

Now lend to me the whole of thee,⁶⁸³—all that thou can'st in mind, all that thou skill'st in penetration.

For that the Reason ⁶⁸⁴of Divinity may not be known except by an intention of the senses like to it. ⁶⁸⁵

'Tis ⁶⁸⁶ likest to the torrent's flood, down-dashing headlong from above with all-devouring tide; so that it comes about, that by the swiftness of its speed it is too quick for our attention, not only for the hearers, but also for the very teachers. ⁶⁸⁷

2. [II. M.] Heaven, then, God Sensible, is the director of all bodies; bodies' increasings and decreasings are ruled by Sun and Moon.

But He who is the Ruler of the Heaven, and of its Soul as well, and of all things within the Cosmos,—He is God, who is the Maker of all things.

For from all those that have been said above, ⁶⁸⁸ o'er which the same God rules, there floweth forth a flood of all things streaming through the Cosmos and the Soul, of every class and kind, throughout the Nature of [all] things.

The Cosmos hath, moreover, been prepared by God as the receptacle of forms of every kind. ⁶⁸⁹

Forth-thinking Nature by these kinds of things, He hath extended Cosmos unto Heaven by means of the Four Elements,—all to give pleasure to the eye of God.

IV

---

⁶⁸² The Latin of this paragraph is very obscure.
⁶⁸³ *Cf. C. H.*, xi. (xii.) 15: "Give thou thyself to Me, My Hermes, for a little while."
⁶⁸⁴ *Ratio*—that is, *Logos*.
⁶⁸⁵ Lit. divine—that is, by a concentration like to the singleness of the Godhead.
⁶⁸⁶ That is, "This Reason is."
⁶⁸⁷ "*Quo efficitur ut intentionem nostram . . . celeri velocitate praetereat.*" Compare with this the description of the instruction of the Therapeuts in Philo's famous tractate, *De Vita Contemplativa*, 901 P., 483 M.—Conybeare's text, p. 117 (Oxford; 1895): "For when in giving an interpretation, one continues to speak rapidly without pausing for breath, the mind of the hearers is left behind, unable to keep up the pace"—ὁ τῶν ἀκροωμένων νοῦς συνομαρτεῖν ἀδυντῶν ὑστερίζει.
⁶⁸⁸ This seems to refer to the Elements.
⁶⁸⁹ *Omniformium specierum*.

1. And all dependent from Above [690] are subdivided into species in the fashion [691] which I am to tell.

The genera of all things company with their own species; so that the genus is a class in its entirety, the species is part of a genus.

The genus of the Gods will, therefore, make the species of the Gods out of itself.

In like way, too, the genus of the daimons, and of men, likewise of birds, and of all [animals] the Cosmos doth contain within itself, brings into being species like itself.

There is besides a genus other than the animal,—a genus, or indeed a soul, in that it's not without sensation,—in consequence of which it both finds happiness in suitable conditions, and pines and spoils in adverse ones;—I mean [the class] of all things on the earth which owe their life to the sound state of roots and shoots, of which the various kinds are scattered through the length and breadth of Earth.

2. The Heaven itself is full of God. The genera we have just mentioned, therefore, occupy up to the spaces of all things whose species are immortal.

For that a species is part of a genus,—as man, for instance, of mankind,—and that a part must follow its own class's quality.

From which it comes to pass that though all genera are deathless, all species are not so.

The genus of Divinity is in itself and in its species [692] [also] deathless.

As for the genera of other things,—as to their genus, they [too] are everlasting; [for] though [the genus] perish in its species, yet it persists through its fecundity in being born. And for this cause its species are beneath the sway of death; so that man mortal is, mankind immortal.

V

1. And yet the species of all genera are interblended with all genera; some [693] which have previously been made, some which are made from these.

The latter, then, which are being made,—either by Gods, or daimons, or by men,—are species all most closely like to their own several genera.

---

[690] *Omnia autem desuper pendentia.* Compare with this the famous Psalm of Valentius, "All things depending from Spirit I see"—πάντα κρεμάμενα πνεύματι βλέπω—Hippolytus, *Philos.*, vi. 37. For revised text see Hilgenfeld's (A.) *Ketzergeschichte*, p. 304 (Leipzig, 1884), and for a translation, my *Fragments of a Faith Forgotten*, p. 307 (London; 1900). See also end of xix. 4 below, and *C. H.*, xvi. 17.

[691] *Genere.*

[692] That is, the Gods.

[693] *Sc.* species.

For that it is impossible that bodies should be formed without the will of God; or species be configured without the help of daimons; or animals be taught and trained without the help of men. [694]

2. Whoever of the daimons, then, transcending their own genus, are, by chance, united with a species, [695] by reason of the neighbourhood of any species of the Godlike class,—these are considered like to Gods. [696]

Whereas those species of the daimons which continue in the quality of their own class,—these love men's rational nature [and occupy themselves with men], and are called daimons proper.

Likewise is it the case with men, or more so even. Diverse and multiform, the species of mankind. And coming in itself from the association spoken of above, it of necessity doth bring about a multitude of combinations of all other species and almost of all things.

3. Wherefore doth man draw nigh unto the Gods, if he have joined himself unto the Gods with Godlike piety by reason of his mind, whereby he is joined to the Gods; and [nigh] unto the daimons, in that he is joined unto them [as well].

Whereas those men who are contented with the mediocrity of their own class, and the remaining species of mankind, will be like those unto the species of whose class they've joined themselves. [697]

VI

1. [III. M.] It is for reasons such as these, Asclepius, man is a mighty wonder,—an animal meet for our worship and for our respect.

For he doth pass into God's Nature, [698] as though himself were God. This genus [also] knows the genus of the daimons, as though man knew he had a [common] origin with them. He thinketh little of the part of human nature in him, from confidence in the divineness of [his] other part.

How much more happy is the blend of human nature [than of all the rest]! Joined to the Gods by his cognate divinity, a man looks down upon the part of him by means of which he's common with the Earth.

The rest of things to which he knows he's kin, by [reason of] the heavenly order [in him], he binds unto himself with bonds of love; and thus he turns his gaze to Heaven.

---

[694] Cf. C. H., xvi. 18, for the hierarchy of Gods and daimones; and for the "intercourse of souls," C. H., x. (xi.) 22.
[695] That is, one of the immortal species, or a God.
[696] That is, they become Gods.
[697] A suggestion of man's attraction to the various species of the animal nature.
[698] This contradicts somewhat the more careful wording of C. H., x. (xi.) 1, where the term Energy is preferred.

2. So, then, [man] hath his place in the more blessed station of the Midst; so that he loves [all] those below himself, and in his turn is loved by those above.

He tills the Earth. He mingles with the Elements by reason of the swiftness of his mind. He plunges into the Sea's depths by means of its [699] profundity. He puts his values on all things.

Heaven seems not too high for him; for it is measured by the wisdom of his mind as though it were quite near.

No darkness of the Air obstructs the penetration of his mind. No density of Earth impedes his work. No depth of Water blunts his sight. [700]

[Though still] the same [yet] is he all, and everywhere is he the same.

3. Of all these genera, those [species] which are animal have [many] roots, which stretch from the above below, [701] whereas those which are stationary [702]—these from [one] living root send forth a wood of branching greenery up from below into the upper parts.

Moreover, some of them are nourished with a two-fold form of food, while others with a single form.

Twain are the forms of food—for soul and body, of which [all] animals consist. Their soul is nourished by the ever-restless motion of the World [703]; their bodies have their growth from foods [drawn] from the water and the earth of the inferior world. [704]

Spirit, [705] with which they [706] all are filled, being interblended with the rest, [707] doth make them live; sense being added, and also reason in the case of man—which hath been given to man alone as a fifth part out of the æther.

Of all the living things [708] [God] doth adorn, extend, exalt, the sense of man alone unto the understanding of the Reason of Divinity. [709]

---

[699] *Sc.* the mind's.
[700] *Cf. C. H.*, xi. (xii.) 19.
[701] Compare with this the symbolism of the "fire-tree" and the "rootage" of the æons, in the "Simonian" system of the Gnōsis, taken by Hippolytus from the document entitled *The Great Announcement* (Hipp., *Philos.*, vi. 9 and 18). Also the common figure of the Ashvattha tree of Indo-Aryan mythology; for instance, in the *Kaṭhopaniṣhad*, II. vi. 1: "The old, old tree that sees no morrow's dawn, [stands] roots up, branches down" (see Mead and Chaṭṭopādhyāya's *Upaniṣhads*, i. 74—London; 1896). Ashvatthaḥ = *a-shvaḥ-tha*, that is, "which stands not till to-morrow." The idea is that the world-tree (*saṁsāravṛikṣha*) never lasts till to-morrow, for all things are perpetually changing.
[702] Lit. non-animal.
[703] Or Cosmos.
[704] *Cf.* xi. 2.
[705] *Cf. C. H.*, x. (xi.) 13, and Commentary thereon.
[706] That is, animal bodies.
[707] Presumably the rest of the Earth elements.
[708] Lit. animals.
[709] Lit. the Divine Reason, *Ratio*, or *Logos*.

But since I am impressed to speak concerning Sense, I will a little further on set forth for you the sermon on this [point]; for that it is most holy, and [most] mighty, not less than in the Reason of Divinity itself.

VII

1. But now I'll finish for you what I have begun. For I was speaking at the start of union with the Gods, by which men only [710]consciously enjoy [711] the Gods' regard,—I mean whatever men have won such rapture that they have obtained a share of that Divine Sense of intelligence which is the most [712] Divine of Senses, found in God and in man's reason.

Asc. Are not the senses of all men, Thrice-greatest one, the same?

Tris. Nay, [my] Asclepius, all have not won true reason [713]; but wildly rushing in pursuit of [reason's] counterfeit, [714] they never see the thing itself, and are deceived. And this breeds evil in their minds, and [thus] transforms the best of animals into the nature of a beast and manners of the brutes.

2. But as to Sense and all things similar, I will set forth the whole discourse when [I explain] concerning Spirit.

For man is the sole animal that is twofold. One part of him is simple: the [man] "essential," [715] as say the Greeks, but which we call the "form of the Divine Similitude."

He also is fourfold: that which the Greeks call "hylic," [716] [but] which we call "cosmic"; of which is made the corporal part, in which is vestured what we just have said is the divine in man, [717]—in which the godhead of the Mind alone, together with its kin, that is the Pure Mind's senses, findeth home and rest, its self with its own self, as though shut in the body's walls.

3. [IV. M.] *Asc.* What, then, Thrice-greatest one, has caused it that man should be planted in the world, and should not pass his life in highest happiness in that part [of the universe] where there is God?

---

[710] *Sc.* of the animals. *Cf.* xviii. 1 below.
[711] *Per-fruuntur. Cf.*, for the idea, xxii. 1 below.
[712] Lit. more.
[713] *Cf. C. H.*, x. (xi.) 23, 24; iv. (v.) 3; and ix. 3 below.
[714] Lit. image.
[715] The Greek term οὐσιώδης is here retained. *Cf.* viii. 2 below.
[716] The Greek ὑλικὸν being retained in the Latin.
[717] *Cf. C. H.*, xvi. 15.

[*Tris.*] Rightly thou questionest, O [my] Asclepius! And we pray God that He bestow on us the power of setting forth this reason; since everything depends upon His Will, and specially those things that are set forth about the Highest Whole, the Reason that's the object of our present argument. Hear, then, Asclepius!

VIII

1. The Lord and Maker of all things, whom we call rightly God, when from Himself He made the second [God], the Visible and Sensible, [718]— I call him Sensible not that He hath sensation in Himself (for as to this, whether or no He have himself sensation, we will some other time declare), but that He is the object of the senses of those who see;—when, then, He made Him first, but second to Himself, and that He seemed to Him [most] fair, as one filled to the full with goodness of all things, He fell in love with Him as being part of His Divinity. [719]

2. Accordingly, in that He was so mighty and so fair, He willed that some one else should have the power to contemplate the One He had made from Himself. And thereon He made man,—the imitator of His Reason and His Love. [720]

The Will of God is in itself complete accomplishment; inasmuch as together with His having willed, in one and the same time He hath brought it to full accomplishment.

And so, when He perceived that the "essential" [721] [man] could not be lover [722] of all things, unless He clothed him in a cosmic carapace, He shut him in within a house of body,—and ordered it that all [men] should be so,— from either nature making him a single blend and fair-proportioned mixture.

3. Therefore hath He made man of soul and body,—that is, of an eternal and a mortal nature; so that an animal thus blended can content his

---

[718] *Sc.* the Logos as Cosmos. *Cf.* xxxi. 1 below.
[719] The Greek original of this passage is quoted by Lactantius, *Div. Institt.*, iv. 6, and runs as follows in Fritzsche's (O. F.) text (Leipzig, 1842):
"The Lord and Maker of all things (whom 'tis our custom to call God) when He had made the second God, the Visible and Sensible,—I call him Sensible not that He hath sensation in Himself (for as to this, whether or no He have himself sensation, we will some other time enquire), but that He is object of senses and of mind;—when, then, He'd made Him first, and One and Only, He seemed to Him most fair, and filled quite full of all things good. At Him He marvelled, and loved Him altogether as His Son." With the last words, *cf.* Plat., *Tim.*, 37 D.
[720] *Diligentiæ*.
[721] The Greek οὐσιώδης being again, as in vii. 2, retained in the Latin. *Cf.* C. H., i. 15 and ix. (x.) 5.
[722] *Diligentem*.

dual origin,—admire and worship things in heaven, and cultivate and govern things on earth. [723]

By mortal things [724] I do not mean the water or the earth [themselves], for these are two of the [immortal] elements that nature hath made subject unto men,—but [either] things that are by men, or [that are] in or from them [725]; such as the cultivation of the earth itself, pastures, [and] buildings, harbours, voyagings, intercommunications, mutual services, which are the firmest bonds of men between themselves and that part of the Cosmos which consists [indeed] of water and of earth, [but is] the Cosmos' terrene part,—which is preserved by knowledge and the use of arts and sciences; without which [things] God willeth not Cosmos should be complete. [726]

In that necessity doth follow what seems good to God; performance waits upon His will.

Nor is it credible that that which once hath pleased Him, will become unpleasing unto God; since He hath known both what will be, and what will please Him, long before.

---

[723] This sentence is also quoted by Lactantius (*Div. Institt.*, vii. 13) in the original Greek, which reads:
"From the two natures, the deathless and the mortal, He made one nature,—that of man, one and the selfsame thing. And having made the selfsame [man] both somehow deathless and also somehow mortal, He brought him [forth], and set him up betwixt the godlike and immortal nature and the mortal; that seeing all he might wonder at all."
[724] That is, the "things on earth."
[725] That is, the two elements mentioned.
[726] The above paragraph seems to have been very imperfectly translated into Latin.

IX

1. [V. M.] But, O Asclepius, I see that thou with swift desire of mind art in a hurry to be told how man can have a love and worship of the Heaven, or of the things that are therein. Hear, then, Asclepius!

The love of God and Heaven, together with all them that are therein, is one perpetual act of worship. [727]

No other thing ensouled, of Gods or animals, can do this thing, save man alone. [728] 'Tis in the admiration, adoration, [and] the praise of men, and [in their] acts of worship, that Heaven and Heaven's hosts find their delight.

2. Nor is it without cause the Muses' choir hath been sent down by Highest Deity unto the host of men; in order that, forsooth, the terrene world should not seem too uncultured, had it lacked the charm of measures, but rather that with songs and praise of men accompanied with music, [729] He might be lauded,—He who alone is all, or is the Sire of all; and so not even on the earths, [730] should there have been an absence of the sweetness of the harmony of heavenly praise.

3. Some, then, though they be very few, endowed with the Pure Mind, [731] have been entrusted with the sacred charge of contemplating Heaven.

Whereas those men who, from the two-fold blending of their nature, have not as yet withdrawn their inner reason from their body's mass, [732] these are appointed for the study of the elements, and [all] that is below them.

4. Thus man's an animal; yet not indeed less potent in that he's partly mortal, but rather doth he seem to be all the more fit and efficacious for reaching Certain Reason, since he has had mortality bestowed on him as well.

For it is plain he could not have sustained the strain of both, unless he had been formed out of both natures, [733] so that he could possess the powers of cultivating Earthly things and loving Heaven.

X

1. The Reason of a thesis such as this, O [my] Asclepius, I would that thou should'st grasp, not only with the keen attention of thy soul, but also with its living power[734] [as well].

---

[727] *Una est obsequiorum frequentatio.* Cf. Ex. i. 3.
[728] Cf. C. H., xvi. 11: "The duty of mankind is to give worship."
[729] *Musicatis*; or perhaps "Muse-inspired"; a word which, like so many others, occurs only in the Latin of this treatise.
[730] *In terris*, pl.
[731] Cf. vii. 1 and 2 above.
[732] The reading is "*interiorem intelligentiam mole corporis resederunt*," of which I can make nothing; *resederunt* is evidently an error.
[733] There is here a "double" in the text, which the editor has not removed.
[734] *Vivacitate.* Cf. C. H., x. (xi.) 17; and xix. 1 below.

For 'tis a Reason that most men cannot believe; the Perfect and the True are to be grasped by the more holy minds.[735] Hence, then, will I begin.

2. [VI. M.] The Lord of the Eternity [736] is the first God; the second's Cosmos; man is the third. [737]

God is the Maker of the Cosmos and of all the things therein; at the same time He ruleth [738]all, with man himself, [who is] the ruler of the compound thing [739]; the whole of which man taking on himself, doth make of it the proper care of his own love, in order that the two of them, himself and Cosmos, may be an ornament each unto other; so that from this divine compost of man, "World" seems most fitly called "Cosmos" [740] in Greek.

3. He knows himself; he knows the World as well. [741] So that he recollects, indeed, what is convenient to his own parts. He calls to mind what he must use, that they may be of service to himself; giving the greatest praise and thanks to God, His Image [742]reverencing,—not ignorant that he is, too, God's image the second [one]; for that there are two images of God—Cosmos and man. [743]

4. So that it comes to pass that, since man's is a single structure,—in that part [of him] which doth consist of Soul, and Sense, of Spirit, and of Reason, he's divine; so that he seems to have the power to mount from as it were the higher elements into the Heaven.

But in his cosmic part, which is composed of fire, and water, and of air, he stayeth mortal on the Earth,—lest he should leave all things committed to his care forsaken and bereft.

Thus human kind is made in one part deathless, and in the other part subject to death while in a body.

XI

1. Now of that dual nature,—that is to say of man,—there is a chief capacity. [And that is] piety, which goodness follows after. [And] this [capacity] then, and then only, seems to be perfected, if it be fortified with virtue of despising all desires for alien things.

---

[735] *Cf. C. H.*, ix. (x.) 10.
[736] That is, the Æon. *Cf.* xxx. I below.
[737] *Cf.* Ex. i. 8.
[738] Reading *gubernat* for *gubernando*.
[739] That is, the compost, or "cosmic" part of himself, apparently, of v. 2.
[740] The original Greek κόσμος is here retained in the Latin; it means "order, adornment, ornament," as well as "world."
[741] The idea is that man is a microcosm; he is, as to his bodies, "cosmic" ("*mundanus homo*"), for his vehicles are made of the elements; he is thus in these an image or seed (microcosm) of the universe, the macrocosm.
[742] *Sc.* Cosmos. *Cf.* xxxi. I below.
[743] *Cf. C. H.*, x. (xi.) 25, last sentence.

For alien from every part of kinship with the Gods [744]are all things on the Earth, whatever are possessed from bodily desires,—to which we rightly give the name "possessions," in that they are not born with us, but later on begin to be possessed by us; wherefore we call them by the name possessions. [745]

2. All such things, then, are alien from man,—even his body. So that we can despise not only what we long for, but also that from which the vice of longing comes to us.

For just as far as the increase of reason leads our [746] soul, so far one should be man; in order that by contemplating the divine, one should look down upon, and disregard the mortal part, which hath been joined to him, through the necessity of helping on the lower [747] world.

3. For that, in order that a man should be complete in either part, observe that he hath been composed of elements of either part in sets of four;—with hands, and feet, both of them pairs, and with the other [748]members of his body, by means of which he may do service to the lower (that is to say the terrene) world.

And to these parts [are added other] four;—of sense, and soul, of memory, and foresight, by means of which he may become acquainted with the rest of things divine, and judge of them.

Hence it is brought about that man investigates the differences and qualities, effects and quantities of things, with critical research; yet, as he is held back with the too heavy weight of body's imperfection, he cannot properly descry the causes of the nature of [all] things which [really] are the true ones.

4. Man, then, being thus created and composed, and to such ministry and service set by Highest God,—man, by his keeping suitably the world in proper order, [and] by his piously adoring God, in both becomingly and suitably obeying God's Good Will,—[man being] such as this, with what reward think'st thou he should be recompensed?

If that, indeed,—since Cosmos is God's work,—he who preserves and adds on to its beauty by his love, joins his own work unto God's Will; when he with toil and care doth fashion out the species [749] (which He hath made [already] with His Divine Intent), with help of his own body;—with

---

[744] *Ab omnibus divinæ cognationis partibus.*
[745] This seems somewhat tautological. The first clause runs: "*quæcunque terrena corporali cupiditate* possidentur; *quæ merito* possessionem *nomine nuncupantur.*" This *Latin* word-play seems almost to suggest that we are dealing with an embellishment of the translator; it may, however, have stood in the original. *Cf.* xii. 2 below.
[746] Lit. my.
[747] Reading *inferioris* for *interioris*, as immediately below in § 3. *Cf.* vi. 3, last sentence.
[748] This seems very loose indeed; the text or the Latin translation is probably at fault, unless the "other members" are supposed to be grouped in sets of double pairs.
[749] Singular—that is, the species in the Cosmos, according to the type in the Divine Mind.

what reward think'st thou he should be recompensed, unless it be with that with which our forebears [750] have been blest?

5. That this may be the pleasure of God's Love, such is our prayer for you, devoted ones.

In other words, may He, when ye have served your time, and have put off the world's restraint, and freed yourselves from deathly bonds, restore you pure and holy to the nature of your higher self,[751] that is of the Divine!

XII

1. *Asc.* Rightly and truly, O Thrice-greatest one, thou speakest. This is the prize for those who piously subordinate their lives to God and live to help the world.

Tris. [To those], however, who have lived in other fashion impiously,—[to them] both is return to Heaven denied, and there's appointed them migration into other bodies [752] unworthy of a holy soul and base; so that, as this discourse of ours will show, [753] souls in their life on earth run risk of losing hope of future immortality.

2. But [all of this] doth seem to some beyond belief; a tale to others; to others [yet again], perchance, a subject for their mirth. [754]

For in this life in body, it is a pleasant thing—the pleasure that one gets from one's possessions. [755] 'Tis for this cause that spite, in envy of its [hope of] immortality, doth clap the soul in prison, [756] as they say, and keep it down, so that it stays in that part of itself in which it's mortal, nor suffers it to know the part of its divinity.

3. For I will tell thee, as though it were prophetic-ly, [757] that no one after us [758] shall have the Single Love, the Love of wisdom-loving, [759] which consists in Gnosis of Divinity alone,—[the practice of] perpetual contemplation and of holy piety. For that the many do confound philosophy with multifarious reasoning, [760]

---

[750] *Cf. C. H.,* x. (xi.) 5; Lact., *D. I.,* i. 11; and xxxvii. 3 below.
[751] Lit. part.
[752] *In corporalia . . . migratio.*
[753] The Latin here does not construe.
[754] *Cf. C. H.,* i. 29; also xxv. 3 below.
[755] *Cf.* xi. 1 above.
[756] *Obtorto . . . collo.*
[757] *Ego enim tibi quasi prædivinans dixero.* Notice the *dixero,*—the "prophetic" tense, if we may be permitted to coin a term to characterize this use, which reminds us so strongly of the "Sibylline" literature and the allied prophetic centonism of the time.
[758] *Cf.* Ex. ix. 8, and xiv. 1 below.
[759] Lit. philosophy. *Cf.* in Philo, *D. V. C.,* the "Heavenly Love" with which the Therapeuts were "afire with God." *Cf.* xiv. 1, and Ex. i. 3.
[760] *Cf. C. H.,* xvi. 2.

Asc. Why is it, then, the many make philosophy so hard to grasp; or wherefore is it they confound this thing with multifarious reasoning?

XIII

1. *Tris.* 'Tis in this way, Asclepius;—by mixing it, by means of subtle expositions, with divers sciences not easy to be grasped,—such as arithmetic, and music, and geometry.

But Pure Philosophy, which doth depend on godly piety alone, should only so far occupy itself with other arts, that it may [know how to] appreciate the working out in numbers of the fore-appointed stations of the stars when they return, and of the course of their procession.

Let her, moreover, know how to appreciate the Earth's dimensions, its qualities and quantities, the Water's depths, the strength of Fire, and the effects and nature of all these. [And so] let her give worship and give praise unto the Art and Mind of God.

2. As for [true] Music,—to know this is naught else than to have knowledge of the order of all things, and whatsoe'er God's Reason hath decreed.

For that the order of each several thing when set together in one [key] for all, by means of skilful reason, will make, as 'twere, the sweetest and the truest harmony with God's [own] Song. [761]

XIV

1. *Asc.* Who, therefore, will the men be after us [762]?

Tris. They will be led astray by sophists' cleverness, and turned from True Philosophy,—the Pure and Holy [Love].

For that to worship God with single mind and soul, and reverence the things that He hath made, and to give thanks unto His Will, which is the only thing quite full of Good,—this is Philosophy unsullied by the soul's rough curiousness.

But of this subject let what has been said so far suffice.

2. [VII. M.] And now let us begin to treat of Spirit and such things.

There was first God and Matter, [763] which we in Greek [764] believe [to be] the Cosmos; and Spirit was *with* Cosmos, or Spirit was *in* Cosmos, but not

---

[761] *Cf.* "Heaven's harmonious song" in xxviii. 11 below.
[762] *Cf.* xii. 3 above, and notes.
[763] The Greek ὕλη is here retained by the translator.
[764] *Græce.*

in like way as in God [765]; nor were there things [as yet] from which the Cosmos [comes to birth] in God.

They *were* not; just for the very reason that they were not, but were as yet in that [condition] whence they *have had* their birth. [766]

For those things only are not called ingenerable which have not yet been born, but [also] those which lack the fertilizing power of generating, so that from them naught can be born.

And so whatever things there are that have in them the power of generating,—these two are generable, [that is to say,] from which birth can take place, though they be born from their own selves [alone]. For there's no question that from those born from themselves birth can with ease take place, since from *them* all are born.

3. God, then, the everlasting, God the eternal, nor can be born, nor could He have been born. That [767]is, That was, That shall be ever. This, therefore, is God's Nature—all from itself [alone].

But Matter [768] (or the Nature of the Cosmos) [769] and Spirit, although they do not seem to be things born from any source, [770] yet in themselves possess the power of generation and of generating,—the nature of fecundity.

For the beginning [771] [truly] is in [just that] quality of nature which possesses in itself the power and matter both of conception and of birth. [772] This, [773] then, without conception of another, is generable of its own self.

XV

1. But, on the other hand, [whereas] those things which only have the power of bringing forth by blending with another nature, are thus to be distinguished, this Space of Cosmos, [774] with those that are in it, seems not to have been born, in that [the Cosmos] has in it undoubtedly all Nature's potency.[775]

---

[765] The Latin translation is confused. The original seems to have stated that Spirit and Cosmos (or Matter) were as yet *one*, or Spirit-Matter.
[766] That is, presumably, they were in potentiality.
[767] *Hoc.*
[768] Again ὕλη in the Latin text.
[769] *Cf.* "Matter or Cosmos" of xvii. 2.
[770] *Principio,* "beginning" the same word as that used in the Vulgate translation of the Proem of the fourth Gospel.
[771] *Initium.*
[772] This seems to make it clear that the idea "Cosmos" is regarded under the dual concept of Spirit-Matter.
[773] *Sc.* Primal Nature, or Spirit-Matter.
[774] *Cf.* xxx. 1, and xxxiv. 1 below.
[775] The Latin construction is very faulty.

By "Space" I mean that in which are all things. For all these things could not have been had Space not been, to hold them all. Since for all things that there have been, must be provided Space.

For neither could the qualities nor quantities, nor the positions, nor [yet] the operations, be distinguished of those things which are no *where*.

2. So then the Cosmos, also, though not born, still has in it the births[776] of all; in that, indeed, it doth afford for all of them most fecund wombs for their conception.

It, therefore, is the sum of [all that] quality of Matter which hath creative potency, although it hath not been [itself] created.

And, seeing that [this] quality of Matter is in its nature [simple] productiveness; so the same [source] produces bad as well [as good].

XVI

1. I have not, therefore, O Asclepius and Ammon, said what many say, that God *could* not excise and banish evil from the Scheme [777] of Things;—to whom no answer need at all be given. Yet for your sakes I will continue what I have begun, and give a reason.

They say that God ought to have freed the World from bad in every way; for so much is it [778] in the World, that it doth seem to be as though it were one of its limbs.

This was foreseen by Highest God and [due] provision made, as much as ever could have been in reason made, then when He thought it proper to endow the minds of men with sense, [779] and science and intelligence.

2. For it is by these things alone whereby we stand above the rest of animals, that we are able to avoid the snares and crimes of ill.

For he who shall on sight have turned from them, before he hath become immeshed in them,—he is a man protected by divine intelligence and [godly] prudence.

For that the ground-work of [true] science doth consist of the top-stones of virtue.

3. It is by Spirit that all things are governed in the Cosmos, and made quick,—Spirit made subject to the Will of Highest God, as though it were an engine or machine.

So far, then, [only] let Him be by us conceived,—as Him who is conceivable by mind alone, who is called Highest God, the Ruler and Director of God Sensible, [780]—of Him who in Himself includes all Space, all Substance,

---

[776] *Naturas.*
[777] Lit. nature.
[778] *Sc.* evil or bad.
[779] Presumably meaning the higher sense.
[780] That is, Cosmos.

and all Matter, of things producing and begetting, and all whatever is, however great it be.

XVII

1. It is by Spirit that all species in the Cosmos are [or] moved or ruled,—each one according to its proper nature given it by God.

Matter, [781] or Cosmos, on the other hand, is that which holds all things,—the field of motion, [782] and the that which crowds together [783]all; of which God is the Ruler, distributing unto all cosmic things all that is requisite to each.

It is with Spirit that He fills all things, according to the quality of each one's nature.

2. [Now,] seeing that the hollow roundness [784] of the Cosmos is borne round into the fashion of a sphere; by reason of its [very] quality or form, it never can be altogether visible unto itself.

So that, however high a place in it thou shouldest choose for looking down below, thou could'st not see from it what is at bottom, because in many places it confronts [the senses], and so is thought to have the quality [of being visible throughout]. [785]

For it is solely owing to the forms of species, with images of which it seems insculpted, that it is thought [to be] as though 'twere visible [throughout]; but as a fact 'tis ever to itself invisible.

3. Wherefore, its bottom, or its [lowest] part, if [such a] place there be within a sphere, is called in Greek *a-eidēs* [786]; since that *eidein* [787] in Greek means "seeing,"—which "being-seen" the sphere's beginning [788]lacks.

Hence, too, the species have the name *eideai*, [789] since they're of form we cannot see.

Therefore, in that they are deprived of "being-seen," in Greek they are called *Hades*; in that they are at bottom [790]of the sphere, they're called in Latin *Inferi*.

---

[781] Again ὕλη.
[782] *Agitatio*.
[783] *Frequentatio*.
[784] *Cava rotunditas*—that is, presumably, concavity.
[785] *Propter quod multis locis instat, qualitatemque habere creditur*. The Latin translation is evidently faulty. Ménard omits the sentence entirely, as he so often does when there is difficulty.
[786] Ἀ-ειδής—that is, "Invisible"; that is, Hades (Ἀιδής or Ἄδης).
[787] εἰδεῖν—? ἰδεῖν.
[788] *Primum sphæræ*; the top or bottom presumably, or periphery, of the world-sphere.
[789] εἰδέαι—? ἰδέαι—that is, forms, species,—but also used of the highest species, viewed as "ideas."
[790] *Sc.* at the centre.

These, then, are principal and prior, [791] and, as it were, the sources and the heads of all the things which are in them, [792] through them, or from them.

XVIII

1. *Asc.* All things, then, in themselves (as thou, Thrice-greatest one, dost say) are cosmic [principles] (as I should say) of all the species which are in them, [or] as it were, the sum and substance of each one of them. [793]

Tris. So Cosmos, then, doth nourish bodies; the Spirit, souls; the [Higher] Sense (with which Celestial Gift mankind alone is blest) [794] doth feed the mind. And [these are] not all men, but [they are] few, whose minds are of such quality that they can be receptive of so great a blessing.

2. For as the World's illumined by the Sun, so is the mind of man illumined by that Light; nay, in [still] fuller measure.

For whatsoever thing the Sun doth shine upon, it is anon, by interjection of the Earth or Moon, or by the intervention of the night, robbed of its light.

But once the [Higher] Sense hath been commingled with the soul of man, there is at-onement from the happy union of the blending of their natures; so that minds of this kind are never more held fast in errors of the darkness.

Wherefore, with reason have they said the [Higher] Senses are the souls of Gods; to which I add: not of *all* Gods, but of the great ones [only]; nay, even of the principles of these.

XIX

1. [VIII. M.] *Asc.* What dost thou call, Thrice-greatest one, the heads of things, or sources of beginnings?

Tris. Great are the mysteries which I reveal to thee, divine the secrets I disclose; and so I make beginning of this thing [795]with prayers for Heaven's favour.

The hierarchies [796] of Gods are numerous; and of them all one class is called the Noumenal, [797] the other [class] the Sensible. [798]

---

[791] Or principles and priorities (*antiquiora*).
[792] *Sc.* the "ideas."
[793] The Latin text is hopeless.
[794] *Cf.* vii. i.
[795] *Initium facio*, or perhaps perform the sacred rite, or give initiation.
[796] *Genera*.

The former are called Noumenal, not for the reason that they're thought to lie beyond *our* [799]senses; for these are just the Gods *we* sense more truly than the ones we call the visible,—just as our argument will prove, and thou, if thou attend, wilt be made fit to see.

For that a lofty reasoning, and much more one that is too godlike for the mental grasp of [average] men, if that the speaker's words are not received [800]with more attentive service of the ears,—will fly and flow beyond them; or rather will flow back [again], and mingle with the streams of its own source. [801]

2. There are, then, [certain] Gods who are the principals[802] of all the species. Next there come those whose essence [803]is their principal. These are the Sensible, each similar to its own dual source, [804] who by their sensibility [805] affect all things,—the one part through the other part [in each] making to shine the proper work of every single one.

Of Heaven,—or of whatsoe'er it be that is embraced within the term,—the essence-chief [806]is Zeus; for 'tis through Heaven that Zeus gives life to all.

Sun's essence-chief is light; for the good gift of light is poured on us through the Sun's disk.

3. The "Thirty-six," who have the name of Horoscopes, [807] are in the [self] same space as the Fixed Stars; of these the essence-chief, or prince, is he whom they call Pantomorph, or Omniform, [808] who fashioneth the various forms for various species.

The "Seven" who are called spheres, have essence-chiefs, that is, [have each] their proper rulers, whom they call [all together] Fortune and Heimarmenē, [809] whereby all things are changed by nature's law; perpetual stability being varied with incessant motion. [810]

---

[797] *Intelligibilis* (= οἱ νοητοί); lit. that which can be known by intellect (alone).

[798] *Sensibilis* (= οἱ αἰσθητοί); lit. that which can be known by the senses.

[799] That is, the "Sense" of those who have reached the "Trismegistic" grade, though of course beyond the range of the normal senses.

[800] The text is faulty.

[801] *Cf.* x. 1 above; and *C. H.*, x. (xi.) 17.

[802] *Principes.*

[803] The Greek original οὐσία being retained.

[804] That is, presumably, essence and sensibility.

[805] That is, presumably, their power of affecting the senses.

[806] The Greek οὐσιάρχης is retained in the Latin.

[807] *Horoscopi* (= ὡροσκόποι); generally called Decans; *cf.* Ex. ix., where the Decans are explained.

[808] Παντόμορφον *vel omniformem*; see xxxv. below; also *C. H.*, xi. (xii.) 16, Comment.

[809] That is, Fate, εἱμαρμένη.

[810] Quoted in the original Greek by Ioan. Laurentius Lydus, *De Mensibus*, iv. 7; Wünsch (Leipzig, 1898), p. 70, 22; as follows: "And Hermes is witness in his [book], called 'The Perfect Sermon,' when saying: 'They that are called the Seven Spheres have a Source that is called Fortune or Fate,' which changes all things and suffers them not to remain in the same [conditions].'" The quotation

The Air, moreover, is the engine, or machine, through which all things are made—(there is, however, an essence-chief of this, a second [Air])—mortal from mortal things and things like these. [811]

4. These hierarchies of Gods, then, being thus and [in this way] related, [812] from bottom unto top, are [also] thus connected with each other, and tend towards themselves; so mortal things are bound to mortal, things sensible to sensible.

The whole of [this grand scale of] Rulership, however, seems to Him [who is] the Highest Lord, either to be not many things, or rather [to be] one.

For that from One all things depending, [813] and flowing down from it,—when they are seen as separate, they're thought to be as many as they possibly can be; but in their union it is one [thing], or rather two, from which all things are made;—that is, from Matter, by means of which the other things are made, and by the Will of Him, by nod of whom they're brought to pass.

XX

1. *Asc.* Is this again *the* reason, O Thrice-greatest one?

Tris. It is, Asclepius. For God's the Father or the Lord of all, or whatsoever else may be the name by which He's named more holily and piously by men,—which should be set apart among ourselves for sake of our intelligence.

For if we contemplate this so transcendent God, we shall not make Him definite by any of these names.

For if a [spoken] word [814] is this:—a sound proceeding from the air, when struck by breath, [815] denoting the whole will, perchance, of man, or else the [higher] sense, which by good chance a man perceives by means of mind, when out of [all his] senses, [816]—a name the stuff of which, made of a syllable or two, has so been limited and pondered, that it might serve in man as necessary link between the voice and ear;—thus [must] the Name of God in

---

is continued without a break; the rest of it, however, corresponds to nothing in our context, but is somewhat similar to ch. xxxix. 1, 2.

[811] That is, the region of things subject to death. The text is faulty. *Cf.* with this "engine" the "cylinder" of the *K. K.* Fragments (10).

[812] *Ab imo ad summum se admoventibus*; for *admoventibus* compare "*genus admotum superis*," Silius Italicus, viii. 295.

[813] *Cf.* iv. 1 above, and the note.

[814] *Vox* (= name), presumably λόγος in the original; a play on "word" and "reason," but also referring to the mysterious "name" of a person.

[815] *Spiritu*, or spirit.

[816] *Ex sensibus* = presumably, in ecstasis.

full consist of Sense, and Spirit, and of Air, and of all things in them, or through, or with them.[817]

2. Indeed, I have no hope that the Creator of the whole of Greatness, the Father and the Lord of all the things [that are], could ever have one name, even although it should be made up of a multitude—He who cannot be named, or rather He who can be called by every name.

For He, indeed, is One and All [818]; so that it needs must be that all things should be called by the same name as His, or He Himself called by the names of all.

3. He, then, alone, yet all-complete in the fertility of either sex, ever with child of His own Will, doth ever bring to birth whatever He hath willed to procreate.

His Will is the All-goodness, which also is the Goodness of all things, born from the nature of His own Divinity,—in order that all things may be, just as they all have been, and that henceforth the nature of being born from their own selves may be sufficient to all things that will be born.

Let this, then, be the reason given thee, Asclepius, wherefore and how all things are made of either sex.

XXI

1. *Asc.* Thou speak'st of God, then, O Thrice-greatest one?

Tris. Not only God, Asclepius, but all things living and inanimate. For 'tis impossible that any of the things that are should be unfruitful.

For if fecundity should be removed from all the things that are, it could not be that they should be for ever what they are. I mean that Nature,[819] Sense, and Cosmos, have in themselves the power of being born,[820] and of preserving all things that are born.

For either sex is full of procreation; and of each one there is a union, or,—what's more true,—a unity incomprehensible; which you may rightly call Erōs [821] or Aphroditē, or both [names].

2. This, then, is truer than all truth, and plainer than what the mind ['s eye] perceives;—that from that Universal God of Universal Nature all other things for evermore have found, and had bestowed on them, the mystery of bringing forth; in which there is innate the sweetest Charity, [and] Joy, [and] Merriment, Longing, and Love Divine.

---

[817] The text of this paragraph is very unsatisfactory.
[818] *Cf.* i. 1 above.
[819] Here, presumably, meaning *hyle*.
[820] *Naturam* again.
[821] *Cf.* 1, 2, above.

We might have had to tell the mighty power and the compulsion of this mystery, if it had not been able to be known by every one from personal experience, by observation of himself.

3. For if thou should'st regard that supreme [point] of time when . . .[822] the one nature doth pour forth the young into the other one, and when the other greedily absorbs [it] from the first, and hides it [ever] deeper [in itself]; then, at that time, out of their common congress, females attain the nature of the males, males weary grow with female listlessness.

And so the consummation of this mystery, so sweet and requisite, is wrought in secret; lest, owing to the vulgar jests of ignorance, the deity of either sex should be compelled to blush at natural congress,—and much more still, if it should be subjected to the sight of impious folk.

XXII

1. The pious are not numerous, however; nay, they are very few, so that they may be counted even in the world. [823]

Whence it doth come about, that in the many bad inheres, through defect of the Gnosis and Discernment of the things that are.

For that it is from the intelligence of Godlike Reason, [824] by which all things are ordered, there come to birth contempt and remedy of vice throughout the world.

But when unknowingness and ignorance persist, all vicious things wax strong, and plague the soul with wounds incurable; so that, infected with them, and invitiated, it swells up, as though it were with poisons,—except for those who know the Discipline of souls and highest Cure of intellect.

2. So, then, although it may do good to few alone, 'tis proper to develope and explain this thesis:—wherefore Divinity hath deigned to share His science and intelligence with men alone. Give ear, accordingly!

When God, [our] Sire and Lord, made man, after the Gods, out of an equal mixture of a less pure cosmic part and a divine,—it [naturally] came to pass the imperfections [825] of the cosmic part remained commingled with [our] frames, and other ones [826] [as well], by reason of the food and sustenance we have out of necessity in common with all lives [827]; by reason of which things it needs must be that the desires, and passions, and other vices, of the mind should occupy the souls of human kind.

---

[822] *Quo ex crebro attritu prurimus ut* . . . .
[823] *Cf.* Ex. i. 16.
[824] *Cf.* vii. 1 above.
[825] *Vitia*; lit. vices.
[826] *Sc.* imperfections.
[827] Lit. animals.

3. As for the Gods, in as much as they had been made of Nature's fairest [828]part, and have no need of the supports of reason and of discipline, [829]—although, indeed, their deathlessness, the very strength of being ever of one single age, stands in this case for prudence and for science, still, for the sake of reason's unity, instead of science and of intellect (so that the Gods should not be strange to these),—He, by His everlasting law, decreed for them an order, [830] circumscribed by the necessity of law.

While as for man, He doth distinguish him from all the other animals by reason and by discipline alone; by means of which men can remove and separate their bodies' vices,—He helping them to hope and effort after deathlessness.

4. In fine, He hath made man both good and able to share in immortal life,—out of two natures, [one] mortal, [one] divine.

And just because he is thus fashioned by the Will of God, it is appointed that man should be superior both to the Gods, who have been made of an immortal nature only, and also to all mortal things.

It is because of this that man, being joined unto the Gods by kinsmanship, doth reverence them with piety and holy mind; while, on their side, the Gods with pious sympathy regard and guard all things of men.

XXIII

1. But this can only be averred of a few men endowed with pious minds. Still, of the rest, the vicious folk, we ought to say no word, for fear a very sacred sermon should be spoiled by thinking of them.

[IX. M.] And [831] since our sermon treats of the relationship and intercourse [832] of men and Gods,—learn, Asclepius, the power and strength of man!

[Our] Lord and Father, or what is Highest God,—as He's Creator of the Gods in Heaven, so man's the maker of the gods who, in the temples, suffer man's approach, and who not only have light poured on them, but who send forth [their] light [on all]; not only does a man go forward towards the God[s], but also he confirms the Gods [on earth]. [833]

Art thou surprised, Asclepius; nay is it not that even *thou* dost not believe?

---

[828] *Mundissima*—that is, most cosmic, or "adorned."
[829] Or science.
[830] *Ordinem*—that is, Cosmos. Compare this also with the idea of the Gnostic Horos which "surrounds" the Plērōma.
[831] This sentence and the first half of the next, down to "suffer man's approach," is quoted word for word in Latin by Augustine, *De Civitate Dei*, xxiii.
[832] Cf. C. H., x. (xi.) 22.
[833] The Latin translation of this paragraph seems confused.

2. *Asc.* I am amazed, Thrice-greatest one; but willingly I give assent to [all] thy words. I judge that man most blest who hath attained so great felicity.

Tris. And rightly so; [for] he deserves our wonder, in that he is the greatest of them all.

As for the genus of the Gods in Heaven,—'tis plain from the commixture [834] of them all, that it has been made pregnant from the fairest part of nature, [835] and that the only signs [by which they are discerned] are, as it were, before all else their heads. [836]

3. Whereas the species of the gods which humankind constructs is fashioned out of either nature,—out of that nature which is more ancient and far more divine, and out of that which is in men; that is, out of the stuff of which they have been made and are configured, not only in their heads alone, but also in each limb and their whole frame.

And [837] so mankind, in imaging Divinity, stays mindful of the nature and the source of its own self.

So that, just as [our] Sire and Lord did make the Gods æonian, that they might be like Him; so hath mankind configured its own gods according to the likeness of the look of its own self. [838]

XXIV

1. *Asc.* Thou dost not mean their statues, dost thou, O Thrice-greatest one?

Tris. [I mean their] statues, O Asclepius,—dost thou not see how much *thou* even, doubtest?—statues, ensouled with sense, and filled with spirit, which work such mighty and such [strange] results,—statues which can foresee what is to come, and which perchance can prophesy, foretelling things by dreams and many other ways,—[statues] that take their strength away from men, or cure their sorrow, if they do so deserve.

Dost thou not know, Asclepius, that Egypt is the image of the Heaven [839]; or, what is truer still, the transference, or the descent, of all that are

---

[834] This is, apparently, the "star stuff" of which their bodies are made.
[835] *De mundissima parte naturæ esse prægnatum*—whatever that means; but *cf.* p. 348, n. 1.
[836] *Cf. C. H.*, x. (xi.) 10, 11.
[837] This sentence, together with the first five sentences of the next chapter, down to the words "and constant worship," are quoted in Latin with two or three slight verbal variants by Augustine, *De Civitate Dei*, xxiii.
[838] *Cf.* xxxvii. 2 below.
[839] *Cf.* Comment, on *K. K.*, 46-48.

in governance or exercise in Heaven? And if more truly [still] it must be said,—this land of ours is Shrine of all the World.

2. Further, in that 'tis fitting that the prudent should know all before, it is not right ye should be ignorant of this.

The time will come when Egypt will appear to have in vain served the Divinity with pious mind and constant worship [840]; and all its holy cult will fall to nothingness and be in vain.

For that Divinity is now about to hasten back from Earth to Heaven, and Egypt shall be left; and Earth, which was the seat of pious cults, shall be bereft and widowed of the presence of the Gods.[841]

And foreigners shall fill this region and this land; and there shall be not only the neglect of pious cults, but—what is still more painful,—as though enacted by the laws, a penalty shall be decreed against the practice of [our] pious cults and worship of the Gods—[entire] proscription of them.

3. Then shall this holiest land, seat of [our] shrines and temples, be choked with tombs and corpses. [842]

O Egypt, Egypt, of thy pious cults tales only will remain, as far beyond belief for thy own sons [as for the rest of men]; words only will be left cut on thy stones, thy pious deeds recounting!

And Egypt will be made the home of Scyth or Indian, or some one like to them,—that is a foreign neighbour. [843]

Ay, for the Godly company [844]shall mount again to Heaven, and their forsaken worshippers shall all die out; and Egypt, thus bereft of God and man, shall be abandoned.

4. And now I speak to thee, O River, holiest [Stream]! I tell thee what will be. With bloody torrents shalt thou overflow thy banks. Not only shall thy streams divine be stained with blood; but they shall all flow over [with the same].

The tale of tombs shall far exceed the [number of the] quick; and the surviving remnant shall be Egyptians in their tongue alone, but in their actions foreigners.

XXV

1. Why dost thou weep, Asclepius? Nay, more than this, by far more wretched,—Egypt herself shall be impelled and stained with greater ills.

---

[840] Augustine's quotation ends here.

[841] *Sepulchrorum erit mortuorumque plenissima.* This sentence is quoted verbatim by Augustine, De Civitate Dei, xxvi.

[842] Compare Colossians iii. 11: "Where there is neither Greek nor Jew, circumcision nor uncircumcision, *Barbarian, Scythian,* bond nor free: but Christ is all, and in all."

[843] *Vicina barbaria;* lit. a neighbouring foreign country. Compare this with the previous note. It is strange the two, Scyth and barbarian, coming twice together.

[844] *Divinitas.*

For she, the Holy [Land], and once deservedly the most beloved by God, by reason of her pious service of the Gods on earth,—she, the sole colony [845] of holiness, and teacher of religion [on the earth], shall be the type of all that is most barbarous.

And then, out of our loathing for mankind, the World will seem no more deserving of our wonder and our praise.

All this good thing, [846]—than which there has been fairer naught that can be seen, nor is there anything, nor will there [ever] be,—will be in jeopardy.

2. And it will prove a burden unto men; and on account of this they will despise and cease to love this Cosmos as a whole,—the changeless work of God; the glorious construction of the Good, comprised of multifold variety of forms; the engine of God's Will, supporting His own work ungrudgingly; the multitudinous whole massed in a unity of all, that should be reverenced, praised and loved,—by them at least who have the eyes to see.

For Darkness will be set before the Light, and Death will be thought preferable to Life. No one will raise his eyes to Heaven; the pious man will be considered mad, the impious a sage; the frenzied held as strong, the worst as best.

3. For soul, and all concerning it,—whereby it doth presume that either it hath been born deathless, or that it will attain to deathlessness, according to the argument I have set forth for you,—[all this] will be considered not only food for sport, [847] but even vanity.

Nay, [if ye will] believe me, the penalty of death shall be decreed to him who shall devote himself to the Religion of the Mind.

New statutes shall come into force, a novel law; naught [that is] sacred, nothing pious, naught that is worthy of the Heaven, or Gods in Heaven, shall [e'er] be heard, or [even] mentally believed.

4. The sorrowful departure of the Gods from men takes place; bad angels [848] only stay, who mingled with humanity will lay their hands on them, and drive the wretched folk to every ill of recklessness,—to wars, and robberies, deceits, and all those things that are opposed to the soul's nature. [849]

---

[845] *Deductio* the technical term for leading out a colony from the *metropolis* or mother city. Compare Philo, *De Vita Contemplativa*, P. 892, M. 474 (Conybeare, p. 58): "In Egypt there are crowds of them [the Therapeuts] in every province, or nome as they call it, and especially at Alexandria. For they who are in every way the most highly advanced, lead out a colony (ἀποικίαν στέλλονται), as it were to the Therapeutic father-land"; and also the numerous parallel passages cited by Conybeare from Philo's other writings.

[846] *Sc.* the Cosmos.

[847] *Cf.* xii. 2 above.

[848] *Nocentes angeli*,—usually daimones in our tractates; still, as Lactantius (*D. I.*, ii. 15) says that Hermes calls the daimones "evil angels" (ἀγγέλους πονηροὺς), he most probably took it from the Greek original of our sermon.

[849] *Cf. C. H.*, x. (xi.) 21.

Then shall the Earth no longer hold together; the Sea no longer shall be sailed upon; nor shall the Heaven continue with the Courses of the Stars, nor the Star-course in Heaven.

The voice of every God [850] shall cease in the [Great] Silence that no one can break; the fruits of Earth shall rot; nay, Earth no longer shall bring forth; and Air itself shall faint in that sad listlessness.

XXVI

1. This, when it comes, shall be the World's old age, impiety,—irregularity, and lack of rationality in all good things.

And when these things all come to pass, Asclepius,—then He, [our] Lord and Sire, God First in power, and Ruler of the One God [Visible], [851] in check of crime, and calling error back from the corruption of all things unto good manners and to deeds spontaneous with His Will (that is to say God's Goodness),—ending all ill, by either washing it away with water-flood, or burning it away with fire, or by the means of pestilent diseases, spread throughout all hostile lands,—God will recall the Cosmos to its ancient form [852]; so that the World itself shall seem meet to be worshipped and admired; and God, the Maker and Restorer of so vast a work, be sung by the humanity who shall be then, with ceaseless heraldings of praise and [hymns of] blessing.

2. For this [Re-] birth of Cosmos is the making new [853] of all good things, and the most holy and most pious bringing-back again of Nature's self, by means of a set course of time,—of Nature, which was without beginning, and which is without an end. For that God's Will hath no beginning; and, in that 'tis the same and as it is, it is without an end.

Asc. Because God's Nature's the Determination [854] of the Will. Determination is the Highest Good; is it not so, Thrice-greatest one?

3. *Tris.* Asclepius, Will is Determination's child; nay, willing in itself comes from the Will.

---

[850] *Omnis vox divina*; or, perhaps, the "whole Word of God."
[851] That is, Cosmos.
[852] The above passage is cited in the original Greek by Lactantius (*D. I.*, vii. 8) as from the "Perfect Sermon" of Hermes. As we might expect from what had been already said on this subject, it differs from our Latin translation, and runs as follows:

"Now when these things shall be as I have said, Asclepius, then will [our] Lord and Sire, the God and Maker of the First and the One God, look down on what is done, and making firm His Will, that is the Good, against disorder,—recalling error, and cleaning out the bad, either by washing it away with water-flood, or burning it away with swiftest fire, or forcibly expelling it with war and famine,—will bring again His Cosmos to its former state, and so achieve its Restoration."

[853] *Cf. C. H.*, iii. (iv.) 1.
[854] *Consilium* = βουλή.

Not that He willeth aught desiring it; for that He is the Fullness of all things, and wills what things He has.

He thus wills all good things, and has all that He wills. Nay, rather, He doth think and will *all* good.

This, then, is God; the World of Good's His Image.

XXVII

1. *Asc.* [Is Cosmos] good, Thrice-greatest one?

Tris. ['Tis] good, [855] as I will teach thee, O Asclepius.

For just as God is the Apportioner and Steward of good things to all the species, or [more correctly] genera, which are in Cosmos,—that is to say, of Sense, [856] and Soul, and Life,—so Cosmos is the giver and bestower of all things which seem unto [us] mortals good;—that is to say, the alternation of its parts, of seasonable fruits, birth, growth, maturity, and things like these.

And for this cause God doth transcend the height of highest Heaven, extending everywhere, and doth behold all things on every side.

2. Beyond the Heaven starless Space doth stretch, stranger to every thing possessed of body.

The Dispensator who's between the Heaven and Earth, is Ruler of the Space which we call Zeus [Above].

The Earth and Sea is ruled by Zeus Below [857]; he is the Nourisher of mortal lives, and of fruit-bearing [trees].

It is by reason of the powers of all of these [858] that fruits, and trees, and earth, grow green.

The powers and energies of [all] the other [Gods] will be distributed through all the things that are.

3. Yea, they who rule the earth shall be distributed [through all the lands], and [finally] be gathered in a state, [859]—at top of Egypt's upper part, [860]—which shall be founded towards the setting sun, and to which all the mortal race shall speed.

Asc. But now, just at this moment, where are they, Thrice-greatest one?

---

[855] This seems a *formal* contradiction of *C. H.*, x. (xi.) 10, but is not really so.
[856] Meaning higher sense, presumably; reading *sensus* for *sensibus*.
[857] *Jupiter Plutonius.* Ménard suggests "*Zeus souterrain* (*Sarapis?*)"; the original was probably Zeus Aidoneus.
[858] It is not clear who "these" are; perhaps all that have so far been mentioned, but this does not seem satisfactory. Doubtless the Latin translation is, as usual, at fault.
[859] Or city.
[860] *In summo Ægypti initio.*

Tris. They're gathered in a very large community, [861] upon the Libyan Hill. [862] And now enough concerning this hath been declared.

---

[861] *Civitate.*
[862] *In monte Libyco;* lit. on a (or the) Libycan, or Libyan or African Hill or Mount. Compare with this xxxvii. below.

4. [X. M.] But now the question as to deathlessness or as to death must be discussed.

The expectation and the fear of death torture the multitude, who do not know True Reason.

Now death is brought about by dissolution of the body, wearied out with toil, and of the number, when complete, by which the body's members are arranged into a single engine for the purposes of life. The body dies, when it no longer can support the life-powers [863] of a man.

This, then, is death,—the body's dissolution, and the disappearance of corporeal sense.[864]

As to *this* death anxiety is needless. But there's another [death] which no man can escape, [865] but which the ignorance and unbelief of man think little of.

5. *Asc.* What is it, O Thrice-greatest one, that men know nothing of, or disbelieve that it can be?

Tris. So, lend thy ear, Asclepius!

XXVIII

1. When, [then,] the soul's departure from the body shall take place,—then shall the judgment and the weighing of its merit pass into its highest daimon's power. [866]

And when he sees it pious is and just,—he suffers it to rest in spots appropriate to it.

But if he find it soiled with stains of evil deeds, and fouled with vice,—he drives it from Above into the Depths, and hands it o'er to warring hurricanes and vortices of Air, of Fire, and Water. [867]

---

[863] *Vitalia.*

[864] This passage is quoted in the original Greek by Stobæus, *Florilegium*, cxx. 27 (G. iii. 464; M. iv. 105, 106; Pat. 45, under title "Death"), under the heading "Of Hermes from the [Sermons] to Asclepius." It runs as follows:

"Now must we speak of death. For death affrights the many as the greatest of all ills, in ignorance of fact. Death is the dissolution of the toiling frame. For when the 'number' of the body's joints becomes complete,—the basis of the body's jointing being number,—that body dies; [that is,] when it no longer can support the man. And this is death,—the body's dissolution and the disappearance of corporeal sense."

The directness and the sturdy vigour of the Greek original has clearly lost much in the rhetorical paraphrasing of the Latin translator.

[865] *Necessaria.*

[866] *Cf. C. H.*, x. (xi.) 21.

[867] The substance of these two sentences is contained in a "quotation" from the Greek by J. Laurentius Lydus, *De Mensibus*, iv. 149 (Wünsch, 167, 15): "According to the Egyptian Hermes who, in what is called 'The Perfect Sermon,' says as follows: 'But such souls as transgress the norm

2. 'Twixt Heaven and Earth, upon the waves of Cosmos, is it dragged in contrary directions, for ever racked with ceaseless pains [868]; so that in this its deathless nature doth afflict the soul, in that because of its unceasing sense, it hath the yoke of ceaseless torture set upon its neck.

Know, then, that we should dread, and be afraid, and [ever] be upon our guard, lest we should be entangled in these [toils].

For those who do not now believe, will after their misdeeds be driven to believe, by facts not words, by actual sufferings of punishment and not by threats.

3. *Asc.* The faults of men are not, then, punished, O Thrice-greatest one, by law of man alone?

Tris. In the first place, Asclepius, all things on Earth must die.

Further, those things which live by reason of a body, and which do cease from living by reason of the same,—all these, according to the merits of this life, or its demerits, find due [rewards or] punishments.

[And as to punishments] they're all the more severe, if in their life [their misdeeds] chance to have been hidden, till their death. [869] For [then] they

---

of piety, when they do leave their body, are handed over to the daimones and carried downwards through the air, cast forth as from a sling into the zones of fire and hail, which poets call Pyriphlegethon and Tartarus.'" That this is a "quotation," however, I doubt very much, for if we compare it with *D. M.*, iv. 31 (W. 90, 24), which very faintly echoes the teaching of our chaps, iv., v., xxvii., we shall find that Tartarus and Pyriphlegethon are entirely due to Laurentius himself. The passage runs as follows:

"For the Egyptian Hermes, in his Sermon called Perfect, says that the Avenging of the daimones, being present in matter itself, chastise the human part [of us] according as it has deserved; while the Purifying ones confined to the air purify the souls after death that are trying to soar aloft, [conducting them] round the haily and fiery zones of the air, which the poets and Plato himself in the *Phædo* call Tartarus and Pyriphlegethon; while the Saving ones again, stationed in the lunar space, save the souls." *Cf. Ex.* ix. 6.

[868] Ménard here quotes a couple of lines from Empedocles (*c.* 494-434 B.C.), cited by Plutarch, but without giving any reference. They are from the famous passage beginning ἔστιν ἀνάγκης χρῆμα κ.τ.λ. (369-382), of which the following is Fairbanks' translation. See Fairbanks (A.), *The First Philosophers of Greece* (London, 1898), p. 205:

"There is an utterance of Necessity, an ancient decree of the Gods, eternal, sealed fast with broad oaths: Whenever any one defiles his body sinfully with bloody gore or perjures himself in regard to wrongdoing,—one of those spirits who are heir to long life (δαίμων οἵτε μακραίωνες λελάχασι βιοῖο),—thrice ten thousand seasons shall he wander apart from the blessed, being born meanwhile in all sorts of mortal forms (φυόμενον παντοῖα διὰ χρόνου εἴδεα θνητῶν) changing one bitter path of life for another. For mighty Air pursues him Seaward, and Sea spews him forth on the threshold of Earth, and Earth casts him into the rays of the unwearied Sun, and Sun into the eddies of Air: one receives him from the other, and all hate him. One of these now am I too, a fugitive from the gods and a wanderer, at the mercy of raging Strife."

[869] *Cf.* the Vision of Thespesius (Aridæus) in Plutarch, *De Sera Numinis Vindicta*: "Thus he had to see that the shades of notorious criminals who had been punished in earth-life were not so hardly dealt with . . . ; whereas those who had passed their lives in undetected vice, under cloak and

will be made full conscious of all things by the divinity, just as they are, according to the shades of punishment allotted to their crimes.

XXIX

1. *Asc.* And these deserve [still] greater punishments, Thrice-greatest one?

Tris. [Assuredly;] for those condemned by laws of man do lose their life by violence, so that [all] men may see they have not yielded up their soul to pay the debt of nature, but have received the penalty of their deserts.

Upon the other hand, the righteous man finds his defence in serving God and deepest piety. For God doth guard such men from every ill. [870]

2. Yea, He who is the Sire of all, [our] Lord, and who alone is all, doth love to show Himself to all.

It is not by the place where he may be, nor by the quality which he may have, nor by the greatness which he may possess, but by the mind's intelligence alone, that He doth shed His light on man,—[on him] who shakes the clouds of Error from his soul, and sights the brilliancy of Truth,[871] mingling himself with the All-sense of the Divine Intelligence; through love [872] of which he wins his freedom from that part of him o'er which Death rules, and has the seed of the assurance of his future Deathlessness implanted in him.

3. This, then, is how the good will differ from the bad. Each several one will shine in piety, in sanctity, in prudence, in worship, and in service of [our] God, and see True Reason, as though [he looked at it] with [corporal] eyes; and each will by the confidence of his belief excel all other men, as by its light the Sun the other stars. [873]

For that it is not so much by the greatness of his light as by his holiness and his divinity, the Sun himself lights up the other stars.[874]

Yea, [my] Asclepius, thou should'st regard him as the second God, [875] ruling all things, and giving light to all things living in the Cosmos, whether ensouled or unensouled.

For if the Cosmos is a living thing, and if it has been, and it is, and will be ever-living,—naught in the Cosmos is subject to death.

For of an ever-living thing, it is [the same] of every part which is; [that is,] that 'tis [as ever-living] as it is [itself]; and in the World itself [which

---

show of virtue, were hemmed in by the retributory agents, and forced with labour and pain to turn their souls inside out."
[870] Compare the Fragment quoted in Greek by Lactantius, *D. I.*, ii. 15, and by Cyril, *C. J.*, iv. 130.
[871] *Cf.* xiii. (xiv.) 7-9, Comment.
[872] *Cf.* xii. 3 above.
[873] *Astris.*
[874] *Stellas.*
[875] *Cf. C. H.*, xvi. 5. ff.

is] for everyone, and at the self-same time an ever-living thing of life,—in it there is no place for death.[876]

5. And so he [877]should be the full store of life and deathlessness; if that it needs must be that he should live for ever.

And so the Sun, just as the Cosmos, lasts for aye. So is he, too, for ever ruler of [all] vital powers, or of [our] whole vitality; he is their ruler, or the one who gives them out.

God, then, is the eternal ruler of all living things, or vital functions, that are in the World. He is the everlasting giver-forth of Life itself. [878]

Once for all [time] He hath bestowed Life on all vital powers; He further doth preserve them by a law that lasts for evermore, as I will [now] explain.

XXX

1. For in the very Life of the Eternity [879]is Cosmos moved; and in the very Everlastingness [880]of Life [itself] is Cosmic Space. [881]

On which account it [882]shall not stop at any time, nor shall it be destroyed; for that its very self is palisaded [883]round about, and bound together as it were, by Living's Sempiternity.

Cosmos is [thus] Life-giver unto all that are in it, and is the Space of all that are in governance beneath the Sun.

The motion of the Cosmos in itself consisteth of a two-fold energy. 'Tis vivified itself from the without by the Eternity, [884] and vivifies all things that are within, making all different, by numbers and by times, fixed and appointed [for them].

---

[876] The text of this paragraph is very corrupt.
[877] That is, the Sun.
[878] See Comment on *C. H.*, xvi. 17.
[879] *Æternitatis*, doubtless αἰῶνος in the original Greek,—that is, the Æon; *cf.* x. 2 above. For the general Æon-doctrine, see chap. xi. in the Prolegomena, and xxxii. 1 below.
[880] *Æternitate*; Æon again.
[881] Lit. the Space of Cosmos; *cf.* xv. 1 above.
[882] *Sc.* Cosmos.
[883] *Circumvallatus et quasi constrictus.* Compare with this the idea of the Horos or Boundary in the æonology of "Them of Valentinus," as set forth by Hippolytus (*Philosophumena*, vi. 31):

"Moreover that the formlessness of the Abortion should finally never again make itself visible to the perfect Æons, the Father Himself also sent forth the additional emanation of a single Æon, the Cross [or Stock, τὸν σταυρόν], which being created great, as [the creature] of the great and perfect Father, and emanated to be the Guard and Wall of protection [lit. Paling or Stockade—χαράκωμα, the Roman *vallum*] of the Æons, constitutes the Boundary (ὅρος) of the Plērōma, holding the thirty Æons together within itself. For these [thirty] are they which form the divine creation." See *F. F. F.*, p. 342.
[884] That is, the Æon.

2. Now Time's distinguished on the Earth by quality of air, by variation of its heat and cold; in Heaven by the returnings of the stars to the same spots, the revolution of their course in Time.

And while the Cosmos is the home [885] of Time, [886] it is kept green [itself] by reason of Time's course and motion.

Time, on the other hand, is kept by regulation. Order and Time effect renewal of all things which are in Cosmos by means of alternation.

3. [XI. M.] All things, then, being thus, there's nothing stable, nothing fixed, nothing immoveable, of things that are being born, in Heaven or on the Earth.

Immoveable [887] [is] God alone, and rightly [He] alone; for He Himself is in Himself, and by Himself, and round Himself, completely full and perfect.

He is His own immoveable stability. Nor by the pressure of some other one can He be moved, nor in the space [of anyone].

4. For in Him are all [spaces], and He Himself alone is in them all; unless someone should venture to assert that God's own motion's in Eternity [888]; nay, rather, it is just Immoveable Eternity itself, back into which the motion of all times is funded, and out of which the motion of all times takes its beginning.

XXXI

1. God, then, hath [ever] been unchanging, [889] and ever, in like fashion, with Himself hath the Eternity consisted,—having within itself Cosmos ingenerate, which we correctly call [God] Sensible. [890]

Of that [transcendent] Deity this Image [891] hath been made,—Cosmos the imitator of Eternity.

Time, further, hath the strength and nature of its own stability, in spite of its being in perpetual motion,—from its necessity of [ever] from itself reverting to itself.

2. And so, although Eternity is stable, motionless, and fixed, still, seeing that the movement of [this] Time (which is subject to motion) is ever being recalled into Eternity,—and for that reason Time's mobility is circular,—it comes to pass that the Eternity itself, although in its own self, is motionless, [yet] on account of Time, in which it is—(and it *is* in it),—it seems to be in movement as all motion.

---

[885] *Receptaculum.*
[886] *Cf. C. H.*, xi. (xii.) 2.
[887] That is, changeless.
[888] That is, again, in the Æon.
[889] *Stabilis.*
[890] *Cf.* viii. 1 above.
[891] *Cf.* x. 3 above.

So that it comes to pass, that both Eternity's stability becometh moved, and Time's mobility becometh stable.

So may we ever hold that God Himself is moved into Himself by [ever-] same transcendency of motion. [892]

For that stability is in His vastness motion motionless; for by His vastness is [His] law exempt from change. [893]

3. That, then, which so transcends, which is not subject unto sense, [which is] beyond all bounds, [and which] cannot be grasped,—That transcends all appraisement; That cannot be supported, nor borne up, nor can it be tracked out.[894]

For where, and when, and whence, and how, and what, He is,—is known to none. [895] For He's borne up by [His] supreme stability, and His stability is in Himself [alone],—whether [this mystery] be God, or the Eternity, or both, or one in other, or both in either.

4. And for this cause, just as Eternity transcends the bounds of Time; so Time [itself], in that it cannot have bounds set to it by number, or by change, or by the period of the revolution of some second [kind of Time],—is of the nature of Eternity.

Both, then, seem boundless, both eternal. And so stability, though naturally fixed, yet seeing that it can sustain the things that are in motion,—because of all the good it does by reason of its firmness, deservedly doth hold the chiefest place.

XXXII

1. The principals of all that are, are, therefore, God and Æon. [896]

The Cosmos, on the other hand, in that 'tis moveable, is not a principal. [897] For its mobility exceeds its own stability by treating the immoveable fixation as the law of everlasting movement.

The Whole Sense, [898] then, of the Divinity, though like [to Him] in its own self immoveable, doth set itself in motion within its own stability.

'Tis holy, incorruptible, and everlasting, and if there can be any better attribute to give to it, ['tis its],—Eternity of God supreme, in Truth

---

[892] *Eadem immobilitate.* The whole is an endeavour to at-one the "Platonic" root-opposites "same" (ταὐτόν) and "other" (θάτερον)—the "Self" and the "not-Self," *sat-asat, ātmānātman,* of the Upaniṣhads.
[893] Lit. motionless.
[894] *Cf. C. H.,* xiii. (xiv.) 6; also xxxiv. 3 below.
[895] Compare the Hymn in *C. H.,* v. (vi.) 10, 11.
[896] Or Eternity.
[897] Lit. does not hold the chief place.
[898] *Cf.* 3 below.

itself subsisting, the Fullness of all things, of Sense, and of the whole of Science, consisting, so to say, with God. [899]

2. The Cosmic Sense is the container [900] of all sensibles, [all] species, and [all] sciences.

The human [higher sense consists] in the retentiveness of memory, in that it can recall all things that it hath done.

For only just as far as the man-animal has the divinity of Sense [901] descended; in that God hath not willed the highest Sense divine should be commingled with the rest of animals; lest it should blush for shame [902] on being mingled with the other lives.

For whatsoever be the quality, or the extent, of the intelligence of a man's Sense, the whole of it consists in power of recollecting what is past.

It is through his retentiveness of memory, that man's been made the ruler of the earth.

3. Now the intelligence of Nature [903] can be won by quality of Cosmic Sense,—from all the things in Cosmos which sense can perceive.

Concerning [*this*] Eternity, which is the second [one],—the Sense of this we get from out the senses' Cosmos, and we discern its quality [by the same means].

But the intelligence of Quality [itself], the "Whatness" of the Sense of God Supreme, is Truth alone,—of which [pure] Truth not even the most tenuous sketch, or [faintest] shade, in Cosmos is discerned.

For where is aught [of it] discerned by measurement of times,— wherein are seen untruths, and births [-and-deaths], and errors?

4. Thou seest, then, Asclepius, on what we are [already] founded, with what we occupy ourselves, and after what we dare to strive.

But unto Thee, O God most high, I give my thanks, in that Thou hast enlightened me with Light to see Divinity!

---

[899] *Consistens, ut ita dixerim, cum deo.* Is there possibly here underlying the Latin *consistens cum deo* the expanded form of the peculiar and elliptical πρὸς τὸν θεὸν of the Proem to the Fourth Gospel (the *apud deum* of the Vulgate)? This was explained by the Gnostic Ptolemy, somewhere about the middle of the second century, as "at-one-ment with God," in his exegesis of the opening words, which he glosses as: "The at-one-ment with each other, together with their at-one-ment with the Father" (ἡ πρὸς ἀλλήλους ἅμα καὶ ἡ πρὸς τὸν πατέρα ἕνωσις). So that the first verse of the Proem would run: "In the Beginning was the Logos, and the Logos was (one) with God; yea, the Logos was God. He was in the Beginning (one) with God"—? *consistens cum deo.* See Irenæus, *Ref. Om. Hær.*, I. viii. 5—Stieren (Leipzig; 1853), i. 102; also *F. F. F.*, p. 388.

[900] Or receptacle.

[901] That is, the divine or higher sense, connected with memory in its beginnings and with the Platonic "reminiscence" (the Pythagorean *mathēsis*) in its maturity.

[902] *Cf. C. H.*, x. (xi.) 19.

[903] That is, Cosmos.

And ye, O Tat, Asclepius and Ammon, in silence hide the mysteries divine within the secret places of your hearts, [904] and breathe no word of their concealment [905]!

5. Now in our case the intellect doth differ from the sense in this,—that by the mind's extension intellect can reach to the intelligence and the discernment of the quality of Cosmic Sense.

The Intellect of Cosmos, on the other hand, extends to the Eternity and to the Gnosis of the Gods who are above itself.[906]

And thus it comes to pass for men, that we perceive the things in Heaven, as it were through a mist, as far as the condition of the human sense allows.

'Tis true that the extension [of the mind] which we possess for the survey of such transcendent things, is very narrow [still]; but [it will be] most ample when it shall perceive with the felicity of [true] self-consciousness.

XXXIII

1. [XII. M.] Now on the subject of a "Void," [907]—which seems to almost all a thing of vast importance,—I hold the following view.

Naught is, naught could have been, naught ever will be void.

For all the members of the Cosmos are completely full; so that Cosmos itself is full and [quite] complete with bodies, diverse in quality and form, possessing each its proper kind and size.

And of these bodies—one's greater than another, or another's less than is another, by difference of strength and size.

Of course, the stronger of them are more easily perceived, just as the larger [are]. The lesser ones, however, or the more minute, can scarcely be perceived, or not at all—those which we know are things [at all] by sense of touch alone.

Whence many come to think they are not bodies, and that there are void spaces,—which is impossible.

2. So also [for the Space] which is called Extra-cosmic,—if there be any (which I do not believe),—[then] is it filled by Him with things Intelligible, that is things of like nature with His own Divinity; just as this Cosmos which is called the Sensible, is fully filled with bodies and with animals, consonant with its proper nature and its quality;—[bodies] the proper shape of which we do not all behold, but [see] some large beyond their proper measure, some very small; either because of the great space which lies between [them and ourselves], or else because our sight is dull; so that they seem to us

---

[904] Lit. breasts.
[905] Cf. C. H., xiii. (xiv.) 22.
[906] The super-cosmic Gods, or beings of the Intelligible Cosmos; the Æons of the Gnostics.
[907] Cf. C. H., xi. (xii.).

to be minute, or by the multitude are thought not to exist at all, because of their too great tenuity.

I mean the daimones, who, I believe, have their abode with us, and heroes, who abide between the purest part of air above us and the earth,—where it is ever cloudless, and no [movement from the] motion of a single star [disturbs the peace].

3. Because of this, Asclepius, thou shalt call nothing void; unless thou wilt declare of what that's void, which thou dost say is void;—for instance, void of fire, of water, or things like to these.

For if it should fall out, that it should seem that anything is able to be void of things like these,—though that which seemeth void be little or be big, it still cannot be void of spirit and of air.

XXXIV

1. In like way must we also talk concerning "Space," [908]—a term which by itself is void of "sense." [909]

For Space seems what it is from that of which it is [the space]. For if the qualifying [910] word is cut away, the sense is maimed.

Wherefore we shall [more] rightly say the space of water, space of fire, or [space] of things like these.

For as it is impossible that aught be void; so is Space also in itself not possible to be distinguished what it is.

For if you postulate a space without that [thing] of which it is [the space], it will appear to be void space,—which I do not believe exists in Cosmos.

2. If nothing, then, is void, so also Space by its own self does not show what it is unless you add to it lengths, breadths [and depths],—just as you add the proper marks [911] unto men's bodies.

These things, then, being thus, Asclepius, and ye who are with [him],—know the Intelligible Cosmos (that is, [the one] which is discerned by contemplation of the mind alone) is bodiless; nor can aught corporal be mingled with its nature,—[by corporal I mean] what can be known by quality, by quantity, and numbers. For there is nothing of *this* kind in that.

3. This Cosmos, then, which is called Sensible, is the receptacle of all things sensible,—of species, qualities, or bodies.

But not a single one of these can quicken without God. For God is all, and by Him [are] all things, and all [are] of His Will.

---

[908] *Cf.* xv. 1 above.
[909] *Intellectu caret.*
[910] *Principale,*—lit. principal.
[911] *Signa*; characteristics, presumably.

For that He is all Goodness, Fitness, Wisdom, unchangeable,—that can be sensed and understood by His own self alone.

Without Him naught hath been, nor is, nor will be.

4. For all things are from Him, in Him, and through Him,—both multitudinous qualities, and mighty quantities, and magnitudes exceeding every means of measurement, and species of all forms;—which things, if thou should'st understand, Asclepius, thou wilt give thanks to God.

And if thou should'st observe it [912]as a whole, thou wilt be taught, by means of the True Reason, that Cosmos in itself is knowable to sense, [913] and that all things in it are wrapped as in a vesture by that Higher Cosmos [914] [spoken of above].

XXXV

1. Now every single class of living thing, [915] Asclepius, of whatsoever kind, or it be mortal or be rational, whether it be endowed with soul, or be without one, just as each has its class, [916] so does each several [class] have images of its own class.

And though each separate class of animal has in it every form of its own class, still in the selfsame [kind of] form the units differ from each other.

And so although the class of men is of one kind, so that a man can be distinguished by his [general] look, still individual men within the sameness of their [common] form do differ from each other.

2. For the idea [917]which is divine, is bodiless, and is whatever is grasped by the mind.

So that although these two, [918] from which the general form and body are derived, are bodiless, it is impossible that any single form should be produced exactly like another,—because the moments of the hours and points of inclination [when they're born] are different.

But they are changed as many times as there are moments in the hour of that revolving Circle in which abides that God whom we have called All-formed. [919]

3. The species, [920] then, persists, as frequently producing from itself as many images, and as diverse, as there are moments in the Cosmic

---

[912] *Sc.* the Cosmos.
[913] *Sensibilem*; probably referring to the *sensus par excellence*; that is, the higher or cosmic sense.
[914] That is, the Intelligible Cosmos; presumably the Æon.
[915] *Animalium.*
[916] *Genus.*
[917] *Species*; meaning here apparently the *genus* or class.
[918] Apparently the idea and mind.
[919] *Cf. C. H.*, xi. (xii.) 16; and *C. H.*, xvi. 15; also xix. 3 above, and xxxvi. 2 below.
[920] That is, apparently, the "divine species," or idea, the *genus.*

Revolution, [921]—a Cosmos which doth [ever] change in revolution. But the idea [922] [itself] is neither changed nor turned.

So are the forms of every single genus permanent, [and yet] dissimilar in the same [general] form.

XXXVI

1. *Asc.* And does the Cosmos have a species, O Thrice-greatest one?

Tris. Dost not thou see, Asclepius, that all has been explained to thee as though to one asleep?

For what is Cosmos, or of what doth it consist, if not of all things born?

This, [923] then, you may assert of heaven, and earth, and elements. For though the other things possess more frequent change of species, [still even] heaven, [by its] becoming moist, or dry, or cold, or hot, or clear, or dull, [all] in one kind [924] of heaven,—these [too] are frequent changes into species. [925]

2. Earth hath, moreover, always many changes in *its* species;—both when she brings forth fruits, and when she also nourishes her bringings-forth with the return of all the fruits; the diverse qualities and quantities of air, its stoppings and its flowings [926]; and before all the qualities of trees, of flowers, and berries, of scents, of savours—species.

Fire [also] brings about most numerous conversions, and divine. For these are all-formed images of Sun and Moon [927]; they're, as it were, like our own mirrors, which with their emulous resplendence give us back the likenesses of our own images.

XXXVII

1. [XIII. M.] But [928]now let this suffice about such things; and let us once again return to man and reason,—gift divine, from which man has the name of rational animal.

Less to be wondered at are the things said of man,—though they are [still] to be admired. Nay, of all marvels that which wins our wonder [most] is

---

[921] *Cf.* xl. 3 below.
[922] *Species.*
[923] That is, that there are genera embracing many species.
[924] *Specie.*
[925] The construction is here confuted and elliptical.
[926] This clause seems to be out of place.
[927] Presumably of the ideal Sun and Moon; for "all-formed," *cf.* xxxv. 2 above.
[928] The first six paragraphs of this chapter are quoted in Latin, with two slight verbal variants, by Augustine, *De Civitate Dei*, xxiv., xxvi.

that man has been able to find out the nature of the Gods and bring it into play.

2. Since, then, our earliest progenitors were in great error, [929]—seeing they had no rational faith about the Gods, and that they paid no heed unto their cult and holy worship,—they chanced upon an art whereby they made Gods [for themselves]. [930]

To this invention they conjoined a power that suited it, [derived] from cosmic nature; and blending these together, since souls they could not make, [they set about] evoking daimons' souls or those of angels; [and thus] attached them to their sacred images and holy mysteries, so that the statues should, by means of these, possess the powers of doing good and the reverse.

3. For thy forebear, Asclepius, the first discoverer of medicine, to whom there is a temple hallowed on Libya's Mount, [931] hard by the shore of crocodiles, [932] in which his cosmic man [933]reposes, that is to say his body; for that the rest [of him], or better still, the whole (if that a man when wholly [plunged] in consciousness of life, [934] be better), hath gone back home to heaven,—still furnishing, [but] now by his divinity, the sick with all the remedies which he was wont in days gone by to give by art of medicine.

4. Hermes, which is the name of my forebear, whose home is in a place called after him, [935] doth aid and guard all mortal [men] who come to him from every side. [936]

As for Osiris' [spouse]; how many are the blessings that we know Isis bestows when she's propitious; how many does she injure when she's wrath!

For that the terrene and the cosmic Gods are easily enraged, in that they are created and composed of the two natures.

5. And for this cause it comes to pass that these are called the "sacred animals" by the Egyptians, and that each several state [937]gives service to the

---

[929] Ménard thinks he can distinguish the hand of a Christian scribe in this sentence, which he translates with great freedom, "*qui s'égaraient dans l'incrédulité.*" A more careful translation, however, does not seem to favour this hypothesis. Hermes says simply that primitive mankind were ignorant of the Gods, and so in error.

[930] That is, images. *Cf.* xxx. above; and *C. H.*, xvii.

[931] *Cf.* xxvii. 3 above.

[932] *In monte Libyæ circa littus crocodilorum.* Does this refer to a Crocodilopolis (κροκοδείλων πόλις, Ptol., iv. 5, § 65)? And if so, to which of these cities, for there were several? The best known of these is Arsinoë in the Faiyyūm; but there was also another down south, in the Thebaid, on the W. bank of the Nile, lat. 25° 6′, of which remains are still visible at Embeshanda, on the verge of the Libyan desert. See Smith's *Dict. of Gk. and Rom. Geography* (London, 1878), *sub voc.*

[933] Presumably his mummy.

[934] *In sensu vitæ.*

[935] Hermopolis therefore (compare Lact., *D. Instit.*, i. 6); that is to say, Hermopolis Magna (Ἑρμοῦ πόλις μεγάλη), the modern Eshmūn, on the left bank of the Nile, about lat. 27° 4′.

[936] To get wisdom. Augustine's quotation ends here.

[937] Or city. For the animal cult of the Egyptians, see Plutarch, *De Is. et Os.*, lxxii. ff.

souls of those whose souls have been made holy, [938] while they were still alive; so that [the several states] are governed by the laws [of their peculiar sacred animals], and called after their names.

It is because of this, Asclepius, those [animals] which are considered by some states deserving of their worship, in others are thought otherwise; and on account of this the states of the Egyptians wage with each other frequent war.

XXXVIII

1. *Asc.* And of what nature, O Thrice-greatest one, may be the quality of those who are considered terrene Gods?

Tris. It doth consist, Asclepius, of plants, and stones, and spices, which contain the nature of [their own] divinity.

And for this cause they are delighted with repeated sacrifice, with hymns, and lauds, and sweetest sounds, tuned to the key of Heaven's harmonious song. [939]

2. So that what is of heavenly nature, [940] being drawn down into the images by means of heavenly use and practices, may be enabled to endure with joy the nature of mankind, and sojourn with it for long periods of time.

Thus is it that man is the maker of the Gods.

3. But do not, O Asclepius, I pray thee, think the doings of the terrene Gods are the result of chance.

The heavenly Gods dwell in the heights of Heaven, each filling up and watching o'er the rank he hath received; whereas these Gods of ours,[941] each in its way,—by looking after certain things, foretelling others by oracles and prophecy, foreseeing others, and duly helping them along,—act as allies of men, as though they were our relatives and friends.

XXXIX

1. [XIV. M.] *Asc.* What part of the economy, [942] Thrice-greatest one, does the Heimarmenē, or Fate, then occupy? For do not the celestial Gods rule over generals [943]; the terrene occupy particulars?

Tris. That which we call Heimarmenē, Asclepius, is the necessity of all things that are born, [944] bound ever to themselves with interlinked enchainments.

---

[938] Or consecrated.
[939] *Cf.* "God's song" in xiii. 2 above.
[940] Namely, the nature of the Gods.
[941] The terrene Gods; the daimones of *C. H.*, xvi. 14.
[942] *Rationis*; lit. reason.
[943] *Catholicorum.*

This, then, is either the effector of all things, or it is highest God, or what is made the second God by God Himself,—or else the discipline [945]of all things both in heaven and on earth, established by the laws of the Divine.

2. And so these twain, Fate and Necessity, are bound to one another mutually by inseparable cohesion. [946]

The former of them, the Heimarmenē, gives birth to the beginnings of all things; Necessity compels the end of [all] depending from these principals.

On these doth Order follow, that is their warp-and-woof, and Time's arrangement for the perfecting of [all] things. For there is naught without the interblend of Order. [947]

That Cosmos [948] is made perfect in all things; for Cosmos' self is vehicled [949]in Order, or totally consists of Order.

XL

1. So, then, these three, Fate, [and] Necessity, [and] Order, are most immediately effected by God's Will, who rules the Cosmos by His Law and by His Holy Reason.

From these, accordingly, all willing or not-willing is altogether foreign, according to God's Will. [950]

They are not moved by wrath nor swayed by favour, but are the instruments of the Eternal Reason's self-compulsion, which is [the Reason] of Eternity, [951] that never can be turned aside, or changed, or be destroyed.

2. First, then, is Fate, which, as it were, by casting in the seed, supplies the embryo of all that are to be.

Follows Necessity, whereby they all are forcibly compelled unto their end.

Third, Order [comes], preserving warp-and-woof of [all] the things which Fate and [which] Necessity arrange. [952]

---

[944] Or borne, *quæ geruntur*.
[945] *Disciplina* = ? *gnōsis*.
[946] *Glutino*.
[947] *Cf.* J. Laurentius Lydus, *De Mensibus*, iv. 7 (Wünsch, 70); the rest of the quotation following on what has been already quoted in the note to xix. 3. The Greek is either a very much shortened form or the Latin a very much expanded one, for the former may be translated as follows: "And Fate is also fated Activity (or Energy), or God Himself, or the Order that doth follow that Activity set over all things in the heaven and all things on the earth, together with Necessity. The former (Fate) gives birth to the very beginnings of things, the latter compels the ends also to come into existence. And on them there follow Order and Law, and there is naught that's orderless." *Cf.* Ex. i. 15, and Ex. xi. 1.
[948] *Mundus* = cosmos, meaning also order in Greek.
[949] *Gestatur*.
[950] *Divinitus*.
[951] That is, the Æon.

This, then, is the Eternity, which neither doth begin nor cease to be, which, fixed by law unchangeable, abides in the unceasing motion of its course.

3. It rises and it sets, by turns, throughout its limbs [953]; so that by reason of Time's changes it often rises with the very limbs with which it [once] had set.

For [its] sphericity,—its law of revolution, [954]—is of this nature, that all things are so straitly joined to their own selves, that no one knoweth what is the beginning of their revolution [955]; since they appear for ever all to go before and follow after their own selves.

Good and bad issues, [956] [therefore,] are commingled in all cosmic things.

4. [XV. M.] And now it hath been told you on each several point,—as man hath power [to tell], and God hath willed it and permitted it.

This, then, alone remains that we should do,—bless God and give Him praise; and so return to taking thought for body ['s comfort].

For now sufficiently have we been filled with feast of mind by our discourse on sacred things. [957]

XLI

1. Now when they came forth from the holy place, [958] they turned their faces towards the south [959] when they began their prayers to God.

For when the sun is setting, should anyone desire to pray to God, he ought to turn him thitherwards [960]; so also at the rising of the same, unto that spot which lies beneath the sun. [961]

As they were just beginning to recite the prayer, Asclepius did whisper:

[*Asc.*] Let us suggest to father, Tat,—what he did bid us do, [962]—that we should say our prayer to God with added incense and with unguents.

Whom when Thrice-greatest heard, he grew distressed and said:

---

[952] Fate thus seems to be regarded as the Creator, Order as the Preserver, and Necessity as the Destroyer or Regenerator.
[953] *Membra*; that is, parts, presumably constellations.
[954] *Cf.* xxxv. 3 below.
[955] *Volubilitatis*; that is, their turning into themselves; the symbol of which was the serpent swallowing its tail.
[956] *Eventus et fors.*
[957] *Cf.* the conclusion of *C. H.*, xvii.
[958] *De adyto*; "down from," literally.
[959] This is apparently an error for south-west or west.
[960] That is, to the setting sun or the west. *Cf. C. H.*, xiii. (xiv.) 16, Comment.
[961] *Subsolanus*, lying beneath the sun; that is to say, eastern.
[962] *Cf.* xxxviii. 1 above.

2. [*Tris.*] Nay, nay, Asclepius; speak more propitious words! For this is like to profanation of [our] sacred rites,—when thou dost pray to God, to offer incense and the rest.

For naught is there of which He stands in need, in that He is all things, or all are in Him.

But let us worship, pouring forth our thanks. For this is the best incense in God's sight,—when thanks are given to Him by men. [963]

---

3. [We give] Thee grace, Thou highest [and] most excellent! For by Thy Grace we have received the so great Light of Thy own Gnosis.

O holy Name, fit [Name] to be adored, O Name unique, by which the Only God [964] is to be blest through worship of [our] Sire,—[of Thee] who deignest to afford to all a Father's piety, and care, and love, and whatsoever virtue is more sweet [than these], endowing [us] with sense, [and] reason, [and] intelligence;—with sense that we may feel Thee; with reason that we may track Thee out from the appearances of things [965]; with means of recognition that we may joy in knowing Thee.

4. Saved by Thy Power divine, let us rejoice that Thou hast shown Thyself to us in all Thy Fullness. Let us rejoice that Thou hast deigned to consecrate us, [still] entombed in bodies, to Eternity.

For this is the sole festival of praise worthy of man,—to know Thy Majesty.

We have known Thee; yea, by the Single Sense of our intelligence, we have perceived Thy Light supreme,—O Thou true Life of life, O Fecund Womb that giveth birth to every nature!

5. We have known Thee, O Thou completely filled with the Conception from Thyself of Universal Nature!

We have known Thee, O Thou Eternal Constancy!

For in the whole of this our prayer in worship of Thy Good, this favour only of Thy Goodness do we crave;—that Thou wilt keep us constant in our Love of knowing Thee, [966] and let us ne'er be cut off from this kind of Life.

With this desire we [now] betake us to [our] pure and fleshless meal. [967]

---

[963] For the three preceding paragraphs, see Lact., *D. I.*, vi. 25.
[964] The Cosmos, presumably, as the One God.
[965] *Suspicionibus*; hints, perhaps, and so phenomena.
[966] Or of Thy Gnosis.
[967] *Cænam.*

COMMENTARY
THE TITLE

The titles in the Latin MSS. vary. The heading preferred by Hildebrand is "Asclepius, or a Dialogue of Thrice-greatest Hermes"; while in the Bipontine edition, the title stands: "Thrice-greatest Hermes Concerning the Nature of the Gods; A Sermon addressed to Asclepius." Ménard, the French translator, prefers: "A Sermon of Initiation, or Asclepius."

The treatise begins with a transparent gloss, in all probability originally the marginal note of some scribe, or student, which has improperly crept into the text. It runs: "This Asclepius is my Sun-god"; that is to say, apparently: "This Sermon 'Asclepius' has illumined me"; from which it is evident that the title lying before the scribe was "Asclepius" simply, as may be seen from § 2: "It is, however, with *thy* name I will inscribe this treatise." Stobæus, moreover, in quoting from the original Greek (of xxvii. 4), heads his extract simply, "Of Hermes from the [Sermons] to Asclepius."

On the other hand, the Church Father Lactantius, writing at the beginning of the fourth century, and quoting from the Greek original, says twice, categorically (*D. I.*, iv. 6 and vii. 8): "*Hermes in illo libro qui* λόγος τέλειος *inscribitur*"; that is, "Hermes in the Book entitled 'The Perfect Sermon,' or 'The Sermon of Initiation'"; while Johannes Laurentius Lydus on three occasions quotes from this "Perfect Sermon" of Hermes, and on each occasion so names it.

I have accordingly preferred this as the main title, and added "The Asclepius" as an alternative.

THE OLD LATIN TRANSLATION AND THE GREEK ORIGINAL

Of the Greek original we have quotations or references by Lactantius (see viii. I and 3; xxv. 4: xxvi. I; xli. 2), Johannes Laurentius Lydus (see xix. 3; xxviii. I; xxxix. I, 2), and Stobæus (see xxvii. 4).

If we compare these Greek quotations with our Latin translation, we shall find, not only that the Latin is an exceedingly free rendering of the Greek, showing many expansions and contractions, and often missing the sense of the original, but also that even in Greek there were probably several recensions of the same text.[968]

Indeed, the free rendering of our translation is of such a nature that it is impossible to base upon it any certain conclusions as to the date of the original or its precise worth in the history of religion.[969]

---

[968] See R. 195, 2.
[969] The so-founded opinions of Bernays and Zeller are characterized by Reitzenstein (p. 195) as of as little value as the opinions which made the whole of our literature dependent on New Platonism.

That, however, our Latin translation is an ancient one is proved by Augustine's verbal quotations from it (see xxiii. 1; xxiii. 3-xxiv. 2; xxiv. 3; xxvii. 1-4). It was thus in existence about 400 A.D. at least.[970]

Tradition, however, has assigned to it a far higher antiquity, attributing it to no less distinguished a writer than Appuleius, and so referring it to the first half of the second century.

This attribution has, of course, for long been questioned by modern criticism, and Reitzenstein, though he does not discuss the subject, accepts the adverse verdict and refers us to a "Pseudo-Appuleius."

Hildebrand, whose minute acquaintance with Appuleius' peculiar style and neologisms is a guarantee of his competence, has thoroughly gone into the matter; and though he sums up against tradition, it is in a half-hearted way. The translation, if not by Appuleius, is at any rate in old African Latin, and there is nothing in the style which absolutely forbids the possibility of its being by the author of *The Golden Ass* and the initiate of Isis. The strongest point, other than philological, against tradition is that Augustine *does not say* the translation was by Appuleius; but this seems to me to be unworthy of serious consideration.

It is, of course, difficult to turn possibilities into probabilities, but I see no reason why the Greek original of our Sermon should not be assigned to the earlier Hermes-Asclepian dialogues as well as to any others. That it was one of the most famous is evident by its wide quotation, and by the fact that several recensions of the Greek text were in circulation.

OF THE WRITER AND THE PERSONS OF THE DIALOGUE

The Latin translator retains a number of the original Greek technical terms, and if we could only rely on his translation giving us the substance of the original in all cases, we should be presented in several passages with phenomena which would persuade us that the writer of the original intended his readers to think he was an Egyptian, and that his native nomenclature was other than Greek, as is also the case in *C. H.* (xvi.).

For instance, in vii. 2, "the man 'essential,'[971] as say the Greeks,"— but this may be a gloss of the Latin translator.

Again, in x. 2: "So that . . . 'World' seems most fitly called 'Cosmos' in Greek,"—which seems to be the original.

Yet again, the "multifarious reasoning" of xii. 3 reminds us strongly of "the philosophizing of the Greeks—the noise of words," in *C. H.*, xvi. 2.

On the other hand, the phrase, "which we in Greek (*græce*) believe to be the Cosmos," would seem to make the original author forget his Egyptian rôle.

---

[970] Augustine's date is 354-430 A.D.
[971] *Cf. C. H.*, xiii. (xiv.) 14.

While "its bottom . . . is called in Greek A-eidēs," coupled with "in Greek they are called *Hades* . . . in Latin *Inferi*" (xvii. 3), may be assigned to a gloss of the translator.

In xxiv. 1, however, the sentence, "Dost thou not know, Asclepius, that Egypt is the image of the Heaven? . . . This land of ours is shrine of the whole world"—coupled with the rest of the chapter, and Ch. xxv.—could hardly have been written by a Greek. In xxviii. 1, moreover, the "weighing of the merit" of the soul is strongly Egyptian, and so with the image and animal-cult.

As to the persons of the dialogue, I would suggest that originally the sermon was addressed to Asclepius alone, and that the slight narrative indications were added later to adapt it to wider circles.

The chief disciple is evidently Asclepius; he it is who is already "well versed in Nature," according to *C. H.*, xiv. (xv.) 1; that is to say, he has progressed beyond the stage of Hearer, for he questions Hermes, whereas Tat does not ask questions, but listens only, he is "the one who is to hear" (i. 1). To them is added Ammon on the proposal of Asclepius; and Ammon is admitted on the ground that he had already had much *written* to him, but apparently had not yet been admitted to oral teaching.

The teaching is delivered in solemn surroundings in the holy place or shrine (i. 2), and teacher and pupils constitute the "sacred four." Hermes teaches in a state of exaltation; the place is filled with "God's goodly presence," and "Love Divine" instructs them, through Hermes' lips, in answer to the Pure and Single Love of Philosophy in their hearts (*cf.* xii. 3; xiv. 1).

The same hand that wrote the warning against revealing the sermon to others in i. 2 also probably wrote: "And ye, O Tat, Asclepius and Ammon, in silence hide the mysteries divine within the secret places of your hearts, and breathe no word of their concealment!" (xxxii. 4); he also, presumably, glossed "Asclepius" (xxxiv. 2) with "and ye who are with him," and added the naïve whisper of Asclepius to Tat (xli. 1).

This redactor (if our analysis is correct), moreover, was a member of a select [972]ascetic community, judging at any rate by his last sentence (xli. 5); in which case Ammon can hardly be equated with any King Ammon, but must be taken as standing for some grade of the community. I would suggest that this grade was similar to that of the Exoterici of the Pythagoreans or the outer circles of the Essenes, of which the members still lived in the world, but received instruction. In this case, however, the "we" of the last sentence would have to be taken as referring to Asclepius and Tat, and not to Ammon.

As to the dependence of our sermon on the rest of the literature, I find more points of contact between it and *C. H.*, x. (xi.), "The Key" sermon

---

[972] *Cf.* for references to the "few," xxii. 1; xxiii. 1; xxxiv. 3; xl. 1.

addressed to Tat; none of the references, however, which I have given in the notes, show any literal dependence.

THE DOCTRINE OF THE WILL OF GOD

In the general doctrine the stress laid on the concept of the Will of God[973] is to be specially noticed. This Will seems to be almost personified, and is, of course, a fundamental doctrine of the Trismegistic religio-philosophy. [974]

In xxvi. 1 it is identified with the Goodness [975] of God, and the Nature of God. [976] But what it seems to correspond to most nearly is the Æon or Eternity-idea which is set forth very clearly in xxx.-xxxii.—in fact, more clearly than anywhere else in the Trismegistic literature. God and Æon are the sources of all things; and Æon is "the Eternity of God, in Truth itself subsisting, the Fullness of all things" (xxxii. 1). The Will of God is thus the Æon or Plērōma, the Wisdom, the Energy, the Spouse of the Supreme.

This Will rules Cosmos with Law and Holy Reason (xl.); Cosmos being the Order of things involved in Fate and Necessity the instruments of the Divine Will. [977]

Our sermon is also characterized by the frequent use it makes of the terms Spirit and Sense.

CONCERNING SPIRIT AND THE ALL-SENSE

The Spirit is evidently Cosmic Life (vi. 4; xxvii. 1) and individual life (x. 4). [978] The exposition of it begins with xiv. 2; Spirit and Matter, or the Nature of the Cosmos (xiv. 3), are practically regarded as the Positive and Negative, or Masculine and Feminine Energies of the Divine.

Spirit is the Ruler (xvii. 1) of all things in Cosmos or Nature; it is the immediate Instrument of the Will of God (xvi. 3); and is, indeed, loosely identified with that Will (xix. 4); while in still looser fashion Spirit seems to be symbolized by "Heaven" and the Sensible Cosmos by "Earth" (xix. 2).

It is very probable that this doctrine of Spirit as Divine Breath is fundamentally Egyptian, and owes nothing to immediate Semitic influence. However this may be, the use of the term Sense, as apparently in some way superior to Reason (vi. 4; x. 4), is very striking, and, as in some cases opposed to the exaltation of the Reason found elsewhere in our tractates, under the

---

[973] *Cf.* vii. 3; viii. 2; xi. 4; xiv. 1; xvi. 3; xix. 4; xx. 3; xxii. 4; xxv. 2; xxvi. 1, 2 and 3.
[974] *Cf.* especially *C. H.*, iv. (v.) 1; x. (xi.) i.
[975] In the Greek text of Lactantius this is "the Good."
[976] *Cf.* vi. 1; xiv. 3.
[977] *Cf.* also *C. H.*, xiii. (xiv.) 19, 20, and R. 39, n. 1.
[978] *Cf. C. H.*, x. (xi.) 13, and Commentary.

influence of this leading idea of Greek philosophy, discloses an Egyptian point of view. We have already noticed this use of the term in some of our tractates, but in our present sermon it is brought into great prominence. This Sense is not the differentiated senses, but a Unit or Cosmic Sense.

It is "the Divine Sense of intelligence," and is found only in God and in man's reason (vii. 1; xxxii. 2).

It is the "Higher Sense (with which Celestial Gift mankind alone is blest)"—characterized as the "feeder of the mind" (xviii. 1); yet on the other hand this "Higher Sense" is that "which by good chance a man perceives by mind, when out of all his senses."

This Sense is in some fashion closely connected with Nature and Cosmos (xxi. 1); through it man "disciplines his soul," and "cures his intellect," thus gaining "intelligence of God-like Reason" (xxii. 1), and finally "mingling himself with the All-sense of the Divine Intelligence" (xxix. 2).

This All-sense is the same as the "Whole Sense of Divinity," and is the Likeness of God; it is "in its own self immoveable," and yet "doth set itself in motion within its own stability" (xxxii. 1). Man must make himself like unto this Likeness.

This Likeness is evidently the Æon or Intelligible Cosmos; for the "Cosmic Sense is the Container of all sensibles" (xxxii. 2).

In man its chief normal characteristic is the retentiveness of memory, "through which man is made ruler of the Earth" (xxxii. 2). This Sense is then man's *continuum*, the germ of everlastingness in him, the root-ground of consciousness (xxxii. 3), the Single Sense of the intelligence (xli. 4), which is fully brought to birth only when a man "is wholly plunged in consciousness of life (in *sensu vitæ*)" (xxxvii. 3),—the "spiritual life" of the Christian Gnostics.

The fact that we have only a translation to deal with prevents us laying too much stress on details, but the general idea is clear enough; so too with the rest of this, the longest of our sermons, we must be content to refer only to general points, the chief of which are the "prophetic" utterances.

THE PROPHETIC UTTERANCES

These present us with problems of very great difficulty, and, so far, I have neither seen any solution nor has any occurred to me.

So much work has been done on contemporary prophetic utterances of this nature, especially on the Sibylline Literature, that it may be said that the scholastic mind has reached certain general *criteria* with regard to such pronouncements—the chief of which is that the hypothesis of genuine prophecy is not to be entertained.

In the Sibylline literature, indeed, this is clearly established; for much of it consists of traditional history written in the prophetical tense, so to say; when the history comes to an end the date of the "prophetical" writer is at once detected, for all that follows has no longer any relation to historical events.

In the case of our "prophecies," however, we have nothing of this nature to guide us. All we can say is that they seem to have been written, most probably, at a time when the Trismegistic communities were being persecuted.

That this was in the course of the fourth century, however, as Reitzenstein (p. 213) supposes, seems to me to be, so far, destitute of any sure objective confirmation; it not only compels us to suppose that the prophecies are later interpolations (which they may possibly be), but that these interpolations are later than Lactantius; whereas there is every probability that the Church Father had the text of them before him,[979] and his date is the beginning of the fourth century.

On the other hand, Zosimus, writing somewhere about the end of the third and beginning of the fourth century, breathes no word of persecution, and leads us to suppose that the community was still flourishing. We are thus still in the gravest uncertainty.

The first of our "prophecies" is in xii. 3: "For I will tell thee as though it were propheticly"—addressed to Asclepius, and, therefore, probably not due to the redactor who we have supposed added the narrative sentences.

The lament of the writer is that "the Single Love, the Love of Pure Philosophy," is fast disappearing from the world; he can hardly have had Christianity in mind when writing these words, for he contrasts the "Pure Philosophy" with "multifarious reasoning" and "divers sciences," and the latter can hardly be said to be characteristic of General Christianity.

If, however, his words may be said to include also Gnostic Christianity, then he was clearly not in sympathy with it; but this can hardly be the case, seeing that the resemblances between the Trismegistic and Christian Gnosis are of a very intimate nature.

THE PROSCRIPTION OF THE WORSHIP OF THE GODS

Turning next to xxiv. 2, we meet with the clear statement that the worship of the Gods will be legally proscribed by the "barbarian" masters of Egypt (also xxv. 3).

Such a general proscription in this emphatic sense took place in Egypt only with the destruction of the Serapeum by the Christians themselves in 389 A.D. Of persecutions of the Christians by the Roman authorities in Egypt prior to this we get clear indications in the writings of the Christian Gnostic Basilides, who flourished at Alexandria at the beginning of the second century, and wrote specially of martyrdom. But this will little help us for the

---

[979] See xxv. 4, and note.

proscription of a cult that favoured the worship of the Gods and of their images.

Can it, then, be possible that these prophetic utterances were written at a time when many of the same nature were being penned by Jew and Christian? For our author, as for Jewish and Christian writers, the "End of the World" was at hand; his expectation is in this precisely the same as that of the writers of the New Testament documents.

The cause of this dire event is that Egypt, the "shrine of the whole world," the "Holy Land" [980] *par excellence*, will be polluted with all iniquity and violence. The Cult of the Gods will cease, and the Gods will leave the Earth and mount to Heaven. The man's whole heart is bleeding for Egypt, even as the heart of a Jew for Jerusalem.

If there is any immediate historical references in these heartfelt utterances, we must seek them in such phrases as: "This holiest land, seat of our shrines and temples, shall be choked with tombs and corpses" (xxiv. 3); "the tale of tombs shall far exceed the number of the quick" (*ibid.*, § 4) [981]; and "Egypt shall be made the home of Scyth or Indian, or someone like to them— that is, a foreign neighbour."

It is true that the Christians were ever reproached with worshipping the dead, and building churches over the bones of the dead—an act of utter pollution according to all Pagan notions; but the words of our author, even allowing for all hyperbole, can hardly be construed in this sense.

People like Scyths or Indians, again, if we are to suppose any historical reference, can hardly be imagined to refer to the Romans; while the Goths under Alaric, who ravaged Greece in 395, 396 A.D., are too late even for Reitzenstein. Moreover, we have already in our notes pointed to the strange conjunction of Scyth and Barbarian in our text as being also found in Colossians.

On the other hand, nothing but the entire State suppression of the Pagan Religion in all its forms can satisfy xxv. 3, and this just suits the end of the fourth century.

If, however, we cannot entertain so late a date, and I do not think we can, there seems nothing for it but to give the writer some credit for his prognostication of the future; for eventually things certainly turned out for him and all he held most dear very much as he imagined or feared they would.

THE LAST HOPE OF THE RELIGION OF THE MIND

---

[980] The "image of the Heaven"; cf. *K. K.*, 46-48.
[981] This is very different language from the more moderate tone of *C. H.*, ix. (x.) 4, where we are told about the Gnostics, "they are thought mad and laughed at; they're hated and despised, and sometimes even put to death."

At any rate the last hope of the Pure Love, the Religion of the Mind, is in the Trismegistic Communities, if indeed it is so permitted to interpret xxvii. 3:

"Yea, they who rule the earth shall be distributed [through all the lands], and finally be gathered in a state,—at top of Egypt's upper part,—which shall be founded towards the setting sun, and to which all the mortal race shall speed."

We need not insist upon details, for our translator may have gone wide of the original; for instance, the "race" may, instead of being "mortal" in the original, have been the "Race" of which we have already heard so much in Philo and these tractates; but the similarity of the idea cannot fail to remind us of Philo when, in writing of the Redeemed of Spiritual Israel, he says:

"Those who were but scattered in Hellas and non-Grecian (Barbarian) lands, over islands and over continents, shall rise up with one impulse, and from diverse regions flock together unto the one spot revealed to them."[982]

And with this further compare the famous passage on the Therapeuts:

"Now this Race of men is to be found in many parts of the inhabited world, both the Grecian and non-Grecian world, sharing in the Perfect Good.

"In Egypt there are crowds of them in every province, or nome as they call it, and especially round Alexandria. For they who are in every way (or in every nome) the most highly advanced, come as colonists, [983] as it were, to the Therapeutic fatherland."[984]

Moreover, just as the Therapeuts in the immediately following lines of Philo are said to have their community on a hill, so too in our text we immediately find mention of the Trismegistic communities as having their chief centre on the Libyan Hill,—a community which is spoken of as "very large" in numbers, and so is somewhat of a contradiction to the numbers of the Pious given in xxii. 1, where we are told "they may be counted even in the world," unless the sentence is to be taken as rhetorical.

This Hill is called the Libyan Mount, a vague enough title; nor is this vagueness removed when we find it again referred to (in xxxvii. 3) as the place of burial of the body of the First Asclepius, and obtain the additional information that it is "hard by the shore of crocodiles," for this can hardly refer to Crocodilopolis in the Fayyūm, the most northern of the towns so named, seeing that the Libyan Mount is "at the top of Egypt's upper part," and "towards the setting sun."

---

[982] *De Execrat.*, § 9; M. ii. 435, 436; P. 937 (Ri. v. 255).
[983] *Cf.* in our Sermon, xxv. I: Egypt, "the sole colony of holiness."
[984] *D. V. C.*, C. 56 ff; M. i. 474; P. 892. *Cf. F. F. F.*, 69.

This, however, corresponds admirably with the location of Philo's Therapeut community on the southern shore of Lake Mareotis, just south of Alexandria; but few indeed will be found to entertain the possibility even that Philo and our author may be speaking of the same people from different standpoints and under different names.

As far as I can see, there is no certainty in the matter; and, therefore, I leave it as a problem of immense interest that has not as yet found a solution.

www.ingramcontent.com/pod-product-compliance
Lightning Source LLC
Chambersburg PA
CBHW071155160426
43196CB00011B/2092